"Turbulence is inevitable, misery is optional. I learned that the hard way, taking Braniff International successfully through financial crisis. Jim Feldman lays out a great flight plan for you to fly through turbulence and not only survive, but thrive. He shares his own turbulent experiences as well as real life experiences of others."

Howard Putnam, Former CEO Southwest Airlines
and Braniff International Airways,
Speaker and Author of: *The Winds of Turbulence*

". . . Especially for the rapidly evolving hospitality, tourism, and leisure sector, Jim Feldman's book, *Shift Happens* provides us with a unique and essential way to look at re-inventing ourselves and our businesses when things change, and we are faced with new and unique circumstances. *Shift Happens* is a critical reminder about what is important. . ."

Brian Margulis, Professor
Hospitality & Tourism Management
Roosevelt University, Heller College of Business

"Jim Feldman is a genius on marketing and positioning. This book is chock full of ideas that can move you onwards and upwards in business and in life."

Dr. Nido Qubein, President, High Point University
Chairman, Great Harvest Bread Co.

"I've known Jim Feldman for a generation. I've seen him go through the many phases and shifts in his career and life. He is a man I admire and marvel at. His innovative mind is remarkable. He's also fun to be with. You will enjoy getting to know him through this book, as you get to know yourself even better. Read it cover to cover . . . twice."

Jim Cathcart, Author *Relationship Selling*

"Shift Happens to everyone. Make yours now, read my friend James's insightful book."

Mark Victor Hansen, Co-founder

"Feldman the creator of Shift Happens, does it again!"

Karen Gordon, Former CEO, Activity Planners

"Today, at 39,000 ft., I read your book again. Jim, it is a great collection of great advice—and wisdom. You are a clone of Jim Welch of GE—and the Jewish Mother I never had! Something about the book was just perfect for my mood today. As you have many times, you inspired me. Thanks, Jim, for sharing what I would like to call, 'Jim Feldman's Greatest Hits' with us all."

"James Feldman is tailor made for the difficult business climate that we all face today. His marketing acumen and out-of-the-box approach (often stretching the boundaries of any geographically shaped problem), leave conventional business leaders and consultants in the proverbial dust."

Mark Chellis, Global Alliance Marketing Director, VMware-Motorola

"Warning: This book is only for those people who want to catch fire with enthusiasm and go for it! James has written a rousing manifesto to help you 'Stop Doing Stupid Stuff' and Shift into the life of your dreams now. Loaded with stories and no-nonsense advice, this book is a wonderful guide to success."

Chellie Campbell, Author of
The Wealthy Spirit* and *Zero to Zillionaire

"The book is clever, incisive, useful and irreverent. I have heard Jim speak for years and always imagined that being Feldman is a full-time job. That's a compliment because he makes it clear that living is a full-time job. Never one to step over dimes to pick up nickels, Feldman is right on the money."

Jeff Broudy, Executive Vice President, United Incentives

"If you're down to your last dime—financially or emotionally—this book is the lifeline you hoped to find. Chief Innovation Expert James Feldman knows your distress and responds to your "SOS" with ideas that will get your engines and your spirits sailing again!"

Carole Lieberman, M.D., M.P.H., Beverly Hills
Media Psychiatrist and Bestselling Author

"*Shift Happens! Think Inside the Box Using 3D Thinking*™ is a witty, insightful and valuable tool to help you get from point A to point B. Shift Happens to us all and Jim makes it not only okay, but he helps to re-frame it into an inspiring challenge to be conquered. Had I known before what I know after reading his book, previous "shifts" would have been far less painful! I wholeheartedly recommend this book to anyone who needs to make a change."

Erica H. Haupert, Vice President - Key Accounts,
Motion Picture Licensing Corporation

"Jim is a multi talented individual with a gift of being highly creative and motivational. Wynn Las Vegas has hired him to train, operate key customer events and purchase premium gifts from his unique collection. I find Jim to be ethical, positive and motivational in whatever he undertakes."

Karolyn Graves-Rhodes
Exective Director of Regional Sales at Wynn/Encore

"Jim Feldman is one of the most creative, connection-making, opportunity-creating people I know. Among the many things I admire about Jim in addition to his own creativity and ability to teach others is his hustle and drive—in the best sense of both words. Jim makes things happen and shows others how they can, too."

Mark Sanborn
President at Sanborn & Associates, Inc. | Leadership Keynote Speaker |
Keynote Speaker | Motivational Speaker

"Jim Feldman goes beyond just an entertaining presenter; he reads his audience and captivates you with spot-on examples that hit home, and then moves you to participation and shifting your way of thinking. He is able to demonstrate ideas simply but with relevance to a wide variety of participants—and the take-home tools reinforce the training for days and months to follow."

Betty Grogan
AVP, NA Channels at Ergotron

"It has been a pleasure and joy to work with James Feldman over several years and visits, when he mesmerized Marquis Los Cabos (a Leading Hotel of The World) workforce with very motivating Service & Customer CARE seminars. The results were immediately felt and longlasting, translating into reputation improvement as well as sales growth. I will always have James as my first speaker at any business that I run because he delivers tangible results to a team. Thank you, Jim!"

Ella Messerli
Director at Hotel El Ganzo Grupo Questro

"Jim is one of the most diabolical marketers I know. He is super creative and gets things done. He always has great answer and can see possibilities where others might see walls. Jim is as passionate about life as he is about business."

Giovanni Livera
Lifetime Entrepreneur | Corporate Speaker | Keynote Speaker | Motivational Speaker | Inspirational Speaker

"If your organization has a problem, Jim Feldman has an answer. In fact, he has lots of answers because Jim looks past the obvious into a world of possibilities and comes up with multiple solutions before finding the one that's right for you.

"He is creative, has integrity, and a funny sense of humor. Jim looks at the complex world and finds simple solutions that can be implemented. Bottom line he shows his clients a new pathway to reach the top. If you have lots of 'bad shift' in your life or business give him a call. He makes Shift Happen in a good way."

Dale Irvin
THE PROFESSIONAL SUMMARIZER | CEO, Just Imagine | Humorist | Author | Professional Speaker

Shift Happens!®

THINK INSIDE THE BOX

Using

James D. Feldman

CSP, CITE, CPIM, CPT, CPC, MIP, PCS, REALTOR®

Foreword by Joseph Sugarman,
Marketing Legend & Founder of BluBlocker Sunglasses

Transformation Media Books

Transformation Media Books

Published by Transformation Media Books, USA
www.TransformationMediaBooks.com

An imprint of Pen & Publish, LLC
Saint Louis, Missouri
(314) 827-6567
info@PenandPublish.com
www.PenandPublish.com

Copyright © 2020 James D. Feldman

All rights reserved.
No part of this book may be reproduced, stored in a retrieval system, or transmitted by any means, electronic, mechanical, photocopying, recording, or otherwise, except for brief passages in connection with a review, without written permission from the author.

ISBN: 978-1-941799-88-8
Library of Congress Control Number: 2020940417

This book is printed on acid-free paper.

Printed in the USA

Dedication

*To the more than 40 million (as of 5/28/2020) Americans
who filed for unemployment during COVID-19
and more who are underemployed.*

*To those individuals who have lost their roles
as breadwinners or productive, self-reliant citizens.*

*To the laid off workers in almost every industry—
higher average than the Great Depression.*

*To the new high school and college graduates
whose careers have been stalled by the lack of opportunities.*

*To anyone who is creating a new personal brand,
a new career or simply trying to balance the shifts in life.*

*To anyone who has no job, no money
and asks themselves—Now What?*

Our 2020 Vision is now blurred. Before COVID-19, there was a trend toward independent freelancers and contract work. At that time, it was estimated that 35–40% of work was contracted. Current estimates forecast that 50% or more will never return to their traditional jobs. Can we agree that after we return to "the new normal," there are opportunities to shift how we think, adapt, and accelerate team-building as the struggle for recruitment, retention, and education manifests itself?

The concepts in this book will provide you with thinking tools to prevent Thinkruptcy™. They may be applied to find new opportunities or revise existing products or services. You won't find these principles in most business schools because they don't focus on innovative problem solving. This is one of the reasons that this book can become a valuable reference for students wanting to learn how to become better problem solvers, and innovators. As you read on you will discover that these principles involve Customers, employees, suppliers, competitors, and new discoveries.

I don't expect you to agree with 100% of what is contained in this book. What I do hope is that you will find a few ideas, concepts, or suggestions that help you thrive, not just survive, as we transition from what was to what could be your "new normal."

All of us, no matter who you are, what you did in the past, for most of us, this disruption has given us the challenge—and opportunity—to reshape the world. Technology, economic and social stratifications, our digital footprint, and our support systems are open to "shifts." No one can predict the future with any degree of certainty, which provides all of us with a more level marketplace. I hope you will use this book to help you laser focus on what interests you, what you can leverage from your core competencies, and what you can monetize. It's time to think "inside the box" to reinvent yourself using 3D Thinking.

Acknowledgements

A global pandemic has created the necessity for answers as many of us realize that we have no job, no money and no solution, prompting us to ask, "Now What?"

Shift Happens! and we were not prepared for it. Not all infectious disease terms are created equal. We learned that the pandemic "P" means passport. A pandemic is an epidemic that travels. Unlike an epidemic, which is localized, the pandemic spread worldwide. Shift Happened.

In writing this book there was no precedent. Nothing prepared the world for a global "shutdown." There is no one to ask what they had done. Every industry will be transformed as the pandemic shifts how we work in every sector. The global economy has been dislocated, rearranged, and survivors will have to learn—or relearn—how to build sustainable models in every sector, at every level. It won't be the survival of the fittest but the survival of the most innovative, most responsive, and most receptive to shifts in how we think. In truth we are all in this together but 6 feet apart. This is an attempt to offer insights from the past that can be applicable to your future.

I believe this book is a toolbox. I don't expect you to agree with 100% of what I say. I hope that it will prompt you to ask, *What If? What's Next? What's Possible? Why Not? And what if I don't do something differently so that my tomorrow is better than my yesterday?* We are in a global war for Customers. This book is about how to imagine, how to think big, and how to become unsinkable.

All change comes from the same factors and COVID-19 has leveled the marketplace. Today we must all rethink about human nature, the issues of confrontation, and what matters in the contest of delivering goods and services. Two thousand years ago, Sun Tzu wrote *The Art of War*, a book about how to build a winning plan.

Much of this book is a huge checklist for using many of the tools to build a to-be list.

My thanks to all of you that offered advice and counsel. Michelle Hove enthusiastically believed in this book and offered insightful comments that held me accountable. Not only is she my most helpful critic, she is also my deepest and most enduring supporter. I could have never completed this book without her. Sometimes you have to ride the waves of change to reach the shore when Shift Happens!

When I reflected on some of my business mentors I found that many of them had left a corporate culture and found new directions in their life. Ron Jesselson stopped selling low margin merchandise and started offering high-margin colored mulch; Jerry Bower offers wine on the internet after leaving Apple Computer; Paul Spitzberg left Coach to become a professional poker player; Christopher Perks created an event company after leaving Doral Resorts; and Steve Sturm took early retirement from Toyota then after a few months got restless and became EVP of a large trade show/event management company. To anyone that has, or will create their own shifts I congratulate you and hope you will continue to share your wisdom with others.

The real challenge is leveraging those insights of yesterday and trying to apply them to what's happening NOW. None of them faced the onslaught of intensive care, the shutdown of every state, and the feeling of hopelessness in a time where hope is so desperately needed. We are facing the digitalization of work in every industry, every sector, every person.

Much of how we move forward is into unchartered waters. And that's the good news. We will emerge from this and be more focused. As we undertook self-isolation that brought us together we also recognized that an early warning system will be needed.

Acknowledgements

Nothing is more important than good information. It's essential but often clouded. As I write this book 90–95% of all businesses and 100% of public schools are closed. Most airlines are grounded. Hotels and resorts shuttered.

There are "social distancing" requirements for any trip outside homes where house arrest is still in place. Food, cleaning supplies, toilet paper and other necessities are being hoarded. Hopefully by the time you read this, the restrictions have been reduced or lifted but we will never return to "normal." These limbo days will help us to focus and evolve savoring the "new normal" that will represent the essence of a time when Shift Happens!

A benefit from the pandemic is that it cleared the way for new discoveries. For us, the most important lesson is the philosophy of destruction or survival.

These lessons apply equally for anyone looking for an advantage to winning your battle and positioning. *The Art of War* improved our understanding of military tactics. Make no mistake. What we have faced is a battle. This is a war for our survival in the marketplace as we battle for greater mind and wallet share of consumers.

There is no one-size-fits-all approach, especially as we enter an age of unprecedented uncertainty. Now more than ever, it's critical to know your customers, patients, and guests. You must understand what products and services are resonating with them, and most importantly, solving a problem or filling a need.

To everyone who has offered advice, edits, changes and support, my sincerest gratitude.

And to you, the reader, I wish you all the best in applying what you may learn to whatever you do. I would very much enjoy hearing from you about what works and what doesn't. Text or call (312) 500 4493.

Table of Contents

Foreword xiv
Author's Preface xvii
Author's 2020 Vision xiii

Shift Happened

1. Shift Your Attitude.. 3
2. Can You Handle the Shift? 9
3. Shift Happens and I Don't Have to Take It Anymore 15
4. Shift—When Less Is Really More... 19
5. Everyone Experiences Shifts 27
6. Shift Happens When You Train Your Brain.................................... 35
7. Start Your Shifts Today 49

Shifts in Your Personal Life

8. Shift Your Priorities.. 55
9. Shift Happens! Deal with It... 61
10. Shifting into High Gear 69
11. Some Shifts Are Inspiring 77
12. Shift—When the Light Bulb Goes On.. 83
13. Shifts to Instill Innovative 3D Thinking.. 89
14. Shift—Rebuilding the Hospitality, Casino & Travel Industries..... 105
15. Shifts to Improve Patients' Patience... 129

Jobs Shift

17. Shift—I Owe! I Owe! It's Off to Work I Go!........................141
18. When to Shift Your Job..147
19. When Shift Happens, Where Does the Loyalty Go?........157
20. Shift to High Stakes, High Emotions: Where Are the Jobs?...........161
21. Volunteer a Shift..165
22. Shifts to Create New Opportunities 175
23. Shift What Others Know About You 183

Shift to Thinking Like an Entrepreneur

24. Shift Your Flight Plan for Growth 191
25. Shifting to a New Business..197
26. Shift to Business as Unusual 209
27. Shift Your 2020 Vision 219
28. Shifting the Mind to the Marketplace...........................227
29. Shifts that Are Lost in Translation 235
30. Take Your Shifts to ~~the Bank~~ Investors...................237
31. Shifts to Avoid Thinkruptcy™.......................................247
32. Shifting Your Uncertainty 257
33. The Shift Is Up to You!...263

Website Appendix 273
About the Author 283
Shift Happens AHAs 285
Jim's Reading List...291

Foreword

by Joseph Sugarman

Times are tough. People are losing jobs. It's becoming tougher and tougher to get and hold a job. And yet throughout this period of instability, many are prospering. What separates the winners from the losers? Why is now the time to capture the American dream and create a shift in your life towards abundance and success?

America is unique in many ways. First, we are a country of opportunity. Discover a need, fill a niche and build a business. But America also has a subtle advantage over most other countries. We accept failure as part of the risk taking process. In some countries failure is a disgrace. Fail and you're surrounded by a stigma that follows you for the rest of your life. Not so in America.

We accept failure as part of a journey and without any stigma. We have legal procedures like debt resolution, Chapter 11 or Chapter 13—providing a pathway to ease out of a losing situation in a controlled and legal way.

It is this freedom to fail that provides America with a catalyst for its entrepreneurs to take a chance, to take risks and create that next big success story. And it's in tough times that the greatest opportunities emerge. More millionaires were made during the depression in the 30's and recession in 2008 than any other time. Now is the time to act!

Jim Feldman provides the answers in this excellent book on what you need to do, to achieve the American dream or to dramatically build your career. So much is attitude; much of it is shifting your belief system.

You can learn your best lessons from somebody who has fought the good fight, succeeded and failed and ended up on top. Believe me, there are many self-proclaimed gurus who never ran a business or had to meet a payroll. Jim is not in that category. He's done it all. From being an accomplished speaker, to running and building businesses. And he uses examples from his personal experience to teach you the truth about handling the challenges that face us all.

Jim's recipe for success is not the typical formula you'll find in many books on success. In *Shift Happens: Think Inside the Box Using 3D Thinking*™, he points out how to take the worst situations and turn them into positive events in your life. It's not just a business book, but also a book on life. Chances are you'll walk away with more than one good idea from each chapter—with each idea shifting your perception and motivating you to take action and make the changes you need in both attitude and technique.

Take charge of your life. Realize that Shift Happens and the way you respond to it can make all the difference between success and failure. I have known Jim for over 40 years. I've seen his approach to difficult situations and watched him conquer even the toughest challenges. Here is the opportunity to learn from a master and Jim's unique approach to success, failure and what it takes to make a difference. Yes, follow his advice and, sure enough, a shift will happen in your life, too.

—**Joseph Sugarman, Chairman and Founder of BluBlocker Sunglass Corporation and one of America's top marketing professionals**

Turning Lemonade into Cash

When I was seven years old, I had no job and no money, so I went to my parents and asked for an allowance.

"Go earn it yourself," my father told me. "Walk the dog, mow the yard, wash cars..."

I went to my mother and asked for an allowance, and she suggested I set up a lemonade stand.

Upon looking at the local competition—a lemonade stand on almost every corner—I went back to my air-conditioned bedroom to think about how to make money without going out in the heat and facing the inevitable price war.

I asked my mother to take me to Shoppers World, a warehouse store where I priced out bulk lemonade, sugar, and paper cups. I bounced from my Mother to my Father when I asked for an allowance. Once I got ALL the decision makers in the same room I made progress.

I figured out that I could wholesale this "lemonade kit" to the mothers of my competitors during the cool evenings, thus avoiding the heat and tiresome work operating the lemonade stand. It worked. I purchased the bulk supplies in the cool evening when my mother could take me shopping, took orders, repackaged the items for each "lemonade stand," delivered them, and collected the cash. Guess what? At the end of the summer I had a savings account with over $350.

I learned what I needed to know to be successful... there is no shortcut to hard work and a new idea can be worth a lot of money.

When the Shift hits the fan, what do you know? It's time to learn.

I learned, at seven, when I met with an immoveable object, you can create a win-win. I owe it all to my parents who made me realize that there are no white knights, no Robin Hood and no tooth fairies who leave gifts under your pillow. I don't believe in random events or chance because there is something you can do about it. It's time to Shift your thinking.

—Jim Feldman

Author's Preface

Inside these pages, I offer you insights and examples that will make you uncomfortable, challenge your assumptions and inspire you to see your own potential during these turbulent times.

I have discovered that in life there are paths others have created that can guide you to where you need to go. You may deviate from the road and create a new one for others to follow. Remember: living in the past has no future.

I am just a regular guy trying to enjoy life as I experience challenges and overcome life's obstacles. I have been where you are, no matter where you are, as I struggled with the questions:

"Am I satisfied with everything as it is?"

"What if I could be there, instead of here?"

Asking myself those questions helps me focus on the future instead of the past.

I get up in the morning and ask myself, *"What's next?"*

I am going to share with you what I have learned from others and discovered on my own.

I have lots of fears, but I face them head-on. I am not afraid of dying—I am more concerned with how I live *before* I die.

I expect shifts as I grow older.

I am not only a business owner; I'm a business innovator.

I have created dozens of companies. I've also developed new products, marketed commodities and services for some of the biggest and best companies globally, and helped smaller companies grow to become larger ones. I view the world from a unique perspective. I always capitalize **C**ustomers. It reminds everyone they are important.

I have thrived behind the scenes as well as failed in a very public marketplace.

I have experienced success and failure in both my business and personal life.

I have been labeled "morbidly obese," and now I am a poster child for turn around successful weight management.

I have walked the talk, lost my way and been a visionary. I've written and lectured to diverse audiences like the Department of Defense, AT&T and the Cremation Association.

I have been privileged to be on the speaking platform with some of the greatest motivators and educators of our time. I have addressed an audience in some of the strangest venues imaginable, including a truck garage, an airplane hanger and the workout room of a local housing project.

I have learned how to pilot a plane, fly a hot air balloon and a glider. I am a Certified Underwater Photographer and have logged hundreds of dives. I shoot clay pigeons and empty cans—though I have never been hunting or killed an animal.

I have been a conduit for electrifying shifts and have been electrocuted as I've tried. All of these shifts have taught me valuable lessons. For me it was exciting as well as painful. Either way, it was an AH-HA moment.

As you move through this book, reevaluate and then create your own shifts, perhaps you'll hear yourself saying: "AH-HA!"

In the following chapters, many of you will find AH-HA moments, but they won't be the same for everyone. They may challenge conventional thinking, but all of them have worked for someone. This book will provide a fertile foundation for growth.

As I said, life is about AH-HA moments. It's about getting mad at the situations that you can control and doing something about them.

In 1976, a movie called *NETWORK* introduced us to the concept of being upset with the shifts that were taking place.

Here's what Howard Beale, a newscaster in the movie, told us…

"I'M AS MAD AS HELL AND I'M NOT GOING TO TAKE THIS ANYMORE!!!"

"I don't have to tell you things are bad.

Everybody knows things are bad.

It's a depression.

Everybody's out of work or scared of losing their job."

> **"I'M AS MAD AS HELL AND I'M NOT GOING TO TAKE THIS ANYMORE!!!"**

Six Principles of Conversion and Sales

A successful sales funnel is about building connections across different sites of learning. Everyone is a Suspect. Suspects become Prospects when they express interest. Leads become Customers with one purchase. Customers become clients with multiple purchases.

AWARENESS

In a crowded, commoditized industry like most of us, it's important to differentiate yourself. Messaging should consistently point to the value you offer your suspects so they ask for more information. It's an academic exercise. Most students don't go to class to learn but to be taught the value proposition of why they need the information.

INTEREST

No one likes to be "sold to" but most like to "buy from." By strengthening a value proposition that does a deep dive into the suspects industry helps you become an expert. Your goals is to get the suspect to become someone that says "I need you."

CONSIDERATION

Take inventory of your vision. Understand where you are, where you want to go, and how to get there. Then use those same criteria for your prospect. Everyone has unique strengths and weaknesses. Show them your wisdom by demonstrating the value of your back-end assistance. Elevate yourself to demonstrate why they need you in their life.

INTENT

Be creative with your messaging. Deliver samples of your wisdom with no charge. Focus on providing enlightening information while at the same time continuing to the network through events, social media, and referrals.

EVALUATION

Be cautious of spending before you have secured 'buy-in' from your suspect. Owners don't spend money on things or services before they see how it positively impacts their business. The secret to sealing the first order is staying ahead of prospect expectations. Grow without over-promising. Demonstrate their ROI-Return on your Ideas.

PURCHASE

The first sale is like the first date. Put the client's needs first. Don't take your sale for granted. It's really a test to see how you perform. Under-promise and over-deliver. Create customer insistence. You want them to think: I really need you in my life.

For those of you that are time constrained

Current Situation	Shift Happens
What is the Shift Happens!® Process?	Infographic p. 8
Can you give me some immediate "shifts" I can apply to accelerate my success?	Infographic p. 26
How do you break down a problem?	p. 37-38, Infographic p. 51
3D Thinking: A railroad car filled with 33,000 gallons of spaghetti sauce. Now What?	What was I thinking? p. 42
What is 3D Thinking?	Infographic p. 48
Do you have any immediate tips to grow my business while I drink my coffee?	Infographic p. 52
Can you suggest some qualifying questions to I can focus on decision makers?	Infographic p. 60, 61–63
What is the Circle of Clarity? Can you help me distinguish branding from marketing?	Illustration p. 67
How do I create long-term Customer relationships?	Infographic p. 76
What are some of the issues I should consider to deliver high value to my Customers?	Infographic p. 82
How do I instill 3D Thinking?	3D Thinking Chapter p. 89
I need some thought starters for "shifts" in hospitality and travel.	pp. 121–124
How do I differentiate myself or business?	Infographic p. 174
I need some tools and tips right now.	Infographic p. 190
Tell me about the Seven Forces of Success.	Infographic pp. 250–251
What are some productivity tools for working remotely?	Infographics pp. 262, 268–272
Can you give me some presentation tips?	Infographic pp. 266–267
How do I overcome objections?	Infographic p. 282
I think I need coaching. Do you have a timeline that can help me manage my expectations?	Hardcover book purchasers receive complimentary one-on-one coaching.

Author's 2020 Vision

Shift Happens!® to all of us. This book is written as a kick-start, a mind-stretcher, a sweaty palm and high colonic for your business and personal life. It is not for the faint of heart or those who won't step out of their comfort zone or get off of their pity porches.

It's time to partner with the world of tomorrow and co-create a shift in the universe. I am dedicated to bringing a different perspective to your world. When the Shift Happens term evolved out of S—t Happens, I saw the potential and got the registered trademark.

Everyone needs to think beyond what has happened and use it to create new opportunities or direction. This requires you to participate. It would be best if you were the conduit of change in your own life, but I'll help you down that path.

In 2020, over 40 million Americans lost their jobs. Are you one of them? If you still have your job, the chances are that could shift at anytime. Statistics show that a majority of workers between the ages of 18 and 38 change jobs an average of 10 times. And finding another job in your current career field after 50 is becoming more difficult in today's economy. If you fall into any of these categories, this book is for you.

Perhaps you are now asking yourself, "Why should I listen to Jim? What does he know that is of value to me? I need help right now."

First of all, remember: We are all creatures of habit.

Shifts are changes.

Some shift is right.

Some shift is difficult.

Shift exists and we can't always control the amount of shift we have to encounter.

It's time to find your shift's compass, and then create a roadmap to guide you where you need to be to stabilize your future.

> *"If you don't like something change it; If you can't change it, change the way you think about it."*
> —**Mary Engelbreit, graphic artist and children's book illustrator**

Much of our life is dedicated to the improvement of reliable pathways and habits that will operate predictably to produce the outcomes we seek.

Second, most of us are careful about rocking the boat; as a result, we lose momentum. The problem is that if you don't evaluate and then re-chart your course, you will continue to go nowhere.

Here are some typical reasons we don't control our own shift:
- 💡 We exist in our comfort zone.
- 💡 We think we know what we are doing.
- 💡 We believe the rules are clear.
- 💡 We believe our expectations can remain silent.
- 💡 We don't build upon what has worked in the past.
- 💡 We believe the secrets of others' success are public knowledge, so they must not apply to our situation.

- We think we don't need a role model, shaman or tribal leader.
- No one understands our troubles or cares.
- We ignore premonitions and signals or create our own implications of what will happen if we take control of our shifts.
- Many of us believe that our future has been decided.
- We may have no job.
- We may have little or no money.
- And the future looks bleak.

> *"Obstacles are those frightful things you see when you take your eyes off your goals."*
> **—Author Unknown**

We have to make decisions about how Shift Happens and what we can do about it. Either let shifts take you down or ramp you up.

- Today, don't restrict your possibilities to discover new opportunities. Don't let your strengths become weaknesses.
- Take more risks.
- Failure is the second cousin to success. Learn from it.
- Make more mistakes, and then learn from them.

This book lays the infrastructure for rebuilding your life and achieving your potential because *your future is brighter than ever.*

> **Your future is brighter than ever before**

Fellow speaker and consultant Brian Tracy is one of the best business authors and speakers in the world. He recently said that *"... every 24 seconds someone else becomes a millionaire in the United States. Even in the midst of one of the worst recessions ever, this number grew by 16% to 7.8 million millionaires in 2009." I estimate that amount will be doubled by 2021.

So why are **YOU** not one of them? *"By altering your habits and replacing worn-out, ineffective practices with optimal behaviors, you'll notice dramatic, immediate benefits. Change Your Habits. . . . Change Your Life!"* says Brian.

What I have found is that most self-made millionaires are people with average education (even high school or college dropouts), average intelligence, and for the most part, are as ordinary as you and me. They weren't born with money and didn't inherit any, but they saw opportunity and seized it. They were committed to taking control of their lives. Like Babe Ruth, the king of home runs, they each "swing for the fences." However, it's helpful to realize that Babe Ruth was also the strikeout king the same year he became home run king. You can't expect every idea out to be a hit. So keep on swinging because you never know when you may have the next great business concept and "hit it out of the park."

Before we start on our journey, here are some of the ways you know our lives have shifted in the last several years:

- You haven't played solitaire with real cards in years—if ever!
- You text the person who works at the desk next to you.
- You pull into your own driveway and call to see if anyone is home to help you carry in the groceries.
- Leaving the house without your cell phone is now a cause for panic and you turn around to go and get it.
- You get up in the morning and go online before making your coffee.
- You start tilting your head sideways to smile. :)

- 💡 You have to text your children to tell them dinner is ready. They text you back asking what you are serving.
- 💡 You spend more time and money on your pets than your teenagers . . . and the pets are more grateful.
- 💡 You have so many remotes for your media center, TV, DVD, etc., you actually get up to change channels.
- 💡 You remember life before minivans and SUVs.
- 💡 Androids are now a reality instead of a fantasy in Star Wars.
- 💡 Your iPad now controls your lights, TV, radio, movies and music.
- 💡 You thought Sears, RadioShack, JC Penny, Hertz, J.Crew, Dean & DeLuca, Frontier Communications, and Avianca airlines were too big to fail.

Now that we have shared a few laughs, let's start the journey that will shift your life. No one can do it for you. It is up to you to step out of your comfort zone and embrace the shifts around you.

You have to say to yourself, *"I am not going to take it anymore and I am going to do something about it."*

Get going . . . now!

> *"No problem can be solved from the same perspective that created it."*
> **Albert Einstein**

> Most self-made millionaires are people with average education

I don't worry about dying; I worry about how I *live* before I die.

According to Jim

Shift is good, because we:

- 💡 Get rid of our Standard Operating Procedures (S.O.P.)
- 💡 Read a new compass
- 💡 Rely on the wisdom of others
- 💡 Re-evaluate our strengths and weaknesses
- 💡 Raise our standards
- 💡 Shift our thinking to become more innovative

One-On-One Coaching Registration
(Proof of hard cover book purchase will be required)

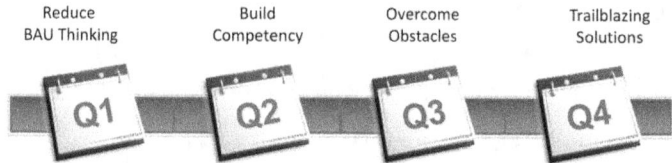

| Reduce BAU Thinking | Build Competency | Overcome Obstacles | Trailblazing Solutions |
| Q1 | Q2 | Q3 | Q4 |

Reinvent Yourself
Our team will support your efforts to create and sustain your 3D Thinking™ with our One-On-One complimentary coaching.

jfa.tips/BookRegistration

Shift
Happened

7 STEPS TO ACHIEVE YOUR GOALS
When Shift Happens!

1. IDENTIFY A PROBLEM
Begin with the end and create the path to reach it. Write it down. List what supports your goal achievement. Be specific. Only one goal. Do not multi-task. Don't create warp speed urgency. Take it slow grasshopper.

2. BRAINSTORM
Build a support group. Look for experts and allies. Meet often. Request their wisdom. Ask for advice. LISTEN...Listen.

3. SET SPECIFIC GOALS
Create clarity and milestones. Challenging yourself to smaller goals with the larger goal in sight increase your chances of achieving your results.

4. DON'T PROCRASTINATE
Write clear, prioritized to-be lists. Focus on one goal at a time. Include time allocations, deadlines, and benefits. Record everything. Adjust steps but keep established finish date.

5. TEST & EVALUATE
Daily goals can be 52 minutes of work and 17 minutes of rest. A customized 52/17 Rule could help you to work smarter, not harder. This approach is not just for athletes.

6. MUSIC HELPS FOCUS
Find music that is suitable background for your focus. Try Classical or New Age with out words that can distract you and your focus.

7. SHARE SUCCESS
If you have allies thank them for their support. Continue to request that they remind not to multitask. Multitasking splits focus. Need a reminder? Go back to #1.

www.jfa.tips/Goals

Shift
Your Attitude

Perhaps you have purchased this book because you have…

> No Job?
> No Money?
> And shift has happened to you faster than you planned.

Well, if you keep an affirmative attitude, it's less of a problem.

I know what you are thinking.

> Who is he kidding?
> This is the REAL WORLD.
> I have bills to pay.
> I have a family to feed.
> I need help now, not later.
> I am upset.
> I need answers.

You may be thinking, *"What does Jim know that I need to know in order to take control of my situation?"*

In the past, I bid on and landed a multi-million dollar contract. I had to immediately: add staff, set up a satellite office closer to the client's city, and expand the amount of products and services to provide them with a new toolbox of goodies for their clients. We spent at least two weeks of each month out of town on-site along with countless hours setting up and servicing the client.

Within two years of our contract, the client slashed their spending to levels far below the agreed upon budget. I had to lay off staff and negotiate with our bank as they demanded full repayment of our business loan. Shift Happens! I realized that the business we worked so hard to earn was going to collapse. The company started to hemorrhage.

> *"If you stick to what you know, you sell yourself short."*
> **—Carrie Underwood**

I encouraged my associates to file for unemployment. I cut expenses and went into survival mode. I negotiated with my creditors, sold off personal assets to pay bills and did what ever I could to "survive." I went to work for someone else in order to earn enough to pay rent and other fixed expenses.

You want to talk about shift? I faced over eleven million dollars in debt and had no revenue stream. After struggling and feeling sorry for myself I said, "I am mad as hell and I am not going to take it anymore."

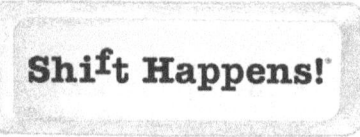

What happened to me is not so different than what may have happened or is currently happening to you—even if you don't own your own business. You may have graduated from school only to find that you have no way to repay student loans, have to move back home with your parents and continually receive rejection letters from dozens of job applications. Even if you have worked enough for unemployment compensation, millions have filed and states are overwhelmed thus delaying benefits. You have no savings and your prospects are not materializing. Shift Happened and we were not prepared!

> Success comes from turning problems into opportunities

Tell yourself that you are not going to take it anymore. Now, I know that this isn't going to change the situation immediately, but at least you're attempting to take control of the shifts that you encounter.

Success comes from turning problems into opportunities. You may only find those AH-HA moments once you get "mad as hell" and stop taking it.

Start shifting your attitude and: Stop whining. No one is listening. All this does is make you weaker. The voice inside your head is reproducing negativity. It spreads like cancer throughout your body, making you more vulnerable. You don't want to get out of bed, you yell at your dog, spouse or children and can't find time to exercise, read or work on Plan A. Stop whining.

Stop complaining and start doing something about it. Write an I OWE ME Promissory Note. Please list what you want, then write down how you will achieve it. Create a plan, a path or a roadmap, whatever you want to call it. It's time to focus on results, not what has happened to you, but what you are going to do about it. Stop complaining.

- Focus is the beginning.
- Focus kicks open the door and unlimited possibilities follow.
- Focus resets everything.
- Focus moves us forward.
- Focus pushes fast forward.
- Focus isn't later. It's now.

> Refocus Your Focus

Ask yourself, right now . . . "What would happen if I refocused my focus? How can I focus on the results and not the effort?"

> Stop Whining.
> Learn from your mistakes; then forget them.

"When it comes to luck, make your own."
—**Bruce Springsteen**

> Start Doing Something.
> Concentrate all your energies on the task.
> Use each moment to maximum productive advantage.

- 💡 Today, say, *"I am mad as hell and I am not going to take it any more."*

- 💡 Today, *I am going to refocus my focus.*

According to Jim

- 💡 Today, *I will create a better tomorrow for myself because there is nothing I can do to change yesterday.*

- 💡 Today, I will write an I OWE ME Promissory Note.

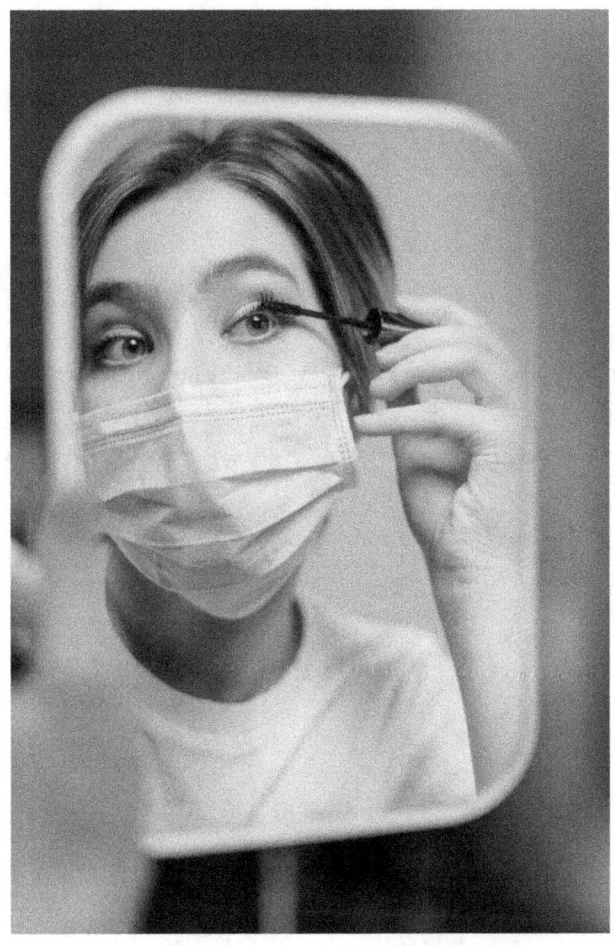

Shift Happens!® Process
Adaptive 'shifts' are methodical and circular.

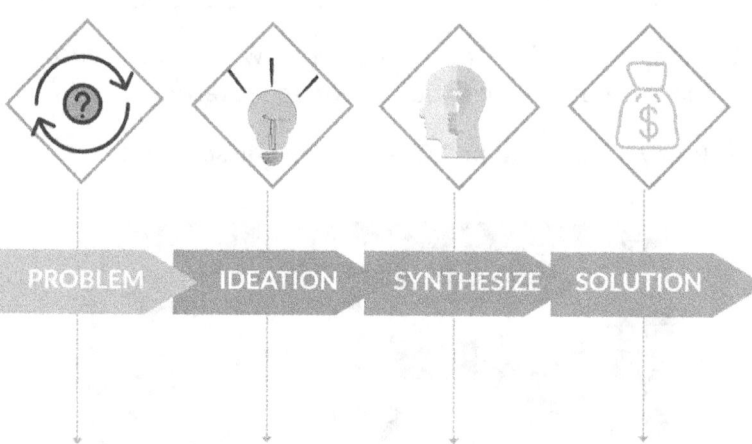

Phase 1 — Customer Need

A well-defined problem will dictate the outcome of your entire project, so you want to ensure that your insight is specific. If you don't define the problem your solution will be ineffective.

Phase 2 — Brainstorming

When someone is able to build upon the idea of someone else, it proves that your exercise is actually inspiring new ways of thinking. Never criticize anyone's idea.

Phase 3 — Small Teams

Collect (100+ ideas): Start with your results from Step 2. Filter (20 ideas): Find the best nuggets! In a smaller team, create clusters. The best ideas serve both you & your customer.

Phase 4 — Implementation

Look deeper than the broadest idea. Find underserved niches of opportunity. Get customer feedback and refinement. It should either make money or save money/time.

Create something that solves a problem for your customers and your solution will have the potential to become viral.

www.jfa.tips/SHProcess

Can You Handle the Shift?

Shift Happens to all of us. At the time I am writing this book there is a grim assessment from the International Monetary Fund (IMF) that the US economy will slide 5.9% this year. Further, the IMF expects the global economy to shrink 3% in 2020—far worse than the 0.1% dip in the Great Recession year of 2009. It forecasts that it'll rebound in 2021 with 5.8% growth.

Let me put this into perspective. The cumulative loss to the global domestic product could reach $9 trillion, more than the GNP of Japan and Germany. Additionally, the IMF projected 7.5% contractions in the European countries that share the euro, 5.2% in Japan, and 6.5% in the United Kingdom. As you review these numbers, I want to point out that the IMG expected China to GROW by 1.2%. What is so amazing is that China was where the pandemic originated. Their growth is due to the fact that China's lockdown was ending earlier than in other countries.

It's time to refocus our focus. We lose our jobs, self-respect, and savings, and the only thing we gain is weight. Shift Happens! Don't stay within the lines that were drawn years ago. Now is the perfect time to pivot. What's stopping you?

What stops most of us is uncertainty. My friend Les Brown, a television personality and motivational speaker, says, *"Leap and *the net will appear!"* Let's set aside uncertainty and start to ask "What If?"

Repeat after me: "It's time to change everything."

Small changes can result in big shifts.

> We are all scared, and fear makes for lousy decisions

> *"Sometimes life is going to hit you in the head with a brick. Don't lose faith."*
> **—Steve Jobs**

Shifts have forced some of the changes, but you have to accept them and not go back to what is "safe." Turn your uncertainty into confidence.

We are in the center of change (shift) and we must accept it. The accumulation of your efforts will create success.

It's time to transcend the conflicts and concerns of the past and create a new future by exploring the widest array of ideas, suggestions, goals, etc. in a logical and controlled process.

Think of an airplane pilot. The pilot determines the final destination and then charts the path to get there. Experienced pilots know that there are unforeseeable conditions that may alter their flight plan, so they have alternate routes. Create Plan A, which is the most direct route, then Plan B, which is only implemented when conditions or circumstances shift.

- Develop outcomes
- Categorize opportunities
- Prioritize opportunities
- Evaluate financial possibilities
- Find relevant, reliable and valid data

> First, establish an end goal or result. Then, create the path you will use to get there!

Shift will happen. *Will you be the cause or the effect?*

"Some people want it to happen, some wish it would happen, others make it happen."
—Michael Jordan

Don't create a shift merely to create a shift. Rather, shift to get to a better position in order to seize your future.

Say "yes" to shift and "no" to the status quo. If you say "yes" to everything there is no way you can accomplish anything. Life is about choices. Make a choice that

> Saying "yes" to one thing is saying "no" to another

has ascertainable results. We can only do so much—say "yes" to the most important things first. Saying "yes" to one thing is saying "no" to another.

"That's one small step for man, one giant leap for mankind," Neil Armstrong said when he first walked on the moon. Plan A turned into Plan B for NASA, but they still reached the goal of landing on the moon. Always have a Plan B.

My business life is about figuring out what promotion, advertising, strategic plan or innovative thinking will lead my Customers and their Customers to spending a few more dollars than they did last week, month or year. (To show their importance, I always capitalize "Customers.")

> Always have a Plan B

As I thought about what I do for my clients, I realized that I could apply some of those same principles to my personal and professional life. For me, as well as you, the answer lies in refocusing and repurposing what we do and how we do it.

For years I was critical of the Kardashians. When they first aired they were bit players in a reality TV show and I often wondered, "Who cares?" Today those sisters and their mother are multi-multimillionaires.

Kylie leveraged her beauty and wealth empire to become the youngest billionaire in history. Guess what? I am not laughing anymore. In fact I am admittedly jealous. Individually, each sister is beautiful, and collectively they build a cultural influence that gets meetings with the President, national media coverage, undeniable influence on the lives of young people, and the idolization by business people. They are a force!

As they navigate social and mainstream media, everything from what they wear and where they eat to who they date and who their kids play with, all influence others with a Tweet or Instagram post.

It's reported that a single Tweet by Kylie Jenner wiped out over one billion dollars off the market value of Snapchat: "sooo does anyone else not open Snapchat anymore? Or is it just me... ugh this is so sad." Shift Happens!

It's important to remember that their lifestyles started off same as you and me. Nobody really paid attention, but then Shift Happened. Now we aspire to Keeping Up with the Kardashians. Learn from their success. Leverage social media. Embrace technology. Zig when others Zag.

What can you learn from them? They earn a living by becoming expert marketers. Their success comes from innovative problem-solving, a close family, love, and being risk-takers. Their goals are clear. You want to keep up with them . . . you can't. But you can learn by studying what they did, how they did it, and how they keep ahead of other media-savy wannabes.

> Let that anger spark your inspiration and drive

When you start reading this book, I recommend using a pocket-sized notebook, which I like to call your **"Little Book of Big Ideas."** Use it to write down your AH-HA moments, your action plans, your roadmap, your recipes for your success, etc. Although I prefer you use a notebook, if you do everything electronically, use apps or programs like Evernote to keep track of your thoughts. The important part is recording your ideas, inspirations, and action items—and then follow up on them.

Keep the notebook with you at all times, as you do your phone. It will become well worn from use, well read from implementation and filled with ideas that you turn into solutions. If you write in it every day, it can become your voice, your diary and your story.

When you write in the notebook, ensure that it is followed by an audible,

"AH-HA! I am now in control of my own SHIFT."

It's the first step to identifying and then actualizing your goals.

> *"By recording your dreams and goals on paper, you set in motion the process of becoming the person you most want to be."*
> **—Mark Victor Hansen**

If you want to share your AH-HA moment with me please:
- 💡 Tweet me: @ShiftHappensNow
- 💡 Post on my Facebook: facebook.com/jamesdfeldman
- 💡 Link at LinkedIn: linkedin.com/in/jamesdfeldman
- 💡 Email me: jfeldman@shifthappens.com

The challenge of life is to debunk our misconceptions and address our realities. Shift Happens and we must take control over our lives rather than let our "shifts" take control of us.

According to Jim

Shift Happens!
and I Don't Have to Take It Anymore!

Repeat after me:

"I'M AS MAD AS HELL, AND I'M NOT GOING TO TAKE THIS ANYMORE!!!"

Now open your Little Book of Big Shifts notebook and write:

"My life has value and
I am not going to take this anymore."

There. You have completed the first step by writing an I OWE ME. You've heard of an I.O.U. When you write an I OWE ME, think of it as a promissory note to yourself. You didn't spend a great deal of money in order to identify your problem, but you did spend some time. It should become an obligation as if you entered into a promise to repay a loan.

So let's ask ourselves, "Now that I have identified a problem, what am I going to do differently tomorrow that will generate better results than what I achieved yesterday?"

There are two simple responses:

1. **Stop the notion of just doing something.**

"Stop doing" is not about cost cutting or strategic planning. It's about finding what frustrates, inconveniences, confuses or annoys you and stopping it.

Start Stopping! Today, Stop The Stupid Stuff!® Stop doing things that don't make you happy; things that drag you down and keep you from creating shift. Stop making excuses.

2. **Start creating your own shift.**

I am not going to candy-coat it. This is tougher than Stopping the Stupid Stuff. Facing the challenge of change means that you let go of what you can't control and learn how to solve problems so that you can grow.

Every problem has a solution, even if the solution isn't in plain sight. It's time to inspire your creative thinking. It's time to reach for the highest goal possible.

It's time to radically shift your behavior; specifically, it's time to start thinking differently.

"Your time is limited, so don't waste it living someone else's life. Don't be trapped by dogma—which is living with the results of other people's thinking. Don't let the noise of other's opinions drown out your own inner voice. And most important, have the courage to follow your heart and intuition. They somehow already know what you truly want to become. Everything else is secondary."

—Steve Jobs

Observe children for any period of time and you will discover that children don't know what they don't know. They take things at face value and they know what makes them happy. It's all about them. They recognize what makes them *happy* and they put that at the top of their list.

Act like children.

> **Make yourself happy**

Today, you and I are in the fast lane. We win or we lose faster.

Most of us say to ourselves, "I should have done this or I should have done that." Those are simply excuses. If it were that important, we would have found the time and resources to complete our task. We tell ourselves we "should" when, in fact, we "could."

It's time to stop ***"shoulding"*** all over ourselves and dare to have fun, dare to dream and dare to believe.

"When they give you lined paper . . . turn the paper sideways and write the wrong way."
—**David Ogilvy, Legendary Advertising Executive**

- Stop the Stupid Stuff.
- Reorder your priorities.
- Face reality.
- Act like children.
- Get mad as hell and stop taking it anymore.
- By truly understanding the marketplace of your products and/or services, you transform your approach from mere *products,* which only *you* care about, to valuable products or services that *others* care about.

According to Jim

Shift
—When Less Is Really More

Sometimes, as parents or friends, we become so good at taking care of other people that we forget how to take care of ourselves. Today, shift your thinking. Start to shift what you do, how you do it and what results you can expect. Spend *less* time devoted to others and *less* time worrying about their problems. Today, it's all about *you*.

In a Synovate survey, 25% of the people surveyed said they were glad the world is having an economic crisis because it helped them realize their priorities. Take the time to reset your own priorities. Figure out what is important to you and your future.

It's time to think differently. It's time to shift from what "was" and "is" to what "could be." To see success you have to think differently about your situation. There are lots of ways to make money if you simply read magazines or surf the web for ideas or inspiration.

> Today, it's all about **you**

For instance, a few years ago *Entrepreneur* offered a contest with $25,000 in cash for the "most savvy home office savings tips." Readers voted for their favorite just like on *American Idol*. So how do the contestants win? They get their friends to vote for them. While this may not be fair in the true spirit of competition, no one said life was fair. And for $25,000 you could have hosted a great "thank you" party. Then have a brainstorming game at the party to get other ideas that you could turn into cash.

So even if you are an "army of one" you can still share ideas by connecting to a network of people that you know and trust for their unbiased suggestions and "brainstorming" ideas.

Take Inventory

I always ask myself some basic questions when I consider keeping an associate in my inner circle, getting rid of physical possessions or opening up to new ideas. While those may all sound extremely different, I view all of them as "inventory." I think my head can only hold so much information; just like my warehouse, office or car trunk can only store so much as well.

So, ask yourself:

- What do I want to do with it?
- Why do I want it?
- Is the space it takes up worth the investment?

No matter how much space you have available, it is not unlimited. We must constantly reorder our priorities, evaluate relationships and alter our goals. If not, we stop growing.

What is the worst result that could take place if I:
  a. Keep the "inventory?"
  b. Move it to a less prominent place?
  c. Remove it all together?

Think of your "inventory" as perishable. Determine the likelihood of the worst and best scenarios and then formulate the next best alternative or option. Take a chance and see what happens. Once you've made the decision, stick to it.

My good friend, speaker, author, and great guy, Tim Gard says: "Rid yourself of Psychic Vampires." Psychic Vampires are people who "suck" the life out of your dreams, goals and desires. Rid yourself of such toxic relationships.

> Once you've made the decision, stick to it

For me, that comes in my yearly evaluation of my life. December is not only the month of parties, celebrations, resolutions and planning, but it is the time to ask myself, "What If?" "Why Not?" "What's Next?" "Now What?" COVID-19 had the same effect without the parties.

When my business lost income, I had to focus on survival. Today millions of business owners face the same situation. For me, my overhead was high and my income could not support it. I started to convert my physical inventory to cash. I sold off the rare coins my father had left me. I reduced my wine collection, cut back on travel and entertainment and put myself on a budget. An amazing result was created. I found that I did not miss the coins or wine; I enjoyed the trips I took more because they were more special; and I had less stress on my earning potential. I lost weight because I could not afford to eat out as often.

COVID-19 reminded me that I liked to read and walk the dogs and allowed me the luxury of developing the concepts for this book.

When Shift Happens, try to harness its power by redirecting it, not fighting it. Surfers ride the waves, sailboats are powered by the same wind that could capsize it. Judo and Aikido uses the opponents own movements. Learn how to leverage the shift.

> Tim Gard says: "Rid yourself of Psychic Vampires."

Like many of you, I did everything I could to make money, negotiate with creditors, pay my mortgage and simply tread water. Times were tough for me and I had to do it or drown. There was no choice. The economy kept slipping, and I had to do what was necessary to make ends meet. No matter whom I talked to, everyone had some serious shift going on in his or her lives.

I reviewed what went right, stopped beating myself up when I sold something, and instead realized that my Return on Investment (R.O.I.) (in this case, return on my ideas) was still more than satisfactory. I reached more decisions, made more progress and planned my next steps in greater detail.

In the past, I made money in real estate selling condos in Chicago. I applied for a Florida Real Estate Broker license, wrote articles for real estate agents, created new content for my speaking by focusing on real estate agents, and landed a significant "coaching" agreement. I found a new revenue stream by applying what I learned from my corporate clients and focused on providing education to Real Estate Agents. Another income stream came from becoming a Licensed Managing Real Estate broker and earning overrides from other salespeople selling condominiums.

The world needs talent that is focused on a single-minded goal. What sets one salesperson apart from another is not only the right attitude but also the proper focus.

Assess your skill sets and find opportunities on which you can capitalize. If you can't sell to yourself how can you sell to anyone else?

> Assess your skill sets and find opportunities on which you can capitalize

During COVID-19, I read some new books and learned more apps for my MacBook Air and iPhone. In anticipation, I created more plans for the "next" unexpected shift, and most importantly, I learned what to stop doing, or as I say: "I stopped the stupid stuff."

For me, stopping the stupid stuff was as simple as a very old joke: A man says, "Doctor, it hurts when I twist my wrist." The doctor replies, "Then stop twisting your wrist!" Now that might sound silly, but think about what causes you pain and how you might eliminate it. In many instances, if we stop doing something the pain goes away.

I'm suggesting the notion opposite of doing something. That is, the art of finding and deciding what things to stop doing. Stop the Stupid Stuff means finding out what annoys, frustrates, inconveniences or confuses you or your target audience—and stopping it. It's about learning what not to do and how to stop doing it.

I even put my Stop the Stupid Stuff logo on my iPhone background as a reminder.

Less is really more, so begin by first managing your shift and then prepare yourself for it. Now set **S.M.A.R.T.** goals. What is a S.M.A.R.T. goal?

When setting goals, answer the following questions:
- 💡 Why is this goal important?
- 💡 What do I need to do to reach this goal?
- 💡 What obstacles do I have to overcome?

S = Specific

M = Measurable

A = Attainable

R = Realistic

T = Time Sensitive

Now is the time to grow your business, find a new job, or come up with an idea that generates some additional income.

Take the time to find a school that works for you. Kaplan University encourages their applicants to "see how life experiences may earn you college credits." Kaplan gives credit similar to "continuing education credits" that can be earned by attending seminars, webinars, etc. It is a life experience that adds to college credits. Will other universities add life experience credits? How can you benefit?

If you need financial assistance, go to the Small Business Administration's website sba.gov. There you can view loan programs which are designed to help small businesses refinance existing loans that will lead to job creation within two years.

Banks are continuing to take money from the government and only offer it to "highly qualified" borrowers. In 2020, numerous high-profile (and some publicly traded) companies admitted they received the emergency loans. So many loans were approved that the Treasury stepped in to remind businesses that they should only apply if they are in dire need.

Didn't our government learn from the 2009 bailout that banks need to be held accountable? Isn't it the banks' obligation, when they accept the funding, to help the 30.7 million small businesses (SBA's 2019 Small Business Profile)? Wasn't that the SBA's intention?

In the US, small businesses account for almost 50% of the economy. Yet, small businesses get significantly less funding than big businesses.

Some relationships are toxic and in order to continue to makes ourselves happy, we have to phase some aspects or people out.

According to Jim

- 💡 Don't let others hold you back from being the happiest and most successful person that you can be.
- 💡 Do whatever it takes today to reach tomorrow.
- 💡 Never give up on yourself—you are all you've got.

Wealth is not gained by perfecting the known, but by **seizing the unknown.**

6 Shifts For Success

Shift Happens!®

When I was 7 years old I asked my mother for an allowance. Talk to your father was her reply. Jointly my parents denied my request and I learned LESSON #1. Get all the decision makers in the same room. Instead of an allowance, they suggested a lemonade stand.

Discovering there was lots of competition I created a 'lemonade supply kit' which I sold at night to the parents of my competitors.

Here's are some of my 'shifts' to motivate, influence, and persuade your 'suspects'. Remember your goal is to identify engageable 'prospects' and then deliver solutions so they become Customers. Repeat Customers become CLIENTS.

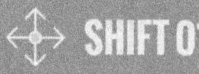
SHIFT 01 — Decide to take action no matter what
Carpe Diem. Seize the day and that's today. Set 'me' time to work on what needs to be done before the day gets rolling. *"The secret of getting ahead is getting started."*

SHIFT 02 — Focus on helping others
Attend live workshops. Join networking groups. Nothing is more effective than a face to face conversation. Your goal is to convert 'suspects' to prospects. Then prospects to Customers. Repeat Customers to CLIENTS.

SHIFT 03 — Send a handwritten note
If you want to break through the clutter send a personal note. Whether it's a thank you or an invitation the written note will get more attention and action.

SHIFT 04 — Take fast action on your ideas
Anything can happen when you take a chance. Failure is the second cousin to success. No one is successful without failures to build upon. *Just do it!* as Nike says.

SHIFT 05 — Get active on social media
Using social helps make it easier to make a personal connection with your followers and fans. You will reach a broader range of people around the globe. It's another way for you to connect with your audience. LinkedIn is #1

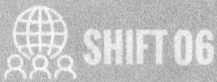
SHIFT 06 — Be honest and trustworthy
We live in an era where people's moral value are under increased scrutiny in a 'shifting' culture of outrage and injury. Honesty. If you can find your moral compass then ask: "What would my mother do or say". Trust is the greatest defense to your selling price erosion.

Everyone Experiences Shifts

Shifts can be enormous—a marriage, new home, baby, new job, divorce, bereavement, etc. Everyone knows that these levels of shift can be very stressful and difficult to manage. Small shifts, which are often underestimated, can have a big impact as well. Things like a new routine to your day, losing or gaining weight, cutting your hair short, changing a room around or not seeing a familiar face any more can affect you for some time.

The pandemic has demonstrated that Shift Happens! It makes no difference whether or not you have chosen the shift, it will still have an impact on you.

> **Point 1: Shift can't be rushed**

Point 1: Imagine deciding on something as small as sleeping without a pillow. At first, it would feel odd and you may not be able to get to sleep. You may wake up in the night with a sense of loss and wonder whether you'd ever get used to it. It might take days, weeks or months before sleeping without a pillow feels normal to you. Eventually, it will. And that's the real point: shift can't be rushed.

> Point 2: It's about the transition from one set of circumstances to another, and that takes time.

Point 2: If you remember that creating value for others is the basis for your success, then you can strategically link your success to what others want or need. Innovation is a discipline that can be accomplished by almost everyone because all it is really about is how to turn an idea into a reality—and everyone has an idea. If you can turn the idea into something people will pay for, then you have an invention. If you can turn an idea into something people want or need, or that saves time, or that saves or makes money, you have an innovation. An invention is a thing; an innovation is a solution or process.

When you think about U.S. universities, most have a long history of education, yet lack innovation. They rely on tuition and graduates to contribute to the maintenance of their campus, but seldom do they innovate the experience or lifestyle of their students. For many of my readers, their college memories may be fresh in their mind. Compare your experience to this shift in traditional learning.

In 1924, High Point University, then High Point College, opened as a cooperative venture between the Methodist Protestant Church and the City of High Point, North Carolina. The campus consisted of three partially completed buildings, there were nine faculty members and student enrollment was 122.

Today, High Point University has undergone a 15-year transformation of campus and culture. HPU has grown from three to nine academic schools and invested $2.1 billion in new facilities and technology, including dozens upon dozens of study abroad opportunities, service learning programs, academic development, student life and experiential learning and programs.

It's a story uncommon in higher education. But it's believable at High Point University, where, in a short amount of time, the campus has quadrupled in size, undergraduate enrollment has tripled, and a $250 million Innovation Corridor flowing with STEM opportunities was completed in fall 2019.

And just recently, HPU President Nido Qubein announced another $1 billion growth plan to lead HPU into the next decade. The growth plan includes another 10-year commitment from Qubein to serve as president and $700 million in scholarships. It also added $300 million in construction, including a new library, academic building, and admissions center. A Town and Gown Think Tank of local leaders committed to ensuring that the city of High Point and HPU continue to thrive together will also be built.

So how did this entire shift take place?

> Consumers don't care about your product; they care about what the product can do for them.

HPU recruited Dr. Qubein, chairman of an international consulting firm and member of the executive committee of BB&T (a Fortune 500 financial corporation with $130 billion in assets and 30,000 employees), to become the President of HPU in 2005. HPU needed distinction to compete with other liberal arts universities and Dr. Qubein was tasked with creating that distinction.

> Reduce the pain and people will pay for it

For Dr. Qubein, the decision was not simple. Becoming involved with HPU would change his life, but the shifts he could create would impact thousands of lives and leave a lasting legacy. Under Dr. Qubein's direction, HPU has undergone a dramatic renovation and revitilization program.

After interviewing students, parents and faculty members and visiting other colleges and universities, Dr. Qubein developed a mission for HPU. He wanted every student to receive an extraordinary education in an inspiring environment with caring people.

And that's how Shift Happened!

Before you try to create a solution, you must first understand the market problems you are trying to solve. Consumers don't care about your product; they care about what the product can do for them, and how your product or service makes them feel. Dr. Qubein did his homework; he conducted research and found that their market advantage could be the college experience. He then created a shift in the thinking of what a university could offer to meet that need. Changing the traditional thinking of an organization that is nearly 100 years old is a difficult challenge. Compared to what HPU had to accomplish, your undertaking should be somewhat easier.

What can you learn from the HPU success? If you think about the problem as a source of pain, then what you want to create is the pain reliever, or even better, the pain eliminator. Reduce the pain and people will pay for it.

Students at HPU had previously complained about the academics, student life programs and facilities. Now, U.S. News & World Report's "America's Best Colleges" 2020 edition ranks HPU

#1 among all regional colleges in the South (the eighth consecutive year at #1). And for the fifth consecutive year, the national list also ranks HPU as the #1 Most Innovative Regional College in the South.

> *"Each of us has the freedom to choose how we will respond to the circumstances in which we find ourselves."*
>
> **Nido Qubein**

HPU is also recognized in Princeton Review's "The Best 385 Colleges: 2020 Edition" for its academic programming, as well as positive survey responses and feedback from students, parents, and higher education leaders across the country. And, data collected by HPU, in accordance with the National Association of Colleges and Employers (NACE) standards, shows 97% of the Class of 2019 launched their careers or continued their education within six months of graduation, 11 points above the national average.

Today, global leaders are attracted to HPU's culture, which fostered Apple Co-Founder Steve Wozniak, HPU's Innovator in Residence; Netflix Co-Founder Marc Randolph, HPU's Entrepreneur in Residence; and Scott McKain and Mark Sanborn, best-selling authors.

This success has helped to increase enrollment, tuition fees and donations.

Seth Godin, one of the most brilliant business writers of this century, writes in his book, *Purple Cow*, "you're either a Purple Cow or you're not. You're either remarkable or invisible. Make your choice." You need to be remarkable to be memorable. Today, it's more important than ever.

> **See a need and fill a need**

Want to be remarkable and make a lot of money? Discover a consumer need, and then address and *solve* that need. See a need and fill a need.

So, today, start to write down some ideas. Target your idea to a market and you are almost there! As you progress, consider these shifts that will take place. Don't be afraid of them—accept them.

What will happen when you make the commitment to create your own shifts?

1. **Expect a Shift in your emotions.** People criticize themselves for crying, laughing or feeling moody and often say: "I don't know why it's affected me so much." Emotions are normal in the face of shift—any shift. Don't beat yourself up. Let it go.

2. **Shift your thinking first.** Shift, no matter how good it is, means loss. When something in your life shifts, you give up the old way of being or the old set of circumstances. And loss means hurt, sorrow and nostalgia. Remember, saying "yes" to something means saying "no" to something else. Instead of thinking outside the box, try thinking inside the box—shift how you approach the problem and you will often find it easier to come up with the right solution. Maybe you are working on the solution to the wrong problem. Shift your approach and you can determine the *real* issue.

3. **Shifts will keep coming.** Think of yourself in the ocean. As the waves hit the boat, you can either turn against the waves and they'll crush you, or you go with them and they'll carry you to shore. In life, if you resist shift, it will be a lot more problematic and laborious to accept. The secret to shift is to be flexible so that you can utilize it more easily. Let the shift carry you to safety.

4. **Hang onto the recognizable Shifts.** All of us resist shift if we are not the one creating it. To accept shift, keep up with as many familiar things as you can—and remind yourself how much in your life isn't changing. Stick to your usual routines and reassure yourself that not everything has to shift just because some things have.

5. **Everyone has Shift Happening.** Don't keep your feelings to yourself or try to deal with shift alone. Talk about it; get a hug, a laugh, a cup of tea and a bit of reassurance. Find the courage to ask for help. Remember: being courageous doesn't always mean managing alone.

6. **Break up your Shifts.** When possible, divide bigger shifts into smaller shifts. When you feel overwhelmed by the enormity of the shift, concentrate on the progress you've made, rather than the bigger picture. For instance, moving, starting a new relationship, learning a new skill or planning a party all involve progressive steps. You don't plan a whole party at one time. You break it into manageable parts: food, theme, décor, event space, invitations, entertainment, etc.

7. **Find the benefit in Shift.** Some shifts feel awful—loss of job, divorce, death, serious illness, financial loss and other shifts can feel like the end of the world. Sometimes you have to look very hard to find the benefits in such shifts, but there always is one. It is through shift that we grow wiser and stronger and learn to make better decisions. Shift Happens to all of us. The only question is: how do we handle it?

8. **Know that all Shifts will end at some point.** All shifts come to an end when the new circumstances are in place and become familiar to you. No matter how big, shift will end and you'll return to a feeling of normality. Keep that in mind when you feel as though you're in the middle of an ocean

with shift hitting you from all directions. Remember: if you let them . . . the waves will carry you to shore.

> Shift your approach and you can determine the **real** issue

- 💡 Expect emotional shifts
- 💡 Shift your thinking
- 💡 Shifts will keep coming
- 💡 Hang onto the shifts
- 💡 Find the benefit in shift
- 💡 Know that all shifts will end

According to Jim

Stop telling your BIG DREAM to small-minded people.

Aha

Shift Happens
When You Train Your Brain

This pandemic forced us to look at the world differently. Let's face it, often times, we view shift as a crisis. What do the world's best leaders do in the face of crisis situations? They remain calm, gather information and resources, come up with a plan, execute that plan and then evaluate its success or failure—making any necessary shifts in the process.

You have to give yourself a moment to understand the shift, accept it, and then think about how you are going to use that shift to grow. Now you must find an opportunity, a silver lining and a learning experience in your shift.

Geinrich Altshuller, a Russian Engineer, developed a theory that creative solutions to different problems have similar characteristics. He discovered that most creative solutions are similar to the most conventional or uncreative solutions. Most ideas describe solutions that do not introduce any new kind of components into the problem.

From my standpoint, I have found that going *"inside the box"* helps me to break up the elements of the problem.

> The value of any solution is in its implementation.

"Going inside the box" means deconstructing the problem into several components, and then reorganizing those components to find a simple solution. You may have to redefine the problem to find the solution. I often find that the solution is simply reordering the components. And *that* can lead you to creative solutions. This could save time, make money, and find new opportunities to use existing resources.

Think for a minute about how some inventions changed the way we live and then extended their impact to other parts of our lives. For example, the electric screwdriver was invented to permit the torque of a small motor to rotate a screw. When it was created, it served one purpose. Then, someone recognized how the handheld motor could be used to rotate other tools such as a saw, grinder, wire brush, etc. That same concept was moved to the kitchen and Cuisinart was born.

> I often find that the solution is simply reordering the components

A creative solution has common elements. If you train your brain to recognize those elements, you can use them to deal with not only your personal problems, but you can also apply that same process to create something better, faster, smarter, or more efficient. You need to develop a way that works for you to generate ideas and connections. How? Focus.

To truly focus on creativity, you must:
- 💡 Use your imagination and ask "What If?"
- 💡 Liberate your mind.
- 💡 Free yourself of the self-limiting thoughts.

💡 Don't skimp on research. The Internet is free information.

Another example of using resources is to find a free Wi-Fi connection at a coffee shop. Look around the coffee shop and you will see others doing the same thing. Walk up to someone and start a conversation. Why not? They must have time to spend in a coffee shop surfing the net, which may mean that they are looking for a job, same as you. Compare networks and become Facebook friends and LinkedIn associates.

It's time to create your own mastermind group. It's about creating your own opportunities; not finding the ones that are already being exploited by others. Napoleon Hill, one of the earliest personal success authors, defined mastermind groups as a "coordination of knowledge and effort in a spirit of harmony between two or more people for the attainment of a definite purpose." *Think and Grow Rich* is a classic book on personal achievement and should be read if you are really committed to changing your current situation.

Free yourself from the constraints of what you used to do and focus on what you need to do. Create many mastermind groups. The result of this kind of teamwork is amazing.

You may find a tennis partner, a yoga coach, a biking advocate or even a person with a relevant contact for your job search. There is a spirit of harmony that gets created when you are sipping tea or coffee and developing "talking points."

As you look at a problem, let's attempt to break it down. You have probably heard of the Who, What, Where, When and

> It's time to create your own mastermind group

Why of assessing a problem, but let me take a minute to remind you of the principle. The concept I am proposing is that we often start to work on a solution when we have not fully explored the five W's of the problem. If we don't identify the problem correctly we will be working on the solution to the wrong problem.

- Who caused the problem?
- Who says that the situation is really a problem?
- Who is influenced by this problem?
- What will happen if the problem is not solved?
- What are the components of the problem?
- What else will be impacted by the problem going unresolved?
- Where does this problem occur?
- Where does the problem have an impact?
- When did this problem take place?
- When did it start?
- Why do you think this problem is happening?

I have read dozens of books on creativity, thought processes, successes and innovative problem-solving. After many years, I have distilled the volumes to a more implementable process, which I have named **3D Thinking.**

3D Thinking has three dimensions or "D"s:

D = Depth of your knowledge. Go inside the box and break the problem up into pieces. Train your brain to see all of the elements and move them around. Often, the solution is found in the shadows.

D = Distance to market. Is there a market for your solution? Does it reduce or eliminate "pain?" Pain is what keeps people up at night, makes them worry. Rogaine claimed to help reverse or cure hair loss. Yet, Rogaine or Minoxidil, had little effect on receding hairlines. It did not cure baldness; most new hair was lost within a few months after the drug was stopped. Does your product go the distance? It could have been a multibillion-dollar product but failed to deliver.

On the other hand, Viagra has become a multibillion-dollar success because it works, is easy to use, has few side effects and has gained attention from the media, comics and satisfied users. Viagra, in essence, provided the "cure" and went the distance. How far can you take the solution? Can it go the distance? The problem wasn't talked about until the "cure" was readily available. Shift Happened and Pfizer now has a product with over a billion dollars in sales.

D = Determination to succeed. Most people start with great intentions. They have an idea or plan, do some work on it and then talk to others. Often the idea is "shot down" or your friends convince you that you can't accomplish your dream. Once you clarify the problem, discern the marketplace and the opportunity, set your priorities and go for it. You can't learn without being in the center of gravity, which is where the Customer is. Now you can determine what works and what doesn't. Focus on your goals by writing them down, consider the potential obstacles and develop real solutions for which a client will pay.

> **D** = Depth of Your Knowledge
>
> **D** = Distance to Market
>
> **D** = Determination to Succeed

My solutions must meet certain criteria:

- Did it solve the problem completely?
- Did it require limited resources?
- Did it produce any negative effects?
- Is it a solution that others won't discover on their own?
- Does it reduce a source of pain?
- Is it a solution that others will pay for?
- Is there a way to combine several solutions to produce better solutions?

Shifts in thinking are often simple—yet quite complex. Start by spending more time on asking the right questions rather that working on the right solutions to the wrong problems. In life, shifts are the only constant. Shifting your world begins with shifting how you think.

It's not about price. It's about the problem that you solve for others. People will pay for results if you really deliver. To overcome the roadblocks to your success you have to go from failure to failure without any loss of your determination.

One of the questions I have pondered for years is why hot dogs are sold in eight packs and hot dog buns sold by the dozen? After decades of coexistence, why can't the meat packers and bakers agree on a one-bun to one-hot dog ratio? Wouldn't it be remarkable if you didn't end up with extra buns? The only time the two match up is when you purchase three packages of hot dogs (24) and two packages of buns (24). Why can't they get together and "train their brains" to solve this problem? The hot dog maker could sell more hot dogs and two companies could join forces in a marketing campaign or in-store promotions. Not to mention it would reduce packaging and food waste.

Here are some examples relating to "Training Your Brain." Pay attention to the steps that the following people took:

Jennifer K. coached 18–22 year old college women's athletics. As you can imagine, sometimes emotions at that age run high and maturity is contingent on the individual versus the demographic. Over the years, she worked with a diverse group of women. One of the most important skills she taught had nothing to do with their sport, but everything to do with their approach.

> To overcome the roadblocks to your success you have to go from failure to failure without any loss of your determination

Jennifer often had girls running into her office in tears over a situation. What is the first thing that this coach would do in these instances? She did not jump to any conclusions—she kept her cool. She told her athlete to "Sit down," and then she got up, closed the door and asked, "Is everyone okay? Are you hurt? Is anyone hurt?" Why did she ask those questions? She wanted to remind her athletes of just that. As long as everyone is "okay," we can start to learn about and address the issue.

More often than not, the situation was about a grade, a boy, a roommate or a teammate issue—nothing life-threatening. So why did these girls burst into her office in tears? Because they did not yet understand how to take control of their emotions and "Train their Brain." Jennifer taught her athletes to look at the big picture: you—and the people you care about—are safe and healthy, there will be tomorrow and any issue that you are dealing with can be addressed. When they immediately reacted to situations, they had no way of holding on to reality and devising a plan to use to help them through the problem. However, once they were able to control their emotions, they were much better equipped to solve the issues. Nonetheless, when we let our emotions take control, we lose sight of those plans as well as the ability to implement them.

Understanding how to maintain your composure and essentially "Train Your Brain" is a life skill that this coach exemplified to her athletes—and that is the most important skill that they learned from her.

My Own Personal 3D Thinking

One of my law school associates was a part-time insurance claim adjuster. One Wednesday afternoon, he asked if I wanted to go with him to view a railroad boxcar that had been "found" on a sidetrack at the Atchison, Topeka and Santa Fe Railroad yard.

He explained that the railroad boxcar had been declared "lost" and the insurance company paid the claim to American Home Products. His assignment was to recover money for the sale of the "found" product. We went to the railroad yard, cut the lock off the door and found a railroad car full of Chef Boyardee pasta sauce in #10 institutional cans.

Imagine a storage container 60' long, 14' feet high and 4 ½' wide filled with pasta sauce. The first question I asked myself was, "how can I make money from this stuff?"

It's a lot of pasta sauce, but the price had to be worth the risk. I asked my friend what price would permit an immediate sale. $5000 was his instant reply. SOLD!

Now that I had made the offer I needed to come up with a way to pay for it, right? So I called my bank and told them what I wanted to do. They immediately bombarded me with questions like:

"Have you lost your mind?"

"What do you know about surplus food products?"

"What are you going to do with it?"

At the time I owned several cameras and other photographic equipment. I offered to pledge the equipment to secure the loan. The bank agreed only if I brought over the equipment to hold for collateral. The bank gave me $5000 for 60 days.

I paid for the boxcar late Thursday afternoon. Now what to do? Friday morning, my day started with a call from the railroad foreman for the Atchison, Topeka and Santa Fe Railroad.

"Are you James Feldman?" he asked. "Did you purchase railroad box car MDW1967?"

> "Yes!" I said proudly.
> "Move it!" he replied.

To be perfectly candid, the thought of moving the railroad boxcar had never occurred to me.

I told my story and apparently the foreman had the same reaction as my bank, "Are you crazy?"

I quickly learned that you need a permit, a locomotive, an engineer, a caboose, a conductor and easement rights to move the car across the various railroad lines.

Just like the bank, he was in disbelief. I am sure he thought I had lost my mind and needed serious help. After my formal pleading he agreed to delay the paperwork over the weekend because he was going out of town and wouldn't return to work until Wednesday afternoon.

So now . . . I asked myself, "What am I going to do with thousands of gallons of pasta sauce?"

Take the 3D Thinking principles and think about what you would do in the same situation. What is your 3D Thinking plan?

What would you do with a railroad boxcar filled with pasta sauce? After discarding the traditional thinking about trying to find a Customer that could use the sauce I started to make inquiries to my law study group. After all, these were bright people that were being trained to use the Socratic method of problem-solving. It should come as no surprise to you that they did not come up with a solution that was any different than mine. After all we all applied the same logic to the problem-solving.

It was very late Sunday evening. I knew that I had to come up a way to get that railroad boxcar off the tracks at someone else's expense. Who would want that amount of sauce . . . and a railroad boxcar?

Play the "what if" game with me. Stop and write down what you would do. Apply 3D Thinking.

Ask yourself, what happens when you go deep into the problem? What questions can you ask? We know the boxcar is going somewhere. What was its destination? Who was the ultimate consumer?

> **Before you read further, consider what you would do if you had just spent $5,000 which you did not have, to purchase something you did not need, in a railroad boxcar that you could not move. And you think you have problems?**

Got an answer? Are you 3D Thinking?

Here's a hint, the answer is in *the story*.

So maybe you have figured out the solution already, but let's see how I used existing components to solve the railcar full of pasta sauce problem.

If I wanted to repurpose the pasta sauce, I really needed to examine the distribution chain. I knew what it was and who made it, but didn't know where it was going. Now it was just about finding the right people.

As I examined the possible "consumers," I realized that military bases, prisons, and universities were potential users. I found a large military base and contacted them. Unfortunately, without a GSA number (General Services Administration), I couldn't sell to them. A GSA number is issued through the lengthy process of getting a GSA contract. GSA contract award usually takes between 6–8 months after the offer is submitted. Clearly I did not have the time to get a GSA number. And by the way, GSA numbers are also needed for prisons and most state-run universities.

Once I applied 3D Thinking and tracked from the manufacturer to the end user I realized I was working in the wrong direction. I had begun by searching for the end-user or consumer and instead realized that if I could sell it back to the manufacturer for less than it costs them to produce it, then both my Customer and I would win. In addition, if the manufacturer could sell it to one of their local Customers they would also save on freight and production.

I called the pasta sauce company's purchasing department to find out the cost of production of the #10 institutional sized cans of sauce. I was told that the information was confidential. I thought to myself what could be so secret? How can I find out what the product was worth if I didn't know what it cost to make? Let me remind you, I could find out the wholesale cost to the distributor or the consumer because there were printed price lists, but what I really wanted was *manufactured* cost, so I could approach purchasing with a deal they could not refuse.

I phoned the headquarters and asked to speak to the product manager. A cheerful voice informed me that the product manager was unavailable but she would try to assist me. I told her I was a student (which was true) and I was doing some research on the cost of commodities from the manufacturer to the distributor to the consumer (which was also true). She asked why I needed this information and I told her it was a school project (sort of true). In a few minutes she gave me what I needed . . . manufactured cost.

Armed with the cost information, I then contacted purchasing and said that I had a boxcar full of their pasta sauce. I gave them the product code number and expiration date. Within a few hours the company made me a very low offer (from their perspective) and I accepted a fabulous profit (from my perspective).

In less than a week I made over 10 times my real investment. (To learn more about how I made over 10x my ROI, drop me a note at jfeldman@shifthappens.com.) I did so well I paid my friend, the insurance claims adjuster, $5,000 and asked him to take me back to the railroad yard next time he had to "salvage" another railroad boxcar, which he did. I also paid $5,000 to the foreman of the railroad yard to ensure that he gave me a little extra time to move my "stuff." And that's how I got into buying and selling railroad cars of "stuff." Over the next year I purchased three more railroad boxcars and made more money than most first year lawyers.

> Ask the right questions to get the right answers

Only risk what you can afford to lose and only take the risk if you double your money or more.

According to Jim

- 💡 Learn to let go of the things that are out of your control. You will endure significantly less stress that way.

- 💡 If you approach a situation with a clear and open mind, then the results you yield will be far greater than if your mind is consumed with worry.

- 💡 You control your emotions/reactions/outlook.

- 💡 Sometimes you have to take on a high-risk project to get high rewards.

3D Thinking™ "Inside The Box"
Depth • Distance • Determination

7 Insights to manage INNOVATION & TRANSFORMATION Shifts

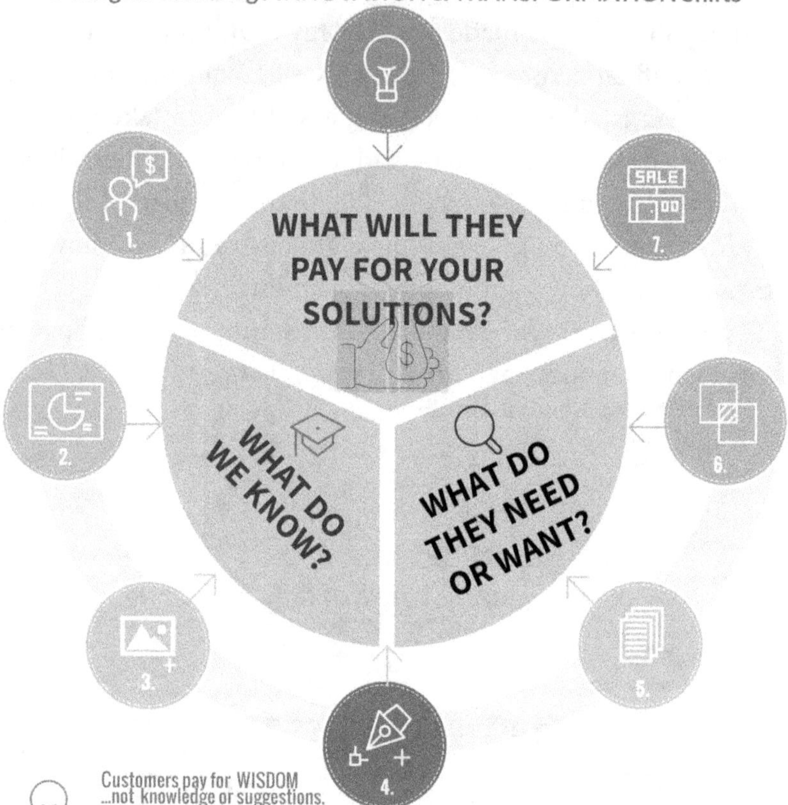

WHAT WILL THEY PAY FOR YOUR SOLUTIONS?
WHAT DO WE KNOW?
WHAT DO THEY NEED OR WANT?

Customers pay for WISDOM ...not knowledge or suggestions.
If your solutions have no monetary value to your Customer then you have not solved their problem and failed to create a value proposition.
Always address the WIIFM*

1. Research & Plan
Dive 'inside' the box to discover the components that make up the problem. Synthesize insight and wisdom.
Beware of Distractions disguised as Opportunities.

7. Develop, Test & Market
Putting your ideas into actions with successful results will help create the value proposition and set the price.
It's not about price, but value.

6. Usability & Layout
Keep your ideas focused and on target. Become a catalyst for innovation and teach others to understand 'shifts'.
It's not what you think, but how you think.

5. New Ideas Come From Old Ones
We learn from our failures. We can't discover the right solutions unless we are working on the real problem.
If nothing changes, nothing changes.

4. Better Tools and Techniques
Uncover relationships 'inside the box.' Move around the components. Add-Subtract-Multiply-Divide for new results. *Rearrange the components to obtain possible solutions.*

3. Become More Persuasive
Great ideas poorly presented will fail in comparison to great presentations with less worthy ideas. Be less informative, more persuasive. *It's not creative if it does not sell.*

2. Marketing & Blogging
Not only write your own but follow others to discover new opportunities. *Never stop learning and sharing your R.O.I***

---

www.jfa.tips/InsideTheBox

Start Your Shifts Today

Want to know how to make this the best year ever? Then repeat after me: "I am mad and I am not going to take it any more." Starting today, instead of simply writing down my goals in the future, I am going to write them in the past, as if I have accomplished them already.

For example, say:

I lost fifty pounds. Not—I'm going to lose the weight.

I reduced my cholesterol to an acceptable level. Not—I'm going to get healthy.

I exercised five times a week. Not—I'm going to exercise.

I am enjoying the way I earn money instead of dreading going to work at a job I did not like. Not—I'm going to find a new job or career.

I increased my take home pay 25% this year. Not—I'm going to make more money.

Make it specific. See a need. Fill a need. Be a problem-solver.

Stop saying I should've done this or should've done that. **Stop Shoulding and Start Doing.** Stop the Stupid Stuff and start to be more innovative in every thing you do. Quit wasting your time on projects, objectives and goals you can't complete. Make a list of accomplishments for this year and make a commitment to achieve them. Take small steps. Don't try to lose 50 pounds all at once. Lose five pounds, and then lose another five pounds. Take small steps to make big leaps. Watch a shot putter or broad jumper. They run in circles or make small skips and jumps before the big push.

Instead of making resolutions, write yourself an I OWE ME. Pay yourself before you pay others.

> **Stop Shoulding and Start Doing**

To be successful, you have to think differently. You have to have a plan. Like a coach with a game plan, you may be forced to shift your thinking as the game progresses. Always have a Plan B. Do the same for your life. If you put on a pound or two, don't beat yourself up, but do commit to lose it right away. Don't let little shifts creep up on you.

Discover some fresh ideas in this book and apply them to your life. Even if only one new idea per chapter captivates your attention, commit to try it out and follow it through to completion.

In a single sentence, determine where you want to go and create the path to get there. Define what you will achieve one year from now and, by that time, even if you fall short, you will still be closer than you are today. You have to create the mindset of a winner. Only you can control what you do . . . no one else. Stop making excuses and start focusing on results.

💡 Determine where you want to go and create the path to get there.

> **Don't let little shifts creep up on you**

 Be specific. Be positive. Create momentum.

- Define what you have achieved one year from now and, by that time, even if you fall short, you will still be closer than you are today.

According to Jim

- You have to create the mindset of a winner.
- Only you can control what you do . . . no one else.
- Stop making excuses and start focusing on results.
- Tell others what you plan to do. This creates a support group.

"Being defeated is often a temporary condition. Giving up is what makes it permanent."
—**Michael Jordan, Basketball Legend**

Disassemble your problem. The components often reveal the solution.

What is your differentiation?
Lowest price is never sustainable. Establish a price/value relationship. If you want transportation a KIA or Hyundai is affordable. If you want status buy a BMW or MB And you pay for the image.

What is the product of your product?
What's in it for them? No one cares about bright shiny stuff. They want solutions!

Are you sustainable?
Are you like Apple that has built a culture of loyal followers? Does your product or service fulfill a need or want that consumers will pay for?

Is your innovative solution relevant?
The speed of opportunity is fleeting. Consumers have many choices. Why do they want to buy from you? Is your solution replicatable by your competitors?

5 Steps To Growing Your Business Over A Cup Of Coffee

TARGET MARKET

Having an identified AND accessible market will make growing your business exponentially easier. It helps to crystalize your message, your product and service offerings and helps you know where you market yourself. FOCUS!

ATTRACT

Going into your target market's community, getting their attention, and attracting them to you. Where does your market hang out? What websites are they visiting, what events are the attending, what social networks are they a part of? Determine where they are and go meet them there - virtually and physically. Then, bring them back to your website by offering them a compelling free gift that has a perceived value and is something they feel they must have. They will exchange their name and email address for that gift so you can continue to communicate and develop a relationship. Become a household name.

NURTURE

Nurture those relationships over time with valuable information that is relevant to their needs. In today's culture, people often need time to get to know you before they will do business with you. You want to keep those who are interested engaged with you so they will consider doing business with you when they have a great enough need.

CONVERT

Make offers that convert your prospects to clients. Strategically plan and promote your products and services, asking your potential clients to hire you or purchase your products. It will take time to brew results.

SERVE

At the end of the day, our success is predicated on our ability to successfully meet a need. *See a need. Fill a need!* Learn from Starbucks. Zappos. Amazon.

SIMPLE IS BEST

www.jfa.tips/BusinessGrowth

Shifts
in Your Personal Life

PITCH STEPS FOR ANY PRESENTATION

01 — Title ATTENTION!
Provide attention getting title. Add in your contact information including email, mobile phone, address, your name & position.

02 — Problem/Opportunity/Pain
Write down the 'pain' you are reducing or eliminating. Think 'inside' the box.

03 — Uncork Value Proposition
Just like enjoying wine. Take your time to engage all the senses to showcase the value you provide.

04 — Smartphone or Land Line
Both allow you to communicate but one has technology, magic, effectiveness. Show your prototype or explain your breakthrough concept.

05 — Bigger Thinking Business Model
Tablets are smartphones on steroids. Leverage your idea on the bigger image to demonstrate your business model? Use high rez images and readable type.

06 — Coffee is a commodity
Explain how your idea will create a competitive differentiation without breaking the bank. Learn from Starbucks, Apple, Rolex, Zappos.

07 — USB Stick
Bring your financial projections and key metrics on a USB instead of printing them. Include your pitch deck, videos, infographics, etc. Brand your USB with your logo, etc. Also a BU of your PowerPoint in JPEG format.

08 — Competitive Analysis
It's just like chocolate. Too much is better than too little. Bring real chocolate as well.

09 — Management Team
Describe your key members and how they will consolidate and focus their wisdom to solve the problem.

10 — Future Predictions
Don't sell--tell. Detail the current status, accomplishments to date, timeline, and use of funds. Answers as many questions as possible before they are asked.

Shift
Your Priorities

Health is the most important shift you can make in life. When you create your I OWE ME you must start with your wellness plan. Without health you can't survive, thrive or prosper. Nothing is more important than good health. While my purpose is not to preach the value of good health, I would be remiss if I didn't tell you about how to take control of your health so that all of the next steps are easier to accomplish.

> "Perhaps the best way to cope with shift is to help create it. That way we control shift rather than having it control us. Since we spend a good portion of our lives working, consider your workplace. What can you shift for the better? Can you accept all aspects of your job that you cannot shift? If not, it may be time for a job shift. But before moving on, make sure it is your job and not your attitude that needs to be shifted."
>
> —**Chuck Gallozzi, Founder, Positive Thinkers Group, Toronto, Ontario, Canada**

After you take control of your health, you can focus on your state of mind. Why? Because it's all about your attitude. That's right. **Attitude.**

It's not about your job, your income, your spouse, your kids or your friends. It all starts with your attitude.

Attitudes Are Caught—Not Taught!

You can't take a class in attitude, but you can see when others have a great attitude. So why is that so important? Shift Happens and there is nothing I can do about it, right? Wrong!

> It's all about your attitude

Success has to be measured and money is the way most of us keep score. There is emotional and intellectual capital for sure, but money is still the medium of exchange—a representative of value. No matter what you seek, everything has a price. Health care, car maintenance and hiring someone to reduce costs or increase productivity all come at a price. Nothing is for free these days, so don't give away your talent or advice for free. I have found that the higher the price for something the greater the perceived value. If something is too cheap then the value diminishes because that's the way we have been educated.

Price = Value. It may not be true but we all think that a haircut at Supercuts for $16.49 can't be as good as a hair styling for $99 at a professional salon. A watch for $19.95 can't keep accurate time compared to a $495 watch and so on. Price is the medium of exchange and the representative of value. Concert tickets in the front row are more than the back but movie tickets in the front are the same price as anywhere in the theater.

> *"We all have two choices;
> we can make a living or we can design a life."*
> —**Jim Rohn**

I use airline flights like a long hot shower. I put on my headphones and think about "shift" for the flight. I wonder about the "What Ifs" in my life. I think about the "What's Next?" and then formulate a "What's Possible?" I try hard to control my attitude. Why? Because it's all I can control these days. And then it hit me. It's all about attitude.

But I am a salesman. A promoter. I have to ask myself, what is it about this product or service that will make others want to buy it? Yes, you guessed it. A little BS. Coupled with hard work and knowledge, a little BS goes a long way. Not too much, but a little. It's like the glue that holds together most sales presentations.

There you have it. Not enough you say? OK, I get it. Not all of you want to have BS in the mix. Not all of you are salespeople. Even though you are always selling something to someone, many of you don't want to be labeled as salespeople.

To be fair, think about any job, any profession or any avocation that does not involve some form of sales. It's your wisdom that you are offering isn't it? Now that's what I am talking about. You need to have hard work, knowledge and the right attitude, but at the end of the day it's about your wisdom.

So look around. Listen to others. Attitudes are caught from others. Knowledge is available for free on the Internet, but wisdom comes from experience. People pay for wisdom coupled with the right attitude.

And it's not about price. Imagine the worst day of your life. You are diagnosed with a brain tumor. The doctor tells you it is operable if done immediately. Each day increases your risk of permanent disability or death. Do you tell the doctor that you are going to create a RFP (Request for a Proposal) and award the procedure to the low bidder? Of course not.

> People pay for wisdom coupled with the right attitude

You simply want to know if the doctor is capable, has done similar procedures and has a track record of success. If all the information is affirmative you don't haggle price. You schedule the procedure to save your life, don't you? So why discount your price when the value is a solution that others will pay for?

Never discount to make the sale. Increase the value you provide. Offer a guarantee, follow up training, or something they would normally need but can't afford. It's called bundling. On the slowest day of the week for attendance a local movie theater offers free popcorn. The cost is small but the value is large. Free refills, free car washes and free examinations all have a low cost but offer value when bundled with other items. Look around at other businesses and get ideas. All you have to do is be open to changing the way you think and how you add value to whatever you do.

> *"A lot of fellows nowadays have a B.A., M.D. or PhD. Unfortunately, they don't have a J.O.B."*
> **—Fats Domino, US musician singer, songwriter**

Refocus your priorities:

💡 Health

💡 Attitude

💡 Income

According to Jim

💡 Understand that managing your shift relies heavily on your willingness to take control of your health and making your attitude a top priority. Once you have those two under control, you can take more control of your shift.

> Knowledge is free.
> People pay for wisdom.
> And they pay a premium for solutions
> that address the WIIFM
> (What's In It For Me?).

THINK INSIDE THE BOX

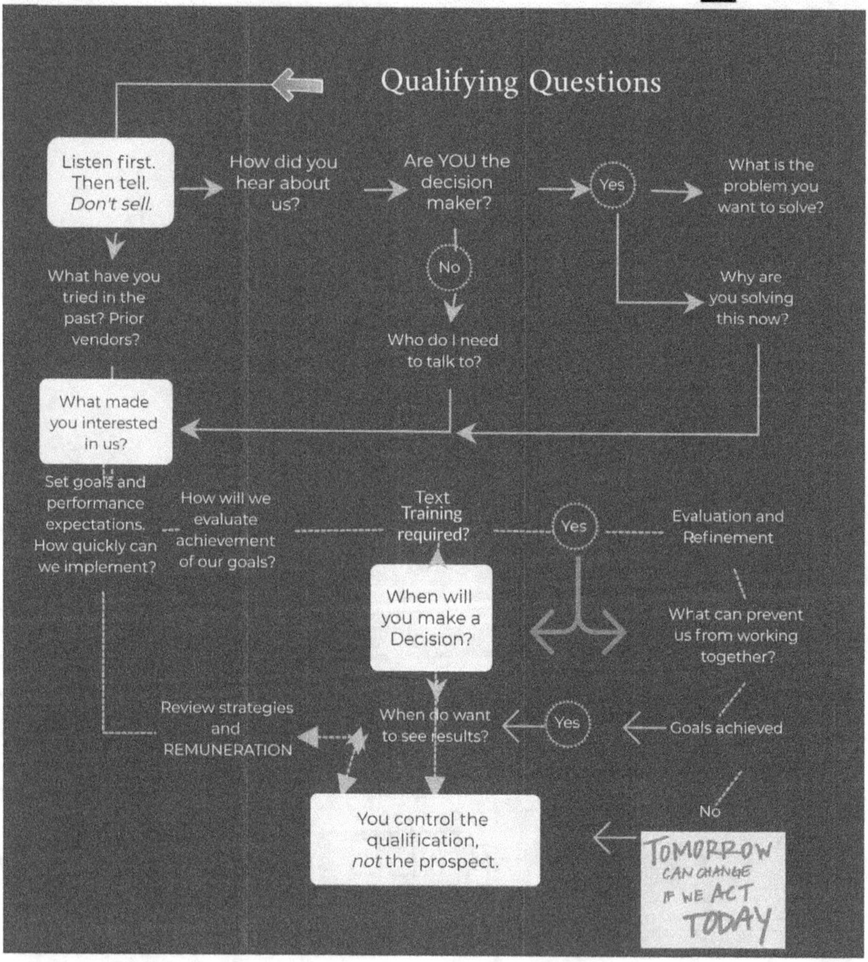

Qualifying Questions

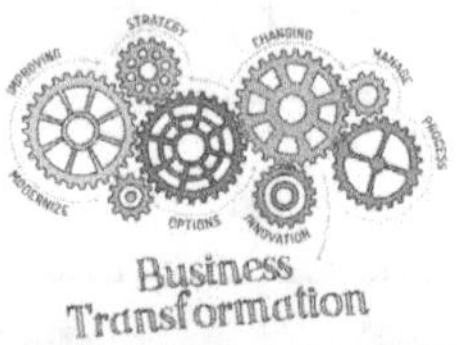

- Listen first. Then tell. *Don't sell.*
- How did you hear about us?
- Are YOU the decision maker?
  - Yes → What is the problem you want to solve? → Why are you solving this now?
  - No → Who do I need to talk to?
- What have you tried in the past? Prior vendors?
- What made you interested in us?
- Set goals and performance expectations. How quickly can we implement?
- How will we evaluate achievement of our goals?
- Text Training required?
  - Yes → Evaluation and Refinement → What can prevent us from working together? → Goals achieved
    - Yes → When do want to see results?
    - No → TOMORROW CAN CHANGE IF WE ACT TODAY
- When will you make a Decision?
- Review strategies and REMUNERATION
- You control the qualification, *not* the prospect.

Shift Happens!
Deal with It

Even before COVID-19 the world was changing every day. The situation is impossible to ignore, and the shift knocked the world on its butt. There is no way to escape the shift that has happened to all of us.

Life involves shift. Shift is inevitable.

There is a lack of jobs, tightened credit, rising food costs, rapidly changing technology, health issues, global warming, and political unrest. Shifts Happen and will continue to happen. Change starts with you and me. Be positive. Even though you may see the negative, make others smile.

Let's shift how you view your current situation and help you discover future opportunities.

Shift 1: Concentrate on what you can improve.

> First and foremost, you have to concentrate on what you can improve.

Shift 2: Identify the real problem.

> I often point out that we work on solutions to the wrong problems. Your second goal is to identify the real problem.

Let's celebrate five COVID shifts. More time for: 1) friends & family 2) community involvement 3) faith 4) strength & resiliency and 5) new opportunities.

Don't confuse impossible with inconvenient. There is always another day and we know that we can put off working on our self-proclaimed promises to stop eating cookies, be kinder to our relatives, help save the manatees, workout more often and save more money.

Shift 3: Pull your perspective into line with your vision.

Alter your vantage point and pull your perspective into line with your vision.

To all of you I say . . . **Your playing field is big.**

Your story is *big*. Your dreams are *big*. There has never been a time when there are more opportunities than right now. I understand that you may be out of work and out of money, but that's when the "tough get going."

Shift 4: Why do I say currently? Shift Happens! It won't be impossible forever.

You must identify what you can improve and what is simply, currently, impossible. Why do I say currently? Shift Happens! It won't be impossible forever.

The search for a COVID-19 vaccine has been expedited in the light of a global threat, compressing years of research, testing, and approval by the FDA into just months. This shifted timeline may become the "norm" for future medical breakthroughs. The tsunami-like impact of a global pandemic has blocked foresight. Right now, it feels impossible to predict what the world will look like next week, let alone next year. Yet behavioral science and the broad sweep of history suggest that COVID-19 will transform our daily lives in the long run. An ongoing University of Southern California study published its first round of results in March, reporting that the coronavirus had already created significant shifts in people's behavior.

Among the top findings: 85% of people reported washing their hands or using sanitizer more often than before, and 61% reported following social distancing guidelines. Twenty-two percent reported building up reserves of food and water.

Our new ways of interacting with each other—"live long and prosper" salutes instead of handshakes, video chats instead of conference-room huddles—are also likely to stick to some degree. "The history of the handshake dates back to the 5th century B.C. in Greece. It was a symbol of peace, showing that neither person was carrying a weapon. . . . Some say that the shaking gesture of the handshake started in Medieval Europe. Knights would shake the hand of others in an attempt to shake loose any hidden weapons" (deepenglish.com/2014/07handshake-history).

But what lingers most after a pandemic, or any large-scale catastrophe, is a pervasive sense that the world is fundamentally unpredictable—that life feels more fragile than it once did.

> Life involves shift.
> Shift is inevitable.

Ask yourself:

- 💡 Are you moving forward, examining and refining your approach to your life?
- 💡 Are you still altering your viewpoint?
- 💡 Are you ready to interact, innovate and reform?
- 💡 Or are you feeling sorry for yourself?

Well, typically, no one is going to ride in and rescue you. You have to do it yourself. **That's why it's called "self-help."**

> Those who act—win.
> Those who don't
> refocus will lose.

Shift will take place the same way the sun rises in the east and sets in the west. It's inevitable. Shift your thinking and, more often than not, the results will be greater than the setbacks. Innovation and shift superseded all problems and solutions. Yet, today, we have so many choices that we often allow shift to become overwhelming.

Today, a typical 21-year-old has played 5,000 hours of computer games, exchanged 25,000 emails, texts and chat messages, has used a cell phone some 10,000 times and spent 3,500 hours online (via Common Sense Media, a nonprofit that promotes safe technology and media for children).

To younger readers this is a constant and not at all unusual. Yet, to many older readers, these are developments that you expect to deal with, but find uncomfortable. Adults can handle 1.7 media channels at the same time, say watching TV and reading a magazine, while kids can pay attention to 5.4 channels at the same time. In other words, children are significantly better at multi-tasking.

> "Without a doubt, technological advances such as the laptop and the smartphone have created the best of times and also the worst of times. It's hardly a surprise that the word 'burnout' and the word 'cyberspace' came into use at about the same time. It can feel like we're at the mercy of technology and that coping with shift is our full-time job.
>
> "What can we do? We can choose how we react. We can whine and complain about our fate and assume the victim posture. Or we can acknowledge our discomfort and say to ourselves, 'OK, this happened and it's not fair, but what can I do about it?'"
>
> **—Edward T. Creagan, M.D. Mayo Clinic Oncologist**

Shift forces you to do things differently. The time to make a shift is *now!*

In this age of global change, personal innovation is more important than ever. The time to be a creative problem-solver is now. Organizations are desperate for creative people who see things differently, who can quickly size up a problem and develop creative solutions to it.

Once you take control of your personal shifts, you can apply that same technique—you can offer that skill set—to create a lifetime of opportunity. Think, for a minute, about why you purchased this book.

Perhaps you are trying to change your life, find a new job, increase your income, lose weight, find a significant other or initiate other worthwhile shifts to your life. It's time to pay attention to what you feel inside and how you think outside. "I can't do that" or

"I could fail" are self-limiting beliefs and will create a self-fulfilling prophecy.

Trying to drive a car is actually the same as driving the car . . . either you do or do not. Here's what others have said to encourage us to take control of the shifts thrust upon us and to teach us how to create our own shifts instead.

Star Wars introduced us to Yoda, the Jedi Master. As he tried to train young Luke Skywalker he said, *"Do or do not. There is no try."*

And Winston Churchill reminded us that *"A pessimist sees the difficulty in every opportunity; an optimist sees the opportunity in every difficulty."*

> Never, never, never, never give up. Never let a good crisis go to waste.

My friend Les Brown, motivational speaker and TV personality, reminds us that, *"Wanting something is not enough. You must hunger for it. Your motivation must be absolutely compelling in order to overcome the obstacles that will invariably come your way."*

The never-give-in principle might not be so easy to apply as the country faces a pandemic, businesses are closed (temporarily or permanently), and 30 million people are unemployed. Give in is not the same as give up. Focus on the end results you want to achieve, not the hurdles you have to jump over. It's about how you think and how you act. The way you respond to challenges helps craft your future.

- Ask yourself, "What can I improve?"
- Assess whether progress is being achieved.
- Unclutter yourself. Get rid of disposable crutches.
- Focus on doing one thing better than anyone else.
- Prosperity is endless and so are the efforts needed to achieve it.
- Remind yourself that, sometimes, courage is saying, "I will try again tomorrow."

According to Jim

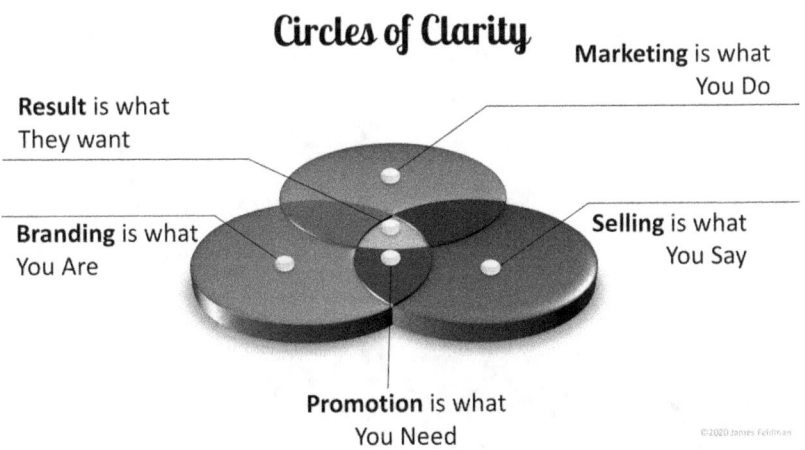

Circles of Clarity

- **Result** is what They want
- **Marketing** is what You Do
- **Branding** is what You Are
- **Selling** is what You Say
- **Promotion** is what You Need

www.jfa.tips/ChangeIntersection

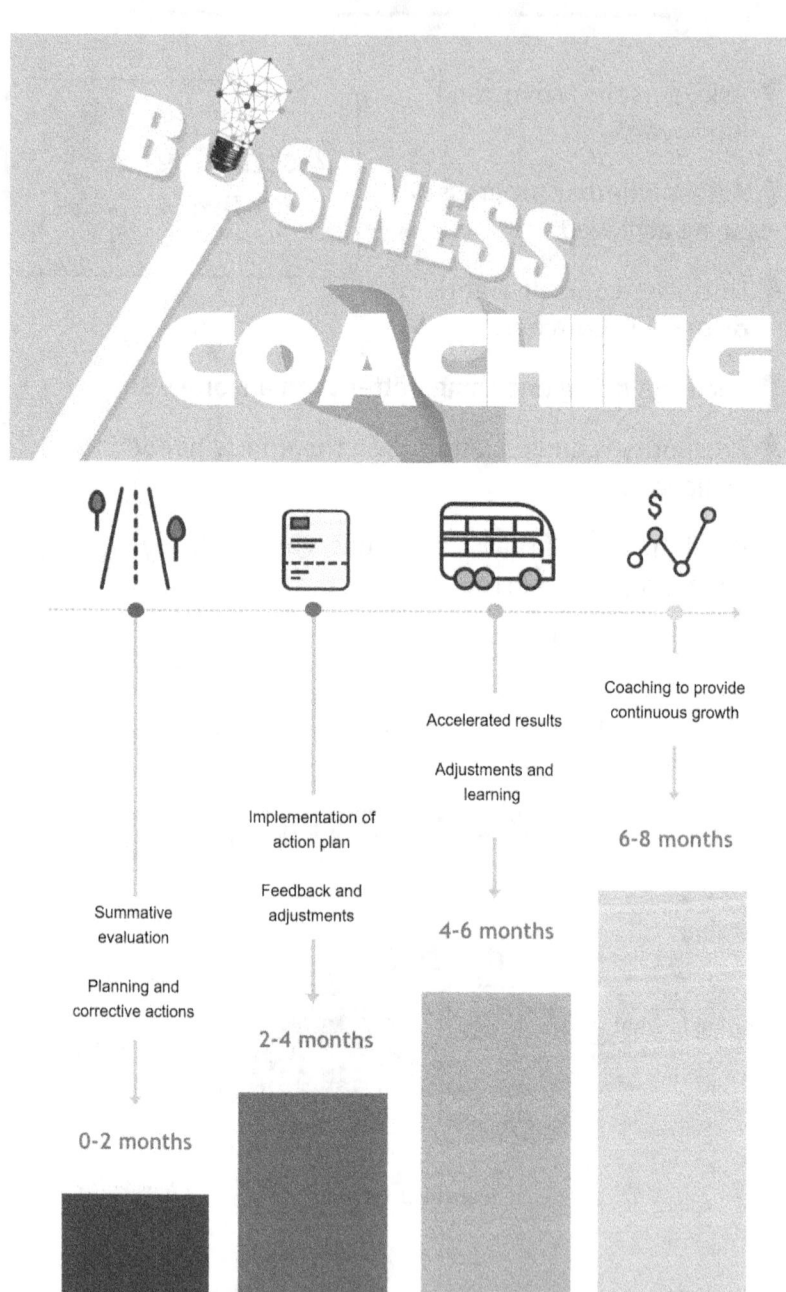

Shifting
into High Gear

I have suffered from overeating my entire life. Unlike addictions to alcohol and drugs, substances which are not necessary for existence, food cannot be quit "cold turkey." Now is the best time to lose weight. If you have no money, perhaps you could save by preparing your own meals rather than takeout or delivery. Eating healthy may cost more upfront but the ROI is significant. You may live longer. You may stay healthier. You may avoid chronic diseases like heart disease, stroke, diabetes, COPD, asthma, Crohn's disease, and even cancer.

In the past, I barely fit behind the wheel of a standard car. My waist was 66 inches. My overeating created high blood pressure, high cholesterol, sleep apnea, stress and Type II Diabetes. In December of every year, I schedule all of my annual tests: dental, eye, physical and my own self-evaluation. I went to see my doctor and upon arrival he said, "You look terrible."

He insisted on a "stress exam," which I failed. After an angiogram showed blockage in my heart, I was told that I should have triple bypass surgery. It was a Friday, so they sent me home and scheduled the procedure for Monday.

Saturday night, an elephant sat on my chest. Sweats, numbness of the arm, rapid heartbeat . . . you get the picture. I called

9-1-1. The fire department was at my 66th floor condo in less than two minutes. I would not let them treat me until I found out how they arrived so quickly. Annoyed, they told me that they were treating someone on the floor above me and simply came down the stairs.

Sunday morning, the doctors advised me that I did not have a heart attack but some kind of stress induced angina. Angina is chest pain or discomfort because your heart muscle does not get enough blood. I learned there are three types of angina: variant, stable and unstable. Unstable angina is the most dangerous. It can happen without physical exertion. I had stable angina, so the risk of a heart attack was not as much of a concern as it was on Friday. It was then that I made my decision.

I made the decision to take control of my weight. I set some goals. Here I was, lying in the hospital bed in the cardiac ward of Northwestern Memorial Hospital making future plans.

What were they? Have a look:

1. **Get a Brioni Suit. Why?** Because Brioni doesn't make big and tall suits. Their suits are cut for men with narrow waists and shoulders.
2. **Drive a NASCAR. Why?** Because you have to climb through the driver's side window to get into the car and at that point it would've been impossible.
3. **Walk 3 miles in an hour. Why?** Because, at the time, I could not walk half a mile without back and leg pain. Walking is great exercise, but at the time my body and mind could not manage the distance.

4. **Learn to drive Exotic Luxury Cars.** Why? Because exotic cars are not made for "morbidly obese" drivers. Yes, morbidly obese. That's the term that they used to describe my condition. 100% over ideal weight is considered severely or morbidly obese.
5. **Play Racquetball.** Why? A sedentary lifestyle, particularly prevalent in affluent societies, such as the United States, contributes to weight gain. Psychological factors, such as shifts that cause depression and low self-esteem may, in some cases, also play a role in weight gain. In my case, it was all of the above. I simply ate to reduce stress. I had played Racquetball in the mid-70s, but my excess weight caused pain on my knees and hips, so I stopped.
6. **Get my chronic medical conditions under control.** Why? Because, after a stress test my Cardiologist said, "Even if you don't have a stroke or heart attack, you are a textbook candidate for amputation or blindness or both." At that time, I was taking 80 units of insulin a day, had cholesterol levels over 300, high blood pressure, hypertension and nerve neuropathy. My first challenge was setting attainable goals. I put on weight over the years so I had to take it off over a long period of time. I set my goal to lose five pounds instead of 200. Five pounds was attainable, 200 was a dream and I would fail. Don't set yourself up for failure. Be honest with yourself and take small steps. You put on the weight one pound at a time, take it off the same way.

I then wanted to address what created the weight gain. Most people that are overweight are not binge eaters. They simply eat the wrong foods at the wrong time. I wrote down what I ate every day for a week, along with the time of day and the portion size, not just the calories. If I ate potato chips I counted them. If I consumed candy I wrote down how many ounces or pieces. What I found out gave me a road map to start to reduce my intake of "bad" food and increase "good" fruits, vegetables, fiber, etc. I noted that I did not eat breakfast, had a small lunch and then ate my way through chips, pretzels and other empty calories by mid afternoon. I then delayed dinner till after 8PM. Once I saw the pattern it was easy to see what I needed to do to shift my habits.

> Once I saw the pattern it was easy to see what I needed to do to shift my habits

These behaviors can have a negative impact on many aspects of your life, including your career, relationships, and personal interests or hobbies. You may find yourself avoiding job opportunities, social events, and even friendships in an attempt to keep your anxiety at bay. What worked for me may not work for you. Don't think of depriving yourself but increasing your overall health and wellbeing.

At the end of each day go to your journal (you got one right?) and look at what you ate, what time you ate it, and if you prepared it yourself or purchased it. Slowly face your behavior and modify it.

Here's a couple of tips that may help you the way they helped me.

- Ignore eating the first food that comes to mind or is in easy reach.
- Eat at the same time each day.
- **Pace your calories throughout the day. Don't have peaks and valleys.**

Shifting into High Gear

- Portion control your meals and snacks. I love to cook so it was easy to create baggies of snacks and pre-plated portions for meals.
- Take multi-vitamins. I started taking a prenatal vitamin and still take it today. It is a horse-size pill that has everything a mother and unborn baby need for proper development. For me it is a "magic pill." I also started taking calcium, 2000 IU of Vitamin D, and two baby aspirin.
- In writing this book I consulted with Anna G. She is a very fit, bright lady that provided some insights that have been instrumental in shifting how I thought about diets vs. lifestyle changes. She said, "I find that diet implies that you have to be perfect, while 'lifestyle change' allows for bumps in the road or like riding a roller-coaster."
- Eat more fiber and reduce red meat, fat and carbohydrates intake. Every morning I enjoy a high protein shake that is low in sugar and carbs.
- Exercise regularly, walk rather than ride, climb stairs rather than take elevators and make it a point to go for walks.
- Drink lots of water—not soft drinks, coffee or alcohol.
- Weigh yourself every Monday morning and measure yourself the first Monday of every month. Losing weight takes a huge commitment.

After some success I came up with my 60-60-60 program: 60 grams of protein, 60 oz of water and 60 minutes of exercise.

After work and commitment, Shift Happened!

1. Today I own a Brioni suit. Only one. It has its own sarcophagus. And when I die I want to wear it so they can say, "He did

take it with him."
2. I have driven NASCARs at four tracks and set a personal best speed time lap of 182mph.
3. I often walk more than 3 miles in less than an hour.
4. I have multiple experiences driving luxury sports cars like: Lamborghini Gallardo, Porsche Turbo, GT and 997, Corvette ZR1 or ZO6, Ferrari F430, Dodge Viper SRT-10, Ford GT, Lotus, BMW R3 and Audi R8 on tracks all over the United States.
5. I play racquetball, for at least an hour, several times a week.
6. I no longer have diabetes. I have cholesterol of 120, a resting heart rate of 58 and I feel great after losing the title of morbidly obese.

So, if I can do it, you can do it. Ask yourself a few questions:

- Why can't I stick to my food and exercise goals and reach my weight goal?
- What are the risk/rewards of losing the weight and keeping it off?
- Where can I find a support group?

Books, weight clinics, support groups, exercise and nutrition resources are available no matter where you live. My suggestion is to experiment and find what works for you. I found not only a better lifestyle, but a new business opportunity as well.

We'll talk more about direct marketing in the Shift to Thinking Like an Entrepreneur section. Direct marketing programs can be either great opportunities for low risk revenue generation or scams. I'll teach you how to tell the difference. Don't sign up or pay for an enrollment until you have done your research.

> **60-60-60 program:**
> **60 grams of protein,**
> **60 oz of water and**
> **60 minutes**
> **of exercise**

If you find that your behaviors are unmanageable and out of control, it may be time to seek professional help. Getting professional help with your lifestyle change is by no means a failure on your part. In fact, many people have found that they shift quicker with treatment.

According to Jim

- 💡 Set some goals.
- 💡 Lets remember how to set goals: S.M.A.R.T. Simple, Measurable, Attainable, Realistic and Timed.
- 💡 Set those goals and go for them!
- 💡 The first sale any of us has to make is to ourselves.
- 💡 Then commit 100%.
- 💡 The time for the important shifts in your life is NOW.

D-A-T-I-N-G Your Customer®
It's about creating a Long-Term Relationship

DAZZLE your Customers with an exceptional level of Service that keeps them Loyal. Get the 2nd "DATE."

ANTICIPATE the needs of your Customers. Listen twice as much as you talk. The right Attitude builds relationships.

NURTURE your employees and they will take care of your Customers. Customer service is not a department.

TREAT each Customer uniquely. One Size does not fit all.

INNOVATE to solve problems better. Innovation & perspiration go hand-hand is sustaining relationships.

After they Buy your product your goal is to help them become a loyal, repeat Customer.

GUARANTEE you have Customers to service by being grateful. You don't do things because everybody will see them, but because the right Customers will see them.

www.jfa.tips/DATING

Some Shifts Are Inspiring

I won't discuss the death of over 1 million people due to the coronavirus. Instead let me share some more uplifting examples of shifts.

Some shifts force you to meet your fears head on and sometimes how you handle the shift is almost as important as the outcome.

Cancer is a scary disease. Sadly, it seems as though almost everyone has been affected by it in some way, shape or form. We all hope that it is a battle that we, and the ones we love, never have to fight, but that is not generally the reality.

The following is a beautiful story of how one woman took control of her life after being diagnosed with lung cancer.

Having never smoked a day in her life, lung cancer was the last thing Karen ever thought she would battle. She was the only person in her family who was a non-smoker—exposing her to secondhand smoke for years.

For five years in a row, she developed pneumonia in the same lung. On the fifth year, when she went to her usual doctor, she learned that he was out of town and she would be seeing a new, young doctor who was filling in for him. This new doctor explained to Karen that, unfortunately, people do not get pneumonia in the same area of the same lung five years in a row. He sent her for more testing.

> Appreciate life

Because Karen was a teacher and was thirsty for knowledge, she wanted to stay awake for the procedure and look at what the doctors were seeing—her tumor. How did she describe it? It was the size of a Ping-Pong ball and looked like a beautiful white pearl with a slight pink tint to it. Beautiful? A tumor? Yes, Karen remained positive.

Again, because she was a teacher, she wanted to put off such an invasive surgery until the summertime, since her students would need her during the year. The doctor refused and told her that they needed to get the tumor out right away.

When she finally came home from the hospital, the doctors told her that it would take a couple weeks to determine the kind of cancer that had been removed from her lung. After two weeks, the doctors still could not figure out what kind of cancer they had removed. They sent the sample to the Mayo Clinic, then to Johns Hopkins, and finally, they pulled a pathologist living in Ireland out of retirement to finally diagnose her cancer. It was one of the less dangerous forms of lung cancer and was completely encapsulated—they had removed it all.

So what effect did having cancer have on Karen? It made her really appreciate life—not that she did not appreciate it before, but now she had a new appreciation. It also made her really understand the value of staying positive and not feeling sorry for herself. It made her realize that she was a person that could bring other people up. When things were down and bad, even if those things were about her, she was the one who would set an example for others and keep a positive outlook.

When you are sick, sometimes people put you in the grave already. Karen was completely happy and positive, but her husband was crying and the people at work couldn't even look her in the eye. One of her third graders came up to her before her surgery, hugged her, and said tearfully, "I know you are telling us that you are going to be alright, but my mom says you're a goner! And I don't think you're coming back!"

> Keep a positive outlook

This reaction incited an entire classroom full of emotional children. What was Karen's response? She stood in the front of the room and addressed her class, "Thank you for the drama. You are all very good actors, but I am going to be fine. I know you don't like to hear that your parents can be wrong, but your mom is wrong about this one. I am going to be fine." And she was.

While she was sick, Karen even joked that having cancer gave her the opportunity to hear everything that people would say to and about her if she were dead, only she got to hear it while she was alive! And she really appreciated how nice it was to know how many people loved her.

Now, at school, when someone has an issue, the administrators send them to Karen. They'd say, "Go talk to Karen. Not only will she make you feel better, she will teach you how to laugh your way through the situation."

What has Karen learned? Life is just the way it is—you can't take it for granted. You have to appreciate it. Because of her situation, she has since become much more patient with people and does not initially react. And she certainly does not overreact about little things.

> **Laugh your way through the situation**

Going through this brought peace to Karen's life. She realized that life is all about how you look at things. The most important thing for Karen: she was able to show her students how to stay positive. Her kids are going to face their parents getting ill and they may even get ill themselves. She was able to show them how to handle illness. Life is all about shifting your attitude so that you can come out on top.

Justin Jacobson, founder and President of Platinum Events, a 15-year-old company, found that when the pandemic spread, the events he had contracts to manage were all canceled. Realizing he did not have time to "sulk," he saw an opportunity.

What's Next? What's Possible? questions were answered brilliantly. He went "inside the box" and realized he already sterilized all of its event furniture and equipment. Justin saw opportunity in the sanitation industry. "This is going to be a need that is going to be forever entrenched in people's minds and business owners' minds," he said.

You have a choice. We don't know how we are going to react until it happens, but you are in control and you have a choice of how you are going to deal with it. Both Justin and Karen decided they didn't want to be miserable or make anyone miserable, so they decided to be happy. If they were going to experience a major shift, they wanted to take advantage of the peaks and weather the valleys. When you are sick, you crack jokes and everyone feels like they have to laugh because they think that, any day, you might die. So they laugh! As Karen said, "I always call my cancer my lucky pearl—it kept all of the bad stuff inside it, and to me, it was just beautiful."

Justin and Karen faced adversity in different ways but both of them understood that they had choices, same as you.

Listen to Karen... she will make you feel better, she will teach you how to laugh your way through the situation.

> You have a choice

I think the most important message from Karen and Justin is that your life is never just about you, it's about the others around you as well.

- 💡 Focus on the present.
- 💡 Follow your curiosity.
- 💡 Learn to play better.
- 💡 Stop procrastinating.
- 💡 Enjoy every moment with those around you.
- 💡 Don't expect different results from doing the same thing.

According to Jim

Hierarchy Of F.E.A.R.

- **EXPERIENCE** — Positive Experience fuels the desire to do more.
- **MOTIVATION** — The reward is worth the risk and effort.
- **CONFIDENCE** — I have the ability to make Shi^{f}t Happen.
- **BELIEF** — If I do this, I would be more successful.
- **UNDERSTANDING** — This is different than what I do today.

How are you going to create and deliver high value to your customers from home?

First time working from home, or not, here are some considerations to be more productive.

Go TO the home office to work!

Work like you are in an office. Be selfish. A home office is a commitment for you and your family.

Comfortable Chair
Invest in an ergonomic chair. Surplus or used office chairs are inexpensive.

Back-up Plans
- Mobile Hotspot
- USB backups
- Cloud backups
- Avoid peak WIFI loads

Work space
Find a location that you can use exclusively for work.

Robust WIFI
It's essential to have a reliable cost-effective provider.

CALL TO ACTION
Make sure you have sufficient upload and download speeds to function.

CALL TO ACTION
Find a spot with peace and quiet.

Creative locations may be a closet, basement, garage, etc.

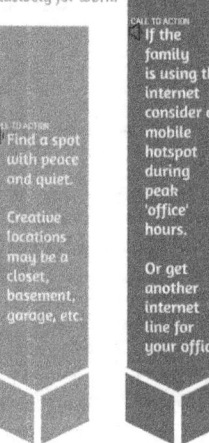

CALL TO ACTION
If the family is using the internet consider a mobile hotspot during peak 'office' hours.

Or get another internet line for your office.

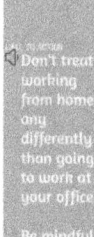

CALL TO ACTION
Don't say 'for now' it's ok.

We have no idea if this turns into many weeks or even a month or more.

You can't be productive if you stop working due to "A Cup" chair for a "D Cup" butt.

CALL TO ACTION
Don't treat working from home any differently than going to work at your office.

Be mindful. You are working not taking a break or a vacation.

Explain to your family and friends you are 'at work.'

Issue 1   **Issue 2**   **Issue 3**   **Issue 4**   **Issue 5**

Shift
—When the Light Bulb Goes On

The first step to managing a shift is recognizing that a shift has occurred. Shift can be welcomed, unwelcomed, expected, unexpected and even—maybe most importantly—engineered. Recognizing that shift has occurred, or is about to occur, is the most important step in starting to manage shift and look for and then find opportunities through that shift.

If you can't recognize change, think of your life as a "reality show." Each episode builds upon the previous one. Ask yourself these questions:

- Do you feel safe?
- Do you feel significant?
- Do you feel loved?
- Do you feel in love?
- Do you feel productive?

Recognizing shifts when they happen: What are some things that help us recognize a shift? Could it be our mood? Health? Status? Position? How we react to others and situations? How others react to our situations? Recognize when to create shifts. What factors in our lives cause us to create shift?

> Do some planning. Don't just shift to shift. Make it mean something.

These can be many of the same factors that we are recognizing when Shift Happens to us. The difference is that we are now recognizing a shift in one area—say, our mood—and using *that* shift to help jumpstart our own shift in another area of our lives.

Recognizing the need for and knowing when to create shift isn't enough—you have to have the follow-through and the foresight to actually make that shift real. You must take the next step and accept that *shift* has happened: Do something about it. Creating *shift* can be accompanied by high risks, but it is also those high risks that often yield the biggest value. You must commit to your shifts.

Just because you have taken an inventory of your shift factors and realized that shift *should* be happening in your life—whether you create it or it happens to you—doesn't mean it will. If you do not wholeheartedly believe and buy into your next steps, then maybe it is time to reevaluate your approach to this shift and come up with a new game plan. Just because all signs are pointing to "yes" and, on paper, it looks like the right time to create shift, doesn't mean that you have shift. Do some planning. Don't just shift to shift. Make it mean something.

Don't make rash decisions just because you are unhappy. Figure out *why* you are unhappy. Then refocus and redefine the issue. Why are you unhappy and what can *you* do to shift into a happier and more positive mindset?

Recognize the *real* issue and refocus your energy and efforts so you can resolve that issue. You should be happy.

> Realization: the "light bulb" goes on

> You must take the next step and accept that **shift** has happened: Do something about it. Creating **shift** can be accompanied by high risks, but it is also those high risks that often yield the biggest value.

Recognizing shift and devising a game plan is sometimes difficult. A lack of progress and lack of change. Realization: the "light bulb" goes on. That sometimes, you have to be sad or upset or unsettled in life in order to make any kind of progress; in order to create shift. If you are always happy and saying that everything around you is good, even when it is not, how often are you really going to seek out new opportunities? Not that often. The best decisions I have made were when I was in my worst state. It was then that I realized a shift needed to happen and I needed to create it.

So how do you execute this shift? Simply act as quickly as possible.

When I was earning my MBA I opened a store. It was in a brand new building that had two stores with a single structure. Each store was 20' wide and 180' deep.

The stores faced one of the busiest streets near the university. The location was perfect for foot traffic. In addition, there was metered parking on the south side of the building for 50 cars.

I decided that I wanted to put a sign on the wall facing the parking lot. I called a sign painter and explained what I wanted to accomplish. He said that I needed to get a permit from the city. My application was denied because it was a sign. I went to the hearing committee and explained that the front of the building was too small and the traffic would not see the sign as they drove by.

I was told that signs were not permitted because they advertised my business but I could put up a billboard if it advertised a different business. WHAT? That made no sense. So I asked if I could put a billboard on my roof and was given the same restriction. If it was advertising my business they would not issue a permit.

I went to the building next door and asked to rent his roof and explained the ridiculous rationale detailing a sign vs. a billboard. "What is going on the billboard" he asked? My business, I explained. Because it was not on my building, I could put up a billboard. The city had no choice but approve my request. However, I was now branded as a disrupter.

One night I noticed I could not see the billboard. I called the sign company and asked for lights. Again, a permit was needed. Surprise: I was denied. Undaunted, I called a light company and installed lights on MY roof aimed at HIS billboard.

No permit was needed, since the lights were not on a sign or billboard, despite the fact that the light illuminated my neighbor's billboard.

I beat the city again. Eventually I won over a dozen of these interpretations for their antiquated rules. Realizing it was better to have me as an advisory rather than an adversary, the city hired me to consult with them to revise and adapt these "shifts" for future business issues. I was paid but also "grandfathered myself" so I was not working against my own interests. Clearly, the light went on and I had the only switch.

When you see people and things in a different light, you realize the importance of the shift. There are three important questions to ask yourself when dealing with shift:

1. *What?*
2. *So What?*
3. *Now What?*

What? refers to the shift. This means recognizing that there is or is about to be a shift and understanding exactly what that shift is. It is the time to correctly identify the shift.

So What? It's your time to think: "Okay, I now know that shift is happening, what does that mean? What can I learn from this shift and what shifts does it bring to my life, work and happiness?"

Now What? refers to your next step. You have just established that shift is happening, defined that shift and dissected it in order to understand its effects on the different aspects of your life. Now, it is time to strategize a game plan that will enable you to manage the shift and discover or create opportunities for yourself *through* that shift. *Now What* is what moves you forward.

> The best decisions I have made were when I was in my worst state. It was then that I realized a shift needed to happen and I needed to create it.

Life is all about:
- Solutions
- Connections
- Leverage

Devising a game plan:

- 💡 What: A shift
- 💡 So What: Recognizing something can/should be done
- 💡 Now What: A roadmap for how to manage that shift and create opportunities for yourself from it.

> "Life is not fair, get used to it . . .
> If you give people tools, [and they use] their natural ability and their curiosity, they will develop things in ways that will surprise you very much beyond what you might have expected."
> **—Bill Gates**

According to Jim

- 💡 The most extraordinary things in life are usually the simple things.

- 💡 Nothing holds you back except yourself.

- 💡 Trying to learn requires doing.

- 💡 Make a decision and go for it. Even if you fail you will learn from the attempt.

- 💡 Have confidence in yourself at all times.

- 💡 Keep a clear focus on your final destination.

Shifts
to Instill Innovative 3D Thinking

Introduction to 3D Thinking

- Do you need to discover new solutions?
- Do you need to overcome challenges?
- Could you benefit with new, improved innovative thinking skills?
- Would you like proven processes and systems that stimulate better ideas in less time?
- Do you need better tools to discover new opportunities (while using existing resources) and the ability to annihilate the competition, deliver new products and services, take charge of your future, all while saving time and money?

3D Thinking can help

Innovation is the quickest, most effective, and most lucrative path to success. Waiting for some other firm to introduce a product first, and then playing catch-up may be fine if you're IBM or Coca-Cola and you can afford to wait. But such companies are notable exceptions in the game of competition. For the majority of businesses, real success comes from their own efforts and from timing—their ability to be there first, instead of feeding off the ideas of others.

So, how does a firm or an individual innovate and think creatively? First, understand that creativity isn't always about inventing products from scratch. Thousands of successful products or services are used in a radically different manner than originally intended. The creativity is in the new method of application, rather than in the unique nature of the original concept.

For example, a creative solution might take the form of redirecting your excess capacity or processes to support your most profitable products or services. Thus, innovation is any creative solution people can use. Innovation is also how you make money from creativity. You sell the idea and show others how to apply it to solve a variety of problems.

Think beyond the profits; think "What if?"

Solutions might be possible, but are they profitable? Often, you don't always know until after the fact. Sometimes profitable solutions aren't developed with the intent of making a profit. For example, take the story of a little girl at her birthday party. Her father was taking photographs, and the girl wanted to see the pictures now. The father thought, "Well, why can't she see the pictures now?"

That father was Edward Land, and his solution was to invent the Polaroid camera. Perhaps we all need to think more like a child and imagine that we can have the picture now.

Fast forward a few years. We see that Polaroid is now in bankruptcy. The company missed the digital revolution because it forgot about its innovative spirit. How could this happen? One common way is when the upper echelons of the corporation stifle creativity throughout the organization.

Centuries ago, kings and other royalty had "yes men" by their sides. But many kings also employed fools, men who had special permission to make fun of and criticize the king's policies without fear. Present-day CEOs have "yes-men," but they are in dire need of someone to give them an honest opinion.

They need someone who can tell those in the royal boardroom that the old ways are no longer effective and that innovation is the way to make money.

Creativity goes hand-in-hand with the courage to embrace the new and the innovative. Organizations are afraid to fail. Failure is the cousin of success. Thomas Edison, Henry Ford, Bill Gates, Steve Jobs, Walt Disney, Albert Einstein all faced numerous failures and obstacles before using what they learned to create substantial successes. Innovation is about disruption of business as usual or standard operating procedures. Innovation creates collisions.

Embrace Innovative "Collisions"

Innovation can occur where you least expect it. Imagine a scientist is trying to produce a stronger glue. He tries and tries, but the glue just doesn't stick. His product is a complete disaster—or is it? Every office in the world now has glue that doesn't stick. The scientist, who worked at 3M, had just invented the raw material for the Post-it® Note. And the Post-it Note is now one of the most profitable products at 3M.

Collisions can sometimes become rare opportunities, and unintended results could have a silver lining. Look for inspiration everywhere.

Think everywhere. Think when you're out walking, when you're in the shower, when you're listening to a boring speaker. Switch off your mind and think about that problem that's been bugging you.

You can't always create on demand. But you can organize your mind to be constantly receptive to new ideas.

For example, in 1941, a scientist went hunting with his dog. When the scientist arrived home, he found burrs were stuck to his wool jacket and trousers. The scientist decided to examine the burrs under a microscope and he found hundreds of little hooks engaging the loops in the material. The scientist, George de Mestral, made a machine to duplicate the hooks and loops in nylon. He called his new product "velcro" and the rest is history. Today, thousands of uses for VELCRO® fasteners exist, all thanks to a man hunting with his dog in the mountains.

The only problem with thinking everywhere is you often don't have a way to record your ideas when they come to you. Then, you forget, someone one else hits on the same idea, and it's too late.

The solution is to keep a pen and paper handy in every room of your home, especially by your bed and near the shower. Or use your smartphone. There are lots of dictations and note-taking apps. When you're driving, you can pull over and dictate into your phone.

Plan Your Luck

Chance discoveries don't really occur by chance. Rather, an environment must be one that allows new ideas to be conceived, recognized for their potential contribution, expanded into tailor-made solutions, and then developed into products for other Customers. And, the best way to arrive at innovative solutions is to use innovative thinking.

To that end, encourage your employees to ask questions, such as, *Why do we do it this way? What If? Why Not? What's Next? What's Possible?*

If management doesn't have a good answer, consider this an invitation for fresh ideas. Nurture the new ideas and welcome the questions as a way to open the channels of communication and to keep the stream of possible solutions flowing.

Beware of Leaks

Because genuinely new ideas are hard to come by and difficult to patent, the shortest route to new ideas can be to get them from someone else. Consequently, be alert to the possibility that others might be listening to the new idea you're sharing with someone. An idle sentence could provide the missing ingredient to a competitor's research and development department. Where innovation is concerned, keep quiet and keep your ears open because you, too, might obtain problem-solving ideas from other markets or businesses.

Perhaps one key to successful innovation is skilful ego-massaging. That is, share your ideas, but use caution when choosing with whom you share them. **Create, Then Innovate!**

Innovation requires more than creative thinking. Innovation is also dependent on the development of ideas into products and services to keep your company on the creative edge. In the end, your determination to succeed is the ultimate stimulus for achievement.

Although many people can come up with innovative concepts, only those who are determined to implement those ideas achieve success.

Once you nurture your ideas into being, charge ahead with the innovative spirit that all successful companies possess. Remember, innovation combines effort and timing, our desire to be first.

Use 3D Thinking to Investigate, Innovate, and Initiate. Your business has every opportunity to achieve success with this IQ.

24 "shifts" in how to think about creative problem-solving

Shift 1. You must truly want to become more creative. Most important, deep down in your heart of hearts, ask yourself: do you want others pestering you with their notions of how to improve something or do you simply need a "push" to demonstrate you have a better solution? Think about it. What's holding you back?

Shift 2. Realize you are creative. All of us have creative potential and lots of ideas. But, unless you actively promote creativity, those ideas are promptly forgotten when you return to the "next normal." You need to set up a safety zone for ideas. In most companies, failure is clearly punished, but success is a vague reward. To succeed after COVID-19 companies must create a system of benefits to innovate success and reduce the penalties created for failures. You can do the same for yourself. Go for it!

Shift 3. Establish trust. No matter how creative you are, you won't share ideas with others if they always say, YES, BUT. Two reasons exist for this:

Sharing a genuinely innovative idea is risky. The idea might be laughed at by people who don't appreciate its value or scorned by those who don't like change. If your friends and family don't trust you completely, don't risk sharing the best ideas with them. OK, now I have said it. Family and friends may not have the same temperment for taking on risk. If that is the case, it may work for them but not for you. Families either support you without reservation or they YES BUT you into thinking you can't take the risk.

Good ideas often have tremendous value. If your people don't trust you or your idea, they won't want you to benefit from your idea. If you are not ready to overcome inherent resistance then don't share the idea with YES BUT and find WHY NOT supporters.

Shift 4. Create a means of communicating ideas. Why Not supporters should also be able to contribute ideas. Remember to take ALL ideas seriously and don't become a YES, BUT. Find a central place where anyone in the group can scribble down his or her idea to add on to your idea. Think of the collaboration of Steve Jobs and Steve Wozniak. A visionary and an engineer. Together they put a dent in the universe. Shift your comments to YES, AND . . .

Shift 5. Create a means for people to collaborate on your ideas. A good idea can often be the tip of the iceberg to a great idea. By getting people to work together to develop ideas, you can turn good ideas into great ideas.

Shift 6. Ensure that people from your WHY NOT community can contribute ideas and the development of ideas. If you assume that only marketing people can have ideas relevant to marketing, you're certain to get the usual marketing ideas. You'd be surprised about the ideas your people in accounting, human resources, and even the staff canteen will have about marketing. Every idea needs a collaboration. However, you do need non-disclosures and non-compete agreements. Don't rely on the "trust me" factor. Even marriages that start with unlimited love can end in destructive divorces. Think of the NDA and NCA as a prenuptial agreement (www.jfa.tips/NDA).

Shift 7. Reward people who give good ideas to the organization. Rewards don't have to be money. They can be small gifts, such as restaurant or movie gift cards. Of course, rewards can also be money or even royalties from the idea (this last option helps ensure people give good ideas to the company, rather than set up their own companies). Remember how I paid for those that helped me with my railroad box car of pasta sauce?

Shift 8. Don't punish people for bad ideas. Even laughing at an idea can seriously de-motivate someone who might have a winning idea tomorrow. Creative people have ideas all the time. Sometimes those ideas stink and sometimes they're brilliant. But, if you de-motivate creative people, you'll soon lose their ideas. Find ways to collaborate using the 3D Thinking methodology.

Shift 9. Don't rely too much on research and analysis. These things have their place, indeed, they're necessary in the twenty-first century. But great ideas usually come from inspiration. Almost nothing in our lifetime will be as disruptive as the coronavirus. It is the perfect time to re-imagine your future.

Shift 10. Creativity is a long-term investment. ROI won't be immediate. Failure is part of the long-term investment. You have to learn from failure. If you are creative now, rethink! There has never been a better time to adopt new ways of thinking, behaving, and producing. Then, once ideas start flowing, they must be implemented. This also takes time. But, over the long term, the pay off can be big. So don't just sit there, go for it!

Shift 11. Listen to classical music. Johann Sebastian Bach does it for me. You might prefer Vivaldi, Mozart, or Beethoven. Music is great stimulation. Find the type of music that encourages, not discourages, your thinking process. Our senses are encouraged by sight, smell, touch, and sound. Music is a powerful way to free your mind of other distractions. Take the time to relax, reflect, refine, and react.

Shift 12. Brainstorm. If properly carried out, collaborative brainstorming can not only help you come up with sacks full of new ideas, but it can also help you decide which idea is best.

Shift 13. Carry a small notebook and a pen or pencil, a tape recorder, your smartphone, tablet around with you. That way, if you think of an idea, you can quickly record it. On rereading your notes, you might discover about 90 percent of your ideas aren't implementable. Don't worry, that's normal. What's important are the 10 percent of your ideas that are brilliant.

Shift 14. If you're stuck for an idea, open a dictionary or magazine. Randomly select a word, and then try to formulate ideas incorporating this word. You'll be surprised how well this works. The concept is based on a simple, but little-known, truth: freedom inhibits creativity. Restrictions can get you thinking.

Shift 15. Go "inside the box" to describe your problem correctly. Grab a sheet of paper, an electronic notebook, your laptop, or whatever you use to make notes, and define your problem in detail. You'll probably find ideas positively spewing out once you do this. You shouldn't spend more time on defining the problem than trying to solve it, however.

The first D in 3D Thinking stands for Depth. Do you understand the problem? Have you defined it properly? Too often, you spend time working on the solution to the wrong problem. Go inside the box because that is where the problem resides. Depth means breaking the problem into components. Moving the components around will often reveal the solution which was hidden in the shadows.

Shift 16. If you can't think, take a break. Go for a walk. Jog around the block. A change of atmosphere is good for you and gentle exercise helps shake up the brain cells. I refer to the process as "incubation." Your brain is working on the problem, even though you might not consciously be thinking about it.

If you think of what's inside the "box," that's what contains the problem. It's made up of the components. Reorder them. Move them apart. The answer is often found in the components and it doesn't require the introduction of new components.

Shift 17. Don't watch NEWS TV. Experience it. If you like TV and find it simulates your brain, then engage it. Think like the writer or the producer. How did they come up with the idea? How did they define the need? Remember, marketing is providing what the consumer wants, not what the factory wants to produce.

Moving outside the box is to determine the second D: Distance.

Is a market here? Will people pay for your solution to the well-defined problem? Is the market large enough to support your innovative concept?

Shift 18. Don't take drugs or drink excessive alcohol. People on drugs think they're creative. To everyone else, they seem like people on drugs. Don't drink excessively. One glass of wine might have a calming effect, but too much of anything reduces your mental sharpness. Do whatever provides some relaxation. Walk, drink a glass of cabernet, enjoy some chocolate, arrange some flowers, do whatever works for you.

Shift 19. Read as much as you can about everything possible. Books exercise your brain, provide inspiration, and fill you with information that enables you to make creative connections easily.

Read about the introduction of new products. Think about how you would have created that new product or service. If you've thought of the right problem to solve and you've come up with the solution, then you need to understand the third D: Determination.

How determined are you to bring this new product or service to your potential consumers? What resources are needed? Have you understood that a market is willing to buy your product or service? Is your product or service unique?

Can others see what you're doing and steal your idea? Have you determined a life cycle of the product? Some products have been around for decades and remain unchanged.

Ketchup is a 100-year-old product, yet Heinz has changed the bottle and the color, added spices, and so forth, and increased market penetration and overall sales to new levels. Apple introduced the iPod, a small device that could hold thousands of songs.

Then, Apple created iTunes, so the iPod user could purchase and download individual songs. In each case, 3D Thinking was used.

Shift 20. Exercise your brain. Brains, like bodies, need exercise to keep fit. If you don't exercise your brain, it will become flabby and useless. Exercise your brain by reading a lot (as just discussed), talking to clever people, and disagreeing with people. Arguing can be a terrific way to give your brain cells a good workout. But, note, arguing about politics or film directors is good for you, but bickering over who should load the dishwasher isn't.

3D Thinking™ = Depth + Distance + Determination

Shift 21. Determine if you have the staying power to deliver the solution to your problem. (Please note, the word "problem" isn't necessarily negative. Your problem could be "We need a new product for the holiday season" or "How can we effectively use our budget surplus for this year?"). Write out your problem concisely and make sure everyone understands the problem and is in agreement with the way it's worded. Putting a lot of restrictions on your problem at this time is unnecessary. What is needed, however, is the correct problem definition.

Spend most of your time defining the problem and your solutions will be easier to reach. **WHAT are you doing NOW and WHAT is the consequence if you do not change (*desirable or not!*)?**

Creativity is the ability of the human mind to come up with ideas and solutions to pressing problems.

The amount of time required to define a problem is approximately three times what you spend on solving the problem. Using the concept of going inside the box, determine the components of the problem. To understand a problem fully, you must break down all the elements that create it.

1. First, write down the problem.
2. Now, write down the desired solution.
3. Then, break down all the elements contained in the problem that could create it in the first place.
4. Understand how to use the components in the solution of the problem-solving process.

If you don't define the problem correctly, you'll be working to reach the solutions to the wrong problem. Take your time. Visualize the end results and see if the problem is articulated correctly.

Shift 22. Give yourself a time limit. I recommend around 30 minutes, but experience will show how much time is required. Larger groups might need more time to get all the ideas on the table.

Shift 23. Shout out solutions to the problem. One person can write out the solutions or enter them into a computer, on a flip chart, and so forth. And, remember: no criticizing of ideas. No matter how off-beat, how impossible, or how silly an idea seems, it must be written down. Laughing should be encouraged, but criticism should not. Why? Because you want to encourage the free flow of ideas and, as soon as participants of the brainstorming session begin to fear criticism of their ideas, they'll stop generating them. Moreover, ideas that seem silly at first might prove to be good or lead to other good ideas.

Shift 24. Select the five best ideas. Make sure everyone involved in the brainstorming session is in agreement, but stick to your time limit.

Anytime you can offer an example that the group understands, the better your solution becomes. Here are a few reminders for team leaders: Identify. Determine. Record. Recycle. Refine. Summarize.

Write down about five criteria for judging which ideas best solve your problem. Criteria should start with the word "should"—for example, "it should be cost effective," "it should be legal," "it should be possible to finish before August 1," and so forth.

Give each idea a score of 0 to 5 points, depending on how well it meets each criterion. Once all the ideas are scored for each criterion, add the scores.

The idea with the highest score will best solve your problem. But keep a record of all your best ideas and their scores, in case your best idea turns out to be unworkable. Exchange ideas. Suggest a "build" to the idea that makes it better. **Don't be negative. Push up not pull down.**

Let's review the process.

D=Depth

Go "inside the box" and move the components around. Break them apart. Do the simple math of dividing them, adding, subtracting or multiplying certain parts. Frequently, the solution is simply how you rearrange the components. Moving them around often reveals a new solution. Innovation is how we make money from creativity.

D=Distance

Now that you are "inside the box," take a 360º look. Do you see a market that will pay for your innovative solution? Are there competitors that are already doing what you suggest? Can you do it better? Cheaper? Faster?

How far can you take the solution? Will you make money from it or save time, materials, etc? This is where you "monetize" your solution. Assuming you are for profit, and even non-profits are for profit, it is here that you start to establish the selling price or the savings value.

D=Determination

Do you have the Determination to move this forward? Did you get enough financial resources to "launch" the solution? Did you keep enough in reserve to promote, market, train, and distribute your solution?

If you have followed the process of 3D Thinking, you will have come up with ideas, products, money saving solutions, etc., that help you to overcome challenges, achieve goals, and/or solve problems.

- 💡 What does the Customer WANT?
- 💡 What does the Customer NEED?

- What does the Customer VALUE?
- What does the Customer EXPECT?

Summary:

1. Define the problem.
2. Gather information.
3. Create alternatives.
4. Evaluate.
5. Choose.

- Customers want better results.
- Customers want better outcomes.
- Customers want the product of your product . . . not the product itself.
- The key to innovation is to become aware of overlooked connections between actions and consequences.
- Discover what other options the Customer is considering.
- Collaborate with the Customer to establish value.
- Listen to what the Customer says they want and deliver what they need.
- Never voluntarily offer to reduce your prices. If you're asked to provide a price reduction, reduce value first.
- Psychologically, higher fees create higher value and naturally greater profits for you.
- Make sure they know the full range of your services.
- Customers like you best when you function as a thinker—An Independent Problem-Solver with Innovative SOLUTIONS!
- 3D Thinking means your business climate is open to innovation and creativity and willing to implement next-generation approaches.

Your challenge is to find ways to deliver it to them.

Qualifying Questions

1. What's most important to you?

2. What's most important about that?

3. To make sure we clearly understand-repeat.

4. What would you pay for #1 & #2?

Shift
—Rebuilding the Hospitality, Travel & Casino Industries

Creative people have a bias toward action. They are often more likely to ask for forgiveness than permission. By shifting how they think, they learn by trying new things, and they live with the uncertainty and the outcomes of those decisions.

The hospitality industry is often mired in the "we have always done it this way" mentality, but it is also quick to learn as much as possible from every mistake, thereby cultivating fertile ground for experiences based on Customer and employee feedback. While it may be easier to embrace familiarity, we must become more resourceful in learning, adapting, implementing "how to think," and inventorying what is wanted, needed, or imagined.

"During periods of discontinuous, abrupt change, the essence of adaptation involves a keen sensitivity to what should be abandoned—not what should be changed or introduced. A willingness to depart from the familiar has distinct survival value."

—Peter Drucker

Nearly 7 out of 10 US hotel rooms were empty as of May 13, 2020, according to the American Hotel and Lodging Association.

Here's a few shifts due to COVID-19 that may create a further change in our business economy:

- 💡 At the time I wrote this book, 62% of employed Americans are working from home. With 60% of American workers preferring a work-from-home policy, what will happen to commercial office space?
- 💡 Companies may limit or reduce business travel which will impact the hospitality industry even further.
- 💡 Working from home with blur the lines between "personal life" and "work life."

Hopefully we will use this crisis to produce something better. Shift Happens and more shift is coming.

Since the public health issue began escalating in mid-February in the US, hotels **have already lost more than $13 billion in room revenue.** This figure is rapidly accelerating with hotels currently on pace to lose more than $500 million in room revenue per day based on current and future reported occupancy rates.

This pace means a loss of $3.5 billion every week and will only further escalate as the situation worsens. Most hoteliers are already reporting projected revenue losses of greater than 50% for the first half of the year. The human toll is equally devastating, with hotel managers already reporting significant layoffs and furloughs. Based on current occupancy estimates for the immediate future and historical employment impact rates, nearly 3.9 million total jobs have either been eliminated or will be reduced in the next few weeks.

With 70% of direct hotel employees laid off or furloughed, hotel workers are losing more than $2.4 billion in earnings each week.

Individual hotels and major operators are projecting occupancies below 20% for the upcoming months. At an occupancy rate of 35% or lower, hotels may simply close their doors, putting 33,000 small businesses at immediate risk.

Travel is typically divided into two groups—business and leisure. Leisure travelers balance tolerance for ambiguity with decisiveness. As travelers become more curious, they intensify their desire to learn and create "meaningful memories."

Business travelers are often driven by an agenda, a specific outcome, and measurable results producing a very distinct price/value/time equation. There is little room for exploration or deviation. They are resisting the unknown and focus on very specific certainties. Ask a business traveler their favorite airline, hotel, resort or rental car company, and they have their preferences clearly in mind. That same person experiencing leisure travel may lean towards their business preferences but can be swayed to more experimentation and discoveries.

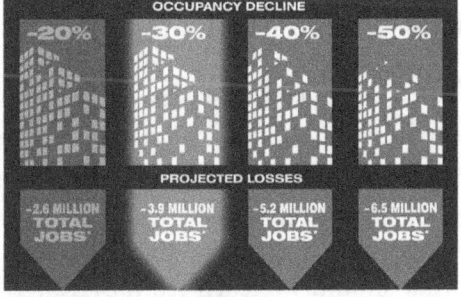

www.jfa.tips/HotelIndustry

When COVID-19 stopped almost all travel, the SOP (standard operating procedure) slate was erased. The hospitality industry, which relies on automobiles, trains, buses or airlines to reach a destination, was hobbled. Business, hospitality, and leisure clients are used to facing extreme adverse weather conditions disrupting travel plans. They move quickly and remain focused on understanding and quantifying the operational and financial impact on their business.

However, the effects of COVID-19 are vast, and not yet entirely predictable, on both revenue and supply chains. We have experienced the shutdown of hotels, restaurants, theme parks, and cinemas—not to mention the disruption of the entire travel ecosystem and forced a paradigm shift in "what's next?"

Hunkered down at home, rarely venturing into hauntingly empty streets, most of us are still at a loss at how life will look afterwards. Will restaurants survive and jobs come back? Will people still travel on airplanes? Do we even need hotels? Will these changes reduce our appetite for fabulous resorts, adventure, and lavish guest rooms?

Does staying at home seem suddenly attractive and at the very least "safe?" Some aspects of our cities and resort areas will be reshaped, depending on how long the current pandemic lasts. Will fear of density and airline travel, plus a desire for safer, more private surroundings, mean we trade travel for staycations?

SARS impacted the industry drastically in 2003. There was a 50% decline in hotel bookings, which led to a drop of nearly $9.4 million in international tourist arrivals, with losses estimated at between $30 billion and $50 billion.

So what should we learn from SARS? After SARS, positive collaborations could have brought about effective preparedness across the health and the tourism sectors for future epidemics.

Regular hygiene surveillance at hotel facilities, developing coordination mechanisms for impending epidemics, the use of screening, swift reporting, and isolation of infected persons should have mitigated the impact of future events.

So what happened? Because preparedness and contingency plans for infectious disease control for the hotel industry required continuous engagement and dialogue, I believe the conversations subsided—despite the fact that after the SARS outbreak in Hong Kong, the health authority established the Guidelines for Hotels in Preventing Severe Acute Respiratory Syndrome (SARS).

The guidelines provided practical information for hotel staff on how to implement measures to prevent communicable diseases. It offered comprehensive information on ways to implement infection control measures, in particular the maintenance of good hygiene on hotel premises (Centre for Health Protection. https://www.chp.gov.hk/files/pdf/105_guideline_on_infection_controland_prevention_in_hotel_industry.pdf).

During SARS, late recognition of the environmental contamination of hotel facilities and the failure of timely intervention with the hotel guests contributed to the spread of the disease internationally. Additionally, the hotel quarantine during the 2009 swine flu exposed gaps in hotel industry partnerships.

Let me acknowledge that you are probably asking yourself, "Didn't our governments, the CDC, WHO, and others understand the potential to establish traveler screening, timely reporting, and isolation for the infected guests before COVID-19?"

Sound familiar? Shift Happens and we did not learn HOW to think. No one seemed to ask What If? What's Next?

Hospitality companies must unlock the power of partnerships to make progress in improving the Customer experience. The question now, with billions of dollars at stake, is whether the current shift will be enough to stimulate a wave of companies to rise to the challenge of putting the Customer at the center.

Despite the facts mentioned above, the travel industry managed to register immense growth by 2006, with a total contribution of $5.16 billion to the global GDP within the year. The recovery from this pandemic will not be as robust. The deficits caused by the "shutdown" gave travelers time to reflect on how they have been treated as Customers.

The ability to provide pleasure by serving a latte with a smile has long provided a safe haven, whether in big cities or local establishments. Will that be enough to get consumers back to their "normal" habits or will it become a treat? Whether you are a hotel, a resort, or a bed & breakfast, traveler suggestions will drive more of the products and services being offered. The only chance to make sure this terrible outbreak can remain a one-time aberration is to invest billions of dollars intelligently in anti-pandemic hospitality infrastructure.

My prediction is that people will strain to get out from lockdown, hungry for the simple joys of being in fearless proximity with one another someplace away from home. After months of being forced to hunker down, they will want to reward themselves.

According to the National Restaurant Association ,before COVID-19, Americans were spending more than 50% of their food budget on meals eaten outside the home.

As we know, restaurants, workplaces and institutions were closed and forced a drastic shift to groceries or packaged meals.

Most studies indicate some of the change will endure even though the reopening of food and beverage in general will be welcomed by the public. The pandemic has shifted the eating habits of Americans.

For example, a recent study by Hunter, a food and beverage consultancy, reports that during the pandemic, over half of American consumers (54%) are cooking more, and almost as many are baking more (46%). Importantly, more than half (51%) of those who are cooking more, reported that they will continue to do so when the coronavirus crisis comes to an end.

While this will impact restaurants in general, it opens up a new revenue possibility for hotels and resorts that can offer home delivery as well as extended room service.

As I write this chapter, the food industry is near the top of any list of those most directly affected by the coronavirus pandemic. From farming and processing to distribution and consumption, shift happened, in many cases dramatically.

Marcum, a NY public accounting and advisory firm, says fresh produce sales in grocery stores rose just 3% from March 2019 to March 2020, compared with a 10% increase in packaged goods (https://www.marcumllp.com/wp-content/uploads/Webinar-FoodBeverage-Forbes-04292020.pdf).

Certainly, everyone hopes that behaviors tied to fear, health policies, and social distancing will not be eliminated as the pandemic threats are reduced. The change in where food is consumed is already having a major impact on what Americans are eating. Prior to COVID-19, we saw trends for fresh and healthy food bolstered by a robust economy. Because 40 million people have lost their jobs and fresh/healthy foods are usually more expensive, we may see a reversal in that trend.

From everything I read, it appears that consumers are flocking to trusted and familiar comfort food, such as peanut butter, spaghetti sauce, rice, canned beans, and pretzels. With forecasters describing an economic recovery in terms of years, not weeks or months, such consumer behavior is likely to continue.

Again, this may provide an opportunity for more of these types of products to become the creative foundation of menus, home delivery items and add-ons that are not being offered today.

I think the biggest losers will be:

- **Fresh** due to short shelf life. People are taking fewer grocery trips and are focused on longer-lasting items. Health and wellness will be traded off for comfort foods.
- **Organic** is a big loser along with foods making dubious health claims not backed by science. Organic won't fit the "fast and frugal" nature of buying.

Restaurants will be able to offer these "loser" items because they can leverage their brand equity to reassure consumers that they can still obtain these products.

The big winners?

- **Frozen** will replace center-aisle staples to some extent. Center-aisle basics are often stocked in the home pantry but not quickly consumed. Frozen is easy to cook with minimal preparation. This is an ideal item for restaurants to offer. It could be that complete meals could be prepared, frozen, and sold.
- **Processed foods** which are simple to cook will help educate consumers. Think about local products that have a following and offer them in your restaurants.

- 💡 **Eggs** will continue to receive a surge in demand because they have a relatively long shelf life and are the easiest protein to cook.
- 💡 **What** products can you add? For instance, I found a fabulous variety bacon that comes as a single slice, ready to eat after 10 seconds in a microwave.

A survey by Shopkick found that with so many consumers finding products out of stock, 69% bought brands new to them when their favorites were sold out. I believe this trend benefits restaurants that offer creative, affordable items that can be prepared at home.

Recovery for all aspects in hospitality needs to focus on any and every path to improve innovative solutions and operational efficiency. Shutdowns to restaurants, workplaces and institutions forced a drastic shift in groceries and packaged meals. As businesses reopen, some of the change will endure. Guests understand that this is a new environment and they understand Shift Happens. Now is the time for you to rethink, reinvent, and revisit how to "wow" your customers.

Let me reiterate: People simply don't care about your company, your products, or your services. One of the standout exceptions is Apple. Under the direction of Steve Jobs, they focused on building a culture. Same with Ritz Carlton, Four Seasons, AM Resorts, Grand Velas, Kempinski.

One of the benefits from COVID-19 is that the hospitality industry has shown its maturity level in working together, revealing their real hospitality commitments in helping out our society where they can. I applaud hotels for making their venue available for hospital beds and hospital employees. The situation brings new business models and opportunities and allows us to apply 3D Thinking. We have seen instances of new delivery concepts, sharing platforms, and "staycation or holistay" concepts. There's also been a shift in the use of the less busy time to work on activities that were customarily pushed forward like asset counts, security plans, defining standard operating procedures, and social media plans.

The hospitality and travel industry must plan for their future by taking steps to diminish resistance to travel once the pandemic has passed. The sector must unify and collaborate on plans to reduce long-term financial losses from coronavirus and drive the sector to recover faster. Airlines and hotels must evaluate the WIIFM (What's in it for me?) for passengers and guests. My suggestion is that upgrades, which cost almost nothing, should be freely offered. The industry must recognize that the early adopters of either business or leisure travel are sacrificing "safety concerns" and should be rewarded, not penalized, for their support. **Hospitality providers should not confuse impossible with inconvenient.**

The travel industry can cultivate a sentiment of reducing tensions, "breaking away" from the fear of contagion, and rediscovering the joys of travel. However, business travel will not resume as quickly as leisure travel because during the shutdown, businesses discovered that virtual meetings could be more time and cost-effective. What changes can the hospitality industry make in shifting the attitudes or actions of business travel, meetings, incentives, education, and networking events? How do they create a more harmonious balance between the poles of virtual versus in-person events?

The meeting industry has been disrupted, along with the escalation of the use of technology, and the increased costs of travel and entertainment. The bottom line is that companies were evaluating the real cost of taking key employees from the marketplace before the pandemic. Travel will diminish everywhere, and international travel will become more expensive. With Zoom, Teams, and other platforms, virtual meetings have gained acceptance.

Overall, many organizations no longer consider conferences, tradeshows, expos, or events as the primary networking resource if they engage in social media. In the past, most meeting attendees roamed the hallway, attended cocktail parties, and took time away from the meeting to set up introductions with those they wanted to interact with in-person or online.

While millions of dollars were previously spent on production, AV, meals, and more to create scholarly output, the attendee often skipped the formal meeting. What was discovered is that attendees often felt the parties and off-site interaction were the highlight of the event. And there is the answer. Create meaningful memories outside of the formal meeting's educational components.

Concentrate on ways to experience greater personal fulfillment with clearly defined goals. Spend more time on the creation of food experiences that are more experiential and less mundane. Review the most anxiety-inducing questions from your attendees' perspective. Remember WIIFM?

Professional Convention Management Association(PCMA), the world's largest, most respected, and most recognized network of business events strategists, summarized shifts in the industry (parentheticals mine):

> **Biodegradable** meeting spaces, artificial intelligence, and serendipity will all play a significant role in the future of meetings and business events.
>
> **Emotional Intelligence:** How to design events with the end-user in mind. (WIIFM)

Orchestrated Serendipity: Engineering, unexpected, but meaningful moments. (Meaningful Memories)

Multi-Modal Design: Creating adaptive spaces such as one that is a biodegradable, and 3D-printed.

Bigger than Oneself: Think about social impact, sustainability . . .

Clear Sense of Place: Leveraging the surroundings where business events are held.

Innovation and creativity will continue to reshape the way we deliver meetings and events. Technology's trajectory was pushed to light speed during COVID-19. What must emerge is more innovation and creativity that partners with others in hospitality.

All meetings must engage attendees and exceed the expectations of influential millennials. Meetings, whether virtual or in-person, will require better ROI evaluation metrics that provide real-time data and a deep dive into the mindsets to assess attendee experience and overall engagement.

Airlines will have to revisit their "add-on" fees for baggage, cancellations, upgrades, and more. The spaces between the reliance on the airlines and hotels/resorts are no longer blurred but inexplicably joined. A coalition between periods of self-serving and the good for the industry must create intensely focused WIIFM.

United Airlines forcibly dragged paying passenger Dr. David Dao off Flight 3411 on April 9, 2017, and suffered the mother of all social media crises. It was the shift in attitudes that became the poster child when CEO Oscar Munoz's response was to blame Dr. Dao for being unwilling to re-accommodate and describe him as "disruptive and belligerent."

The incident highlighted the power of social media, and how one isolated incident could become the global PR disaster overnight. One moment of bad Customer service and the whole airline industry was under a microscope. The airline industry was laser focused on the "necessary cultural and process changes" that were needed. The word "re-accommodate" is forever lodged in the internet lexicon as a United Airlines euphemism for brutally assaulting your Customers.

After COVID-19 and the "next new normal" arrives, airlines need to be reminded that D-A-T-I-N-G Your Customers® requires problem-solving skills and the ability to quickly and accurately assess situations. All airline passengers hope for a seamless, connected journey. We dream of moving smoothly from arrival at the airport, to baggage check and security, to shopping in Duty Free, to checking emails with fast WiFi, and boarding the plane. The bad news is that more often than not, this is a far from seamless experience.

The Airline Quality Ratings (AQR), the most comprehensive study of performance and quality of the largest airlines in the United States, is based on data reported to the Department of Transportation, not loyalty, culture, or Customer service issues. Perhaps the airlines can learn about "hospitality" from hotels and resorts. The airline industry must emerge with above-average Customer service skills and patience.

In one of my books, *D-A-T-I-N-G Your Customer®*, I explain that an extraordinary Customer experience requires the ability to DAZZLE, ANTICIPATE, INNOVATE, NURTURE, and be GRATEFUL. The airline industry must demonstrate that they care about their Customers, not just their wallets. People are ultimately loyal to people. It's either WOW or WHOA.

According to McKinsey & Company, air and travel will have a -44% change in stock price with the potential to restart in Q1/Q2 of 2021. Some people are especially anxious to return to "normal" and venture into the world after the pandemic ends. They are mindful of the outcome, but they are more fearless and will seek "meaningful memories" as soon as possible. They will be price conscious and take advantage of lower prices as they reduce their fears of the virus.

They will be planning their next trip once the restrictions are reduced or removed. They will be mindful of Customer service attitudes. When travel restrictions are lifted, Customers will be more likely than ever before to document their travels. Will the experience be UNIQUE, URGENT, USEFUL, ULTRASPECIFIC and UNDERSTANDABLE from the passenger perspective?

It will all come down to WIIFM? Passengers will vote with their dollars and demand more responsive services. The good news is that airlines can easily transform it to a seamless experience by using data analytics to personalize and perfect each passenger's experience. However, with this transformation also comes a great responsibility to protect the data collected. Cyber security is quickly becoming one of the most pressing issues in the aviation world and it is more important than ever to protect data. And with that data reports on the trends that affect the way airlines do business will influence passenger choices more than price reductions. Safety issues will be targeted optimizations that result in incredible business benefits for airlines. Predictive analytics could transform the consolidation of data for the travel and transportation industries.

Airlines and hotels/resorts should partner in marketing and packaging ways to attract them. Many younger travelers appreciate brands and seek authenticity. Because they are tech-savvy travelers, they want a mobile-first guest experience, personalized messaging, deals, and offers, the 24/7 service, and more. After we return to travel there will be an increased expectation for concierge apps and seamless travel information integration. Hotels and resorts should also rethink meal delivery options for non-guests as well as guests.

In the meantime, I hope that the hospitality industry has used the "downtime" to deep clean everything from their A/C to carpets, beds to showers, and more. They should be making lists of everything that needs to be repaired, repainted, or replaced. Check balconies and railings, pool systems, gyms, hot tubs, swimming pools, and every single light in every room and common area. There is no better time to do this with the mission to improve on everything.

The travel industry should continue to leverage the technologies and analytical tools to connect guests in novel and meaningful ways. Social distancing has separated people by not only physicality, but distances in meetings, travel, and time. However, with this shift came new ways to reduce distance by using video technology. By being available everywhere, video meetings eliminated issues of distance but increased the inherent need for more personal contact. As we return to travel, the hospitality industry needs to find ways to be more accessible, provide insights, and regain their competitive edge. Wireless communications will never replace on-site visits to cities, hotels, resorts, offering real access to assets that have been inaccessible to most people for months.

Hand sanitizers can be offered on flights and as part of the guest room amenities alongside shampoo and conditioner.

Visual cues will now be brought to the forefront to give travelers a sense of security and a sense of safety. Every provider of the hospitality industry will have to establish guest confidence and maintain that trust. Creative innovators will develop a myriad of ways to deliver that experience, make it enjoyable, make it something guests will appreciate, and want to enjoy.

In the past few years, many luxury hotels and resorts pushed the development of Internet of Things (IoT) adoption with smart lights and smart thermostats. Overall, guests won't want to touch a plastic card or thermostat or talk with a front-desk agent face-to-face. They'll want control via their smartphones and tablets. That reliance on IoT could also include keyless entry. The big problem will be funding. The billions of dollars of lost revenue and a wide disparity in investments may delay the IoT implementation.

Post COVID-19 innovative thinking should include how to leverage the benefits and the connections that they can offer their most loyal customers. Think about how casino were used to staying connected to their players. As the market starts to pick up again I think there will be a huge uptick in bookings using loyalty points.

With all of the income losses in the past few months, the hospitality industry will find itself under pressure to balance loyalty redemption with loyalty retention.

The entire hospitality industry will have to think "inside the box" to operationalize what they can afford, offer, and deliver consistently.

The guest experience will be guided by what the changing guest expectations are, starting with incorporating cleanliness and safety into the brand's marketing. I believe that most guests will ask about the safety protocols and cleaning protocols in this particular hotel or resort.

There is no better time than now to review health and safety practices for airlines, restaurants, and hotels. All rely on personal interactions. Consider these changes:

- Orders through mobile applications.
- Complimentary hand-sanitizers at every entrance, exit, passenger seat, restaurant, room, lounge chair, table, and more.
- Self-service pay stations and systems will become a standard.
- Mobile wallets will accept and offer payments from credit cards, debit cards, and bank accounts.
- Cell phones will become a single device for almost all communication and transactions.
- Networking and work meetings will become antiquated as technology replaces their need.
- As automation and technology become more widely accepted, there will be staff reductions.
- Hospitality and travel employees will be monitored more closely to evaluate their health conditions. Same with guests and passengers. When someone enters a hotel, airline, or restaurant, it will be reasonable to check their temperature.
- The hospitality industry will emerge with a new focus on reviews, reflections, and reactions to how they create new processes and policies to ensure they are not spreading infection.
- Sanitation Specialists, formerly called maids or housekeepers, will be elevated to a new professional status. They will implement the disinfection of common areas, tables, chairs, and mirrors to prevent the spread of infection.
- Information Verification Specialists will monitor "fake news" and misinformation. It will be their job to interpret and verify the "facts" and avoid contributing or spreading misinformation.

In the movie, *The Bucket List*, there are several quotes between Edward Cole, an entrepreneur, and Carter Chambers, a car mechanic. Both of these men have been diagnosed with a terminal illness:

"Get busy living or get busy dying."

"If life has taught me anything, it's that 95% of the people are always wrong."

"I envy people who have faith, I just can't get my head around it."

"Maybe because your head's in the way."

What do you want to shift?

At the end of the movie, a mountain climber is ascending to the top and the voiceover says: *"Even now I cannot understand the measure of a life, but I can tell you this. I know that when he died, his eyes were closed and his heart was open. And I'm pretty sure he was happy with his final resting place, because he was buried on the mountain. And that was against the law."* Rent the movie and the message will be clear. Enjoy life today because we don't know about tomorrow.

Take the time to create your own bucket list and then live it.

> It's time to create your own bucket list

Every year when others are making New Year's resolutions I create new goals, dreams and desires to achieve. Some of them are accomplished and others moved to the following year, but every year I accomplish more, enjoy life and make more room in the bucket for additions to the list.

Once I told someone about this project and the response was, "What if you die before you complete your list?"

I replied with a smile, "Then others will know how I lived won't they?" And then it occurred to me that perhaps my survivors wouldn't really know. So I wrote my own eulogy. In thinking about who should deliver the eulogy, I thought, "Who knows me better than I know myself?" So I went into a video recording studio and recorded my own eulogy. It's funny. It's provocative. It's tearful. And it's a celebration of my life and that's all I can ask for.

The hospitality industry is gifted with almost unlimited potential for learning and creativity. The pandemic is a test of their ability to uncover hidden talents, sharpen their guest experience, and think "inside the box." Whether it's the gambling industry or all-inclusive resorts, the hospitality industry worldwide represents the opportunity to create meaningful memories for both business and leisure travelers. The hospitality industry doesn't allow the past to determine the present or the future. Historically, whether a fine dining restaurant or fast food organization, they don't make the same choices in new circumstances. They practice Steven Covey's advice: "I am not a product of my circumstances; I am a product of my decisions."

There is an excellent opportunity for the hospitality industry to encourage leaders to think about how their visions can be translated into something remarkable. It's time to learn about strengths, evaluate opportunities, and discuss how to emerge better, more durable, and more resistant. It will be amazing to see what Determination (the third D in 3D Thinking) can accomplish.

As Darryl Hartley-Leonard, former President of Hyatt Hotels and Resorts, told me: "If all we did is make them feel at home, we have failed."

Here's my AHA to stimulate the return of passengers/guests after a return to the "new normal." Create a package offer that includes free baggage allowances, airline and hotel upgrades, and double loyalty points. The airline has no additional costs for their upgrades except for meal cost. Hotel room inventory that is unoccupied is a lost opportunity to reward those guests who book the packages before 12/31. This becomes a joint creation of a meaningful memory that reminds travelers that the hospitality industry embodies friendliness, warmth, generosity, and cordiality. It truly represents a reminder that the hospitality industry embraces a D-A-T-I-N-G relationship.

There are four options in how these shifts impact us.

- **Option One** is coping, which typically manifests itself in a reduction of momentum and productivity. Lots of time is wasted hoping for the return to normal. It's worth noting that the pandemic seriously impacted the proliferation of Option One. Blame, fear, and resistance have created a new impetus to move forward.
- **Option Two** is adaptation. It's often a "cut your losses" attitude. While begrudging compliance is often accompanied by a failure, a personal effort to drive any kind of shift that deals with change could become positive rather than negative.
- **Option Three** is about the opportunity and exploiting shift. Instead of manifesting resistance, a positive search for the benefits is needed.
- **Option Four** creates shift. Those who drive change are not content waiting for shift; they make it happen. Option Four ensures that SHIFT HAPPENS!® If you want to partner with a post–COVID-19 world, you must create a "success zone" so you can drive change and ignite a spirt of adventure, faith, and optimism.

Option Two

Who: Wants a solution, but doesn't understand problem.
Act: Educate

Risky Customer

Option Four

Who: Wants a solution, and understands the problem.
Act: Contact and Pursue

Model Customer

← Less Cognizant | More Pressing | More Cognizant →

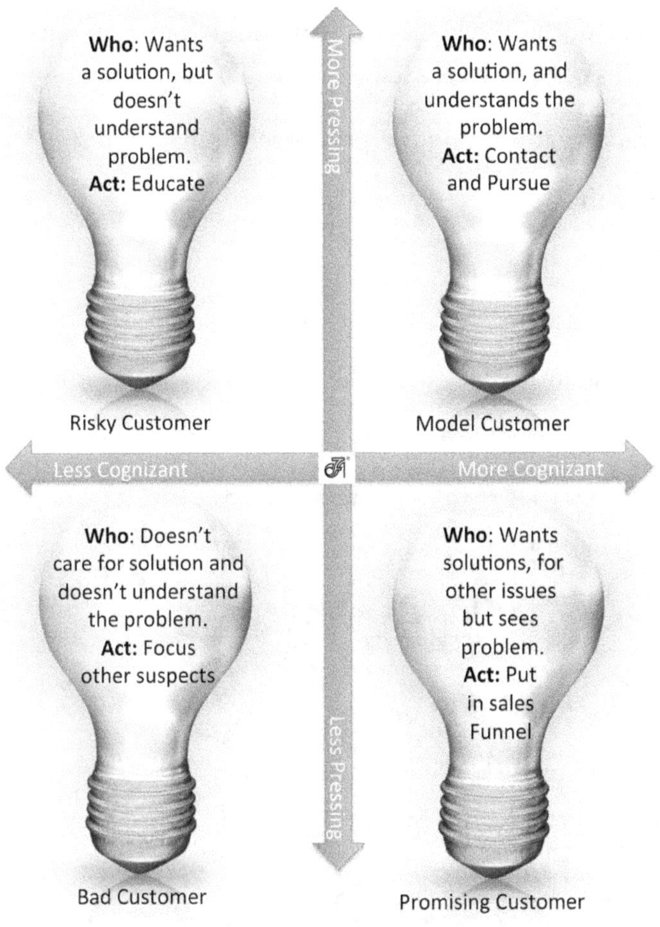

Option One

Who: Doesn't care for solution and doesn't understand the problem.
Act: Focus other suspects

Bad Customer

Option Three

Who: Wants solutions, for other issues but sees problem.
Act: Put in sales Funnel

Promising Customer

Less Pressing

Most people have some idea of what they would like to accomplish in their lifetime. Creating a list helps you turn that vague idea into an action plan. The "bucket list" should be created and achieved in a manner that represents our true desires and interests.

According to Jim

Create categories and the prioritize them.

- 💡 Health
- 💡 Family
- 💡 Finances
- 💡 Personal
- 💡 Work

9 TIPS TO MAKE INTERNATIONAL TRAVEL AND NETWORKING EASIER

1. BUSINESS CARDS
Take 3x the number of business cards you think you will need. Not being able to exchange business cards shows disrespect when attempting to do business or networking. Order cards in the local language if you will be at one destination for a long time. Also, bring thank you cards and leave for hotel staff, drivers, guides, etc. Include your business card and a handwritten note. Learn gratuity preferences prior to tipping.

2. THE SIX-MONTHS PASSPORT RULE
Renew your passport before travel if it expires within six months of your return. Also obtain Visas, travel permits, and any medical inoculations. Start to arrange dining, tours, activities in advance. Don't assume you can just "walk in."

3. GETTING CASH
With ATMs all over the world find out which debit or credit cards waive or reduce fees. If you take cash, ALWAYS divide the cash into three piles that you store in three different places. Don't leave cash in your room. Don't put cash in your luggage.

4. TRAVEL ALERTS
SHIFT HAPPENS! Start checking alerts six months before you travel. Be prepared for changes. Adopt a positive mindset that 'safe' travel often means 'informed' travel. You are not in Kansas anymore.

5. CREDIT CARD
Make photocopies of all your cards. Give one to your companion in a sealed envelope. Leave one at home. Take a few cards as possible. Separate the credit cards into several pockets so that you can't lose all of them through misplacement or pickpocket. Take a photo of your receipt or use an expense app such as Expensify.

6. UNWANTED LOCAL CURRENCY
Go to a local bank, not your hotel or currency exchange to obtain local currency. Discover their conversion rate to 'sell' as well as to 'buy' back. Spend the local currency before returning home. Treat local currency the same as if it were your local currency. Conversion back home will be at a higher cost to you.

7. MEDICINE
Copy your prescriptions or pharmacy labels. Do not put either in your luggage. Get a freezer bag and keep all together, in your carryon. Only buy medicine from legitimate local pharmacies. If you don't know what your buying, don't buy it. Be safe. Take NO risks. Buy sealed bottles if possible. Keep a record of where you bought the medicine. Better safe than sorry!

8. BUSINESS ACUMEN
Prepare materials. Backup on a USB drive and keep in carryon. Bring extra USBs to receive files, photos, etc. Print out extra copies before you leave. Arrange appointments in advance. Understand cultural preferences. Follow up. To order book http://tiny.cc/DoctorTravel

9. HAVE FUN EVERY DAY

5 TIPS FOR SHIFT MANAGEMENT
Phases Of Innovative Problem Solving

With all of the 'shifts' in business competition, government regulations, scarcity of employees, and the lack of loyal Customers many companies reduce their price instead of enhancing the relevant value and Customer/Employee retention. It's all about the *Journey To Bright Ideas* for operational excellence and solutions for YOUR Customers and employees.

DEFINE
Who is the economic customer and what are their needs?
What keeps them 'awake' at night? What's their problem we can solve?

MEASURE YOUR IQ
Your culture's innovative building blocks should...
Instill • Involve • Inspire • Imagine

ANALYZE
What is the relevant differentiation from your competition? Organization effectiveness requires an emotional *connection with your employees.*

IMPROVE
How can get 'buy-in' from management?
Ask: What does it cost your organization to NOT implement innovative solutions?

CONTROL
Has operational excellence and emotional connection unified?

www.jfa.tips/ProblemSolving

Shifts
to Improve Patients' Patience

Health care, like any other business, needs good Customer relations to be successful. Unfortunately, we have few role models of good Customer relations, as every day we deal with companies that don't live up to our expectations. It could be the cable company who tells you their installer will show up "sometime between 8 and 4." Or it could be the bank teller who doesn't know your name, account, or business. Or maybe it's the airline that serves a small bag of pretzels instead of lunch during your midday flight. Are these businesses meeting your needs or their own?

- Under the Affordable Care Act the federal government deducts 2% of certain Medicare payments to many hospitals each year.
- Hospitals can earn none, some, or all of that money back based on performance in four areas, including patient experience. Hospitals that perform particularly well can make more than the 2% again.

Remember that what did not work in the past may work in the future. Health-care costs are going up, service is going down, and personal contact has gone the way of doctors making house calls—virtually non-existent. The time has come to make some changes so you can better meet your patients' needs and attract more patients to your practice. If health care doesn't focus on the experience and the kind of care they provide, they are not going to be able to compete in today's marketplace. Patients tend to focus on not only the outcome, but they also compare their expectations with the experiences they had. When those expectations are not met by the actual situation, the patient may become dissatisfied. **Patients should not be going home just feeling comfortable but with an experience that was successful.**

Be the Patient

EVERYTHING STARTS WITH THEIR CHALLENGES, NEEDS, PREJUDICES, AND CONCERNS.

- To what extent are patients satisfied with the health services being offered at your hospital?
- To what extent can the level of satisfaction with the health services be attributed to between-services and within-service factors?
- To what extent is satisfaction with the health services associated with individual characteristics such as demographic status, education, self-perceived health, use of illegal drugs and type of insurance?
- To what extent can service characteristics such as staffing level, competence and hospital size explain differences in satisfaction levels between services?
- Patients' satisfaction is an important indicator for quality of care. Measuring health-care quality and improving patient satisfaction have become increasingly prevalent, especially among health-care providers and purchasers of health care. This is mainly due to the fact that consumers,

especially during and after the pandemic, are becoming increasingly more knowledgeable about health care.
- 💡 Controlling patients' demands and preferences and adopting correct marketing concepts, while facing intense competition, is essential in order to satisfy the public and build up a competitive edge for medical institutions.
- 💡 Just like the hospitality industry, the quality of service and the satisfaction of "Customers" are key determinants of patient's loyalty.
- 💡 What am I doing differently after COVID-19? What is the new value to my Patients? What is the benefit to my Patients? What are my new expectations for the health-care staff?

"We cannot solve a problem by using the same kind of thinking we used when we created them."
—Albert Einstein

Shift 1. Try "D-A-T-I-N-G" Your Patients. The key to being in tune with your patients' needs is to form better relationships with them. Cultivating patient relationships is much like dating; it requires the right amount of thoughtful planning and preparation, intelligent nurturing, diligent caring—even break-ups at times.

Be authoritative
STAY IN YOUR SWEET SPOT, WHERE THE THINGS YOU UNDERSTAND BETTER THAN ANYONE ELSE INTERSECT WITH THE THINGS YOUR PATIENTS REALLY CARE ABOUT.

Patience pays enormous dividends in your quest for the perfect relationship. Remember when you were in high school, and you wanted to date someone? You thought about it. You imagined being on dates together. You might have even imagined going steady with that person, or maybe even marrying him/her. You realized, however, that the first step was to ask the person out. Patient care is similar. To court your patients, you need to:

Be strategic

ONE-OFF CONVERSATIONS DON'T ADD UP TO A LONG-TERM PATIENT RETENTION STRATEGY.

D – **Dazzle** patients with your service.

A – **Anticipate** your patients' needs by emphasizing caring over costs.

T – **Treat** your patients well by being a problem-solver. Understand their concerns and treat the whole person, not just the symptoms.

I – **Innovate** by understanding most rules should be flexible.

N – **Nurture** your employees and suppliers by giving them the same care and respect you want them to give your patients.

G – **Guarantee** you stay in business by making sure you have a great patient service plan for suppliers, employees, and your patients, and then ensure that your employees understand it and follow it.

Shift 2. Become Problem-Solvers. The key difference between other service providers and health-care providers is that practices and staff need to be "problem-solvers." They need to become interpreters of what patients need and value. Sell your ability to solve your patients' problems. They chose to come to your practice and use your services. Once they're in your facility, prove that you deserve their business. They are now in your hands and dependent on your wisdom to provide a solution.

Too often, administrators, practice executives, and managers stay in their offices sitting at their desks. They may hear of deteriorating conditions in the organizations that they lead, but they do not see the requirements for themselves. No substitute for firsthand information and direct contact exists. To service your patients, you need committed employees, and you need suppliers that can reliably deliver the products you provide to your patients. Practices must listen to their patients, suppliers, and employees to make sure all needs are being met. And remember, just because your training has followed a precise procedure for 30 years doesn't mean it's the best way to handle something. Don't be a slave to tradition.

Here are ten tips to help make your patient relations more personal and productive.

Shift 3. Show what you offer. Dazzle your patients with your knowledge. Show them you know your business and demonstrate your expertise. You need to showcase your expertise as you understand your patients' needs. Identify, individualize, and continuously interact with patients. These personal interactions force you to grow and serve.

Shift 4. Create an individualized patient plan. Patients have heard it all. They want to know why your suggestions are the best solution to their needs. They want to see how you have individualized your treatment plan to them. This is their life. They want to know that you care, that you understand their fears, and that you will treat them as individuals.

Be prolific

D-A-T-I-N-G YOUR PATIENT IS A MARATHON NOT A ONE-TIME EFFORT.

Shift 5. Nurture your patients. No two patients are alike. One-to-one interaction allows personalized, relevant, useful, and nurturing contacts to be managed as a process. Even the most inarticulate nurturer can be supported with an online menu of letters, memos, notes, and other expressions of true sentiments. Treat your patients the way you want to be treated.

Shift 6. Offer targeted, precise solutions. Do not offer a "historical" approach to a problem. When the pilot of a fighter jet has his target in sight, he gets a tone, which tells him that he has locked onto his target. We get "tones" all the time, but do we listen? Most patients will tell you what they want. They provide the information you need to be successful. Unfortunately, most doctors and nurses do not monitor. They say to the patient what they have been programmed to say. Instead, they need to be flexible in their approach. Manage the patients' expectations. Cater to their fears.

Shift 7. Focus on keeping your current patients. Just like any business, you'll spend more money to get a new patient than to keep an old one. So why do we forget about the patients we have and continuously try to get new ones? A simple follow up once a year by email, phone, or a personal meeting with each patient to determine their needs will be rewarding to both patients and staff. At this time, you can ask for a testimonial that you can show to other prospective patients. If they are unhappy with your service, they will now tell you they can't provide a testimony. Here is your chance to hear their tone and react accordingly.

IF YOU DON'T CARE ABOUT THIS STUFF, WHY SHOULD ANYBODY ELSE?

Shift 8. Stay positive. Use emails, phone calls, and personal notes for making "touches that matter." People remember people who intentionally create experiences that make them feel special. Keep the tone positive. Let them know you care.

Shift 9. Take pride in your solutions, but don't take all the credit. An attitude of gratitude with your team shares the results and encourages continued nurturing. Make sure your staff understands their role in keeping your patients satisfied. Nurture this relationship. Dissatisfied employees cannot keep their patients happy.

Shift 10. Don't rest on your successes. Without a regular maintenance program, your patients will not return to your practice when the need arises. Forty percent of all patients probably won't choose you again. As such, you will lose revenue, referrals, and continuity. So stay in touch often.

Be tough on yourself

YOU'LL KNOW IF YOU'RE BEING LAZY. DON'T BE LAZY.

Shift 11. Stop pondering the past and begin nurturing the future. Failure is the second cousin to success. Realize that changes take time. If your patience fails, learn from it.

Shift 12. Remember to DATE your patients. If your organization is going to compete in today's fierce marketplace, you must think progressively. The first place to take action is with your patients. They are no longer loyal. Price being equal, they don't care if you have worked with them for years unless you have formed a relationship and become a problem-solver for them. That will ensure they return to your practice whenever the need arises.

Influencing positive experiences requires that the staff frequently check on patients, as well as enabling good handovers with effective information. This removes the hassle of patients retelling their story to every new staff member.

Be Your Own Patient

CALL YOUR FACILITY AS IF YOU WERE THE UNHAPPY PATIENT.

Doctors and nurses talking outside the patient's room were seen as both a positive and a negative thing. Some thought it indicated seamless and "excellent" care, giving patients privacy when they needed it. Others did not like hearing about a grim prognosis.

ATTITUDE is everything. A Walter Reed hospital survey indicated that 67% of all patients seek other resources because of a poor attitude or indifference from health-care employees.

By creating caring and open relationships with your patients, you will keep the patients you have and attract more. Take the time you need to develop a plan that will improve the practice experience for your patients. Once implemented, your practice will be ready for whatever changes come its way.

Patients, if given a choice, go to caretakers they trust, and they share their experiences with other people they like. Since Millenials are so interconnected through social media, they "like" and "share" their experiences online. Online experiences have the potential to reach much wider audiences than simple face-to-face recommendations.

Commit to these critical AHA's:

> I will deliver patience to my Patients.
> I will provide solutions that address WIIFM.
> I will bolster engagement that encourages loyalty.

Zappos embodies this ethos with their core values: "We know that companies with a strong culture and a higher purpose perform better in the long run. As we continue to grow, we strive to ensure that our culture remains alive and well. . . . We are not an average company, our service is not average, and we don't want our people to be ordinary. We expect every employee to deliver WOW."

> You are now halfway through this book so it's time for an AHA Bonus. **www.slibuy.com** is a Wholesale and Liquidation Online Auction Company. Slibuy hosts consignment auctions offering store returns and other sellers such as bank repossessions, foreclosure cleanouts, business and warehouse closings, municipal inventory, product closeouts and overstock. Read their description carefully and bid cautiously. You can save on almost every type of merchandise imaginable. Some items are brand new, directly from stores like Target.
>
> If you're near Shorewood, Illinois, you can even pick up items locally to save on shipping and test electronics in person.
>
> FYI: I was not paid for this company mention. And some of their reviews are not positive. Caveat Emptor.

OUR TOP REMOTE WORK Tips

Don't work on weekends
Make sure there is a time when you put work away and unplug. It's healthy to have "me time."

Spend time with family
If your family is home, take small breaks to hang out with the kids or your significant other.

Make your own schedule
Find your most productive time of day and work your schedule around it

Take naps
To boost performance, try taking a quick 30-minute power nap during your lunch break.

Build rapport
Check in with those in your team or similar roles just to say hi and build a relationship.

Drink water
Keep a water bottle next to you throughout your work day and stay hydrated.

Keep a clean workspace
Nothing prohibits productivity like clutter. Keep a clean desk free of distractions.

Create a to do list
There's nothing quite like checking off completed tasks. Start each day with a to do list.

Set up a home office
Create your own space exclusively for work with a setup that works for you.

Time yourself
Pomodoro timing can be a great way to improve concentration and get tasks done.

Stick to a schedule
Try to stick to the same schedule or routine each work day to increase productivity.

Get dressed
While it may be tempting to work in pajamas all day, getting dressed can improve productivity.

Jobs

Shift

FOUR STEPS HOW TO VALUATE YOUR COMPANY

1. Present Value Of Future Benefits.
Valuation is the present value of future benefits. Prepare financials that make the business look attractive so the buyer knows what they are buying.

2. Succession Planning
Start thinking about your exit plan now. It's a process not an event. The more you're in front of the process the advantageous your opportunities.

3. Translate Your Data
Owners add the most value to their business by helping buyers understand the value of what you are offering and why you are selling?

4. Selling To Your Children
It's still about planning and starting early. Make sure they are on board during your planning and process.

Shift

—I Owe! I Owe! It's Off to Work I Go

As I write this book more than 5.6 million people around the world have become infected with COVID-19, and more than 350,000 people have died from the disease. The United States, now nearing two million infections with 100,000 deaths, is the new epicenter of the outbreak. More people have applied for unemployment benefits than any other time in history. Entire industries have shut down.

COVID-19 has been the most devastating financial loss to the US Economy in history. The coronavirus has touched every aspect of our lives. Most of us are now working from home, separated from friends and colleagues. Family gatherings, community celebrations, and religious services have either been canceled, postponed, or conducted online.

Most of us have had to master the art of remote working and learning in record time, often under trying circumstances. Office workers have had to reorient their tasks given that many no longer have access to the resources necessary to complete their work assignments.

We have been forced to display resilience and deep commitment to one another. Even amid uncertainty, I am confident that you are in a stronger position to weather this crisis and discover new opportunities using existing resources.

While the extent and nature of the economic impact are not yet fully known as I write this book, we must plan for a range of scenarios.

We will never return to the "old normal." It's no longer what you think, but how you think that, which guides you through the maze of loans, forbearance, banking hurdles, and government shifts in tactics.

For the foreseeable future we will need to engage in shared sacrifice as we work through very real financial challenges. Going forward, we must be creative in envisioning new ways to deliver innovative solutions that we can monetize.

I recognize the strain and the disruption that COVID-19 has caused for everyone. The world has been tested in ways none of us could have anticipated, and challenges will continue to confront us in the days ahead. But I am confident that, together, we will adapt to meet these new challenges as they arise. This book is written with the belief that I can assist you to respond with creativity, so we can emerge stronger.

U.S. officials rushed to contain the spread of disease, the federal government is also grappling with the dramatic—and unprecedented—toll the epidemic has had on the economy. In four weeks, 22 million Americans have filed for unemployment benefits. Technical glitches have prevented millions of Americans from receiving their stimulus checks from the U.S. Department of the Treasury. And the Small Business Administration, which supports U.S. entrepreneurs with loans and funding, has run out of money for its Paycheck Protection Program.

But these efforts have not calmed volatility.

It's up to you to take control of your future. We bailed out the banks in 2008 and I see no signs of them offering reciprocity in 2020. Apply for every forbearance, interest reduction, and late-charge waiving that is offered. Do not tap into your 401K but sell off what you don't use. Everything can be sold to someone for the right price.

The additional uncertainty is whether our banks are willing to support small business to make sure that credit keeps on flowing to the real economy, no matter what. Find a community bank. Chase, Citi, Bank of America, and Wells Fargo are assisting their "big" Customers not small business. Go to a credit union or find a rich relative and offer more interest than they are earning now.

If you think about it, supply is the measure of what we collectively produce, but the virus caused a sudden contraction of the labor supply. The resulting loss of confidence has caused a demand shock. Coronavirus had a direct contraction in our ability to produce goods and services.

However as we return to "normality," there will be new products and services that will fill the void left by unfulfilled surging demand.

My message to you, from my experience, is that you need to intrude on your future as swiftly and uniformly as possible.

- 💡 Identify your skills and expertise to focus on your most profitable specialization.
- 💡 Focus on your ideal Customer and how to find them.
- 💡 Develop a marketing message that addresses "What's In It For Them" (WIIFM)

- What problem are you solving for your Customer?
- What will they pay for your solution? Product? Service?

Here's a step by step plan:

- Identify the current or future situation.
- Create a story: This is what we are doing to solve your problem.
- What do you need? When do you need it?
- Tell a story that encourages your Customer to say: Tell Me More.
- Explain your values and core competencies.

What you want to accomplish is your potential Customer thinking: "I can count on them. I can trust them. I need them in my life. And I am willing to pay for it."

When you can't effectively work, due to the outbreak, it's the best time for you to re-imagine your future.

It's time to shift your thinking to re-imagine the "next normal." Achieving sustainable growth isn't impossible. Ditch that self-limiting belief. We can grow—and here's how.

The two primary ingredients of growth are:

1. **Value to you**
2. **Sustainable opportunity**

You can't have one without the other and expect to grow.

Finding a job that is willing to pay for your work isn't true value. It is only a stopgap measure. You must find something you love to do.

If you are out of work, this is the perfect time to create your own shift. Find what you would *want* to do for the rest of your business life–even if you don't get paid—and figure out *how* to get paid for it!

A job opportunity without any value is not a real opportunity. Only when you continuously align your value with a career willing to pay for that value can you shift your life.

First, let's talk about value

Value can be a pretty complex thing, especially since we tend to have tunnel vision about our value perceptions.

What was really valuable in your market six months ago probably isn't as hot today. That's how quickly today's world shifts and evolves. That means we have to evolve our perspective on our value—or get stuck in gravity. Yet, we fall in love with our value—and often hold onto it far beyond its time. It's not just about us, it's about the world. Everyone has the fear of becoming an early adopter or purchaser of a new computer or software because it becomes obsolete so quickly. We have even coined a phrase for this shift, "planned obsolescence."

Our grandparents never thought about products staying on shelves and being freshened, tweaked or discontinued with the frequency we experience today. Many products today have the lifespan no longer than a child's attention span. This creates lots of opportunities for you. Think about what is of value to you. What would you pay for but you can't find? Then create the solution.

Blockbuster, once a market disrupter, filed for bankruptcy. Netflix shifted the way we all thought about movie rentals, from obscene late fees to no late fees, from physical store rental to mail delivery and then online content you can access from wherever you are. Cable and satellite companies started offering movies instantly.

Blockbuster tried to launch similar programs, but it was too little too late. Plus, the cost of their brick and mortar stores weighed down profits. They couldn't adapt their value to match the dramatic shifts in their market. They tried, but they were just too stuck.

EF Hutton, Compaq, Paine Webber, MCI WorldCom, Eastern, TWA, Woolworth's, J. C. Penney, and even Neiman Marcus may join this list. Boeing is set to lay off 16,000 of its 161,000 employees.

Value lies in the eye of the beholder—and in the case of business, the beholder is our Customer. That means that we have to be constantly tuning in to the requirements and perspectives of our markets. As they shift, so must we—unless we want to crash and burn.

Sometimes you have to:

- Sell assets/skills.
- Rent assets/skills.
- Barter assets/skills.
- Sell yourself.
- Realize life is not about stuff. It's about living with stuff.
- Build value on with values.
- Create an environment for people to buy from you.
- Stop being shy. Shift Happens!

According to Jim

When to Shift Your Job

My friend Mary has worked several different jobs, for many different companies and in a variety of capacities. She has hired, fired and managed people, been an account executive, an entrepreneur and even a CEO. Here's what she had to say about recognizing when a job has run its course.

It is a gradual transition between not wanting to go to work because of the typical reasons; we dislike it, to not wanting to go to work because it completely ruins your day. At this point, you come home and are simply unable to get past the work drama and eventually wake up every morning with dread and the feeling that you are stuck. And the "stay at home" mandates gave us time to think.

It's the point when the paycheck no longer outweighs the negatives and you realize the slim likelihood of improving your situation. You realize you must begin looking for something different. It could be the point at which you no longer care about the quality of your work and it is as though you are almost hoping to get fired so that you can collect unemployment. That is when you know that things have gone south—you are constantly coming up with names for your future company and all you can talk about is how much you hate your job. Recognize the shift.

> *"If you're bored with life and you don't get up every morning with a burning desire to do things—you don't have enough goals."*
> **—Lou Holtz**

We attribute our bad moods to a lot of different things. When one thing is going really, really badly it affects other parts of our life. You come home from work in a bad mood only to pick a fight with your significant other. This translates to enjoying your free time less because all you are thinking about is what the next meeting is going to be like or how your boss is going to respond to the latest project you completed. One thing affects another. Recognize the shift and make the appropriate changes.

When we are miserable at work, we make all kinds of excuses for why we won't look for another job: the economy is bad, nothing will pay me as much, I'll have to relearn everything, the commute is so easy now, etc.

Stop being lazy! It is time to make Shift Happen. We tend to stifle our own growth and advancement in our careers for fear of not being able to get anything else. Fear of being found out.

Look around at job sites to see what other positions are interesting. It could open your eyes to opportunities and allow you to think: "*I wonder about . . .*" "That sounds like a cool company," "This company offers great benefits," or "Oh, well, I could do that!"

While browsing new opportunities, the age-old adage rings true: the grass is always greener on the other side of the fence. However, you must remain realistic and know that no job is going to be perfect. Focus on the real issue. Be

> Recognize the **shift** and make the appropriate changes

> Stop being lazy!
> It is time to make
> SHIFT HAPPEN

realistic! Find the real issue and focus your efforts on that! What is it that makes you unhappy in your work life?

Set realistic goals. Research other opportunities and talk to people to see what else you can find. Get yourself motivated and see if there are careers out there that might make you happier. Go on informational interviews to learn about other companies and other fields of work. Give them a call and say, "I'm not necessarily looking for a position, but I'd like to talk to you and learn how your company functions."

LinkedIn is the main social media for businesses. Paying the fee to join the Sales Navigator is well worth the investment if you want to reach potential employers.

> Be realistic! Find the real issue and focus your efforts on that! What is it that makes you unhappy in your work life?

Today *anything* that is attempted is better than nothing. A "no" is a "no" whether you annoyed them or simply did not get to meet the decision maker. My personal feeling is that you should do everything you can to get a "yes." A negative is still a response that you can learn from. It is not yet the time for the timid to inherit the earth. It's time for those who take control of their own destiny.

When thinking about informational interviews, remember that few people will turn away an opportunity to talk about themselves and their company. And they will certainly question who the person coming to talk to them is and why they don't necessarily want a job with their company—it is a great way to get your foot in the door and learn a little something. Play the game.

If you're out of college and have no job or were recently downsized, so what? Start exploring all of your options and opportunities. If you are at a stage in your life where you think you could open up your own company, research it.

If you don't think you can do it alone, talk to somebody you trust, somebody who has what it takes and, most importantly, somebody whose abilities compliment your strengths and weaknesses.

> A negative is still a response that you can learn from

If you are still employed and unhappy with your job but you don't want to start your own company, then set up informational interviews, search through job sites and talk to your friends. But be careful. People don't always have the respect to keep your job hunt a secret. Don't make it clear to your coworkers that you are looking because, unfortunately, even your closest coworkers may essentially use that against you. Watch your back and don't get caught up in the game.

> Play the game

Check out the websites of other companies. If it is a service industry, check out their client lists. If their clients are companies you could see yourself working for, then take the necessary steps to learn a little more about them. Find out which one of the categories is the most interesting to you. This is the time to start networking. Never quit your job before you have another one lined up. You don't need to add unnecessary stress at this point—you have already established that you are unhappy. Try to work on that part first. Learn, learn and learn. And don't make rash decisions.

Now that you've done some research, it's time to move forward. Weigh your options carefully. If you still have a job, keep in mind that unemployment is at around 15% right now. You are fortunate if you are still working and getting paid.

You don't want to take just anything to change your situation. **Make sure it is a step up or a lateral move in the right direction.** Be smart.

> Learn, learn and learn. And don't make rash decisions.

How do you define "step up?" It is the value that you place on the new opportunity. When you finally get that job, make that move or start your own company, try not to focus on the negative right away. Try to appreciate it for what it is and realize that every job is going to have its "crappy boss" or "cutthroat employee" or its "bad vacation time." Every job is going to have something that you don't like. Don't expect it to be perfect. Be realistic.

If you have experienced a job layoff or need to earn some additional income, network marketing or direct sales may offer you some immediate relief from the cash crunch you now face. As you consider alternate ways to earn money consider direct sales. Consumers who purchase products from direct sales spend over 35.4 billion dollars per year. Avon, Tupperware, The Pampered Chef, Creative Memories, Mary Kay, Cutco and others rely on independent sales people that work from home.

Direct selling is not for everyone. I recognize that it's not for a lack of participation. According to AARP, 20 million Americans participate or have participated in direct selling. Anyone interested in direct selling needs to become as knowledgeable as possible before investing time or money.

> Watch your back and don't get caught up in the game

Direct selling is a $36 billion dollar industry. My goal in this book is to open up ways people can make money. Nothing is a sure thing. I don't gamble but I do know direct-selling top performers that earn seven figures a year from "knowing when to hold 'em and knowing when to fold 'em."

I was a consultant to many direct selling companies. I saw stay at-home-moms earn pink Cadillacs, go on fabulous trips, and build passive income streams. Likewise, I knew many who joined, lacked patience or persistence, and lost money. Whether it is investing in stocks, playing bingo, or joining a direct sales organization, there are both successes and failures.

If everyone liked vanilla, there wouldn't be 36 flavors. No matter what you do after COVID-19, conduct online searches of the company, the industry, the work hours, the investment, and see what others are saying. The smartest people I know focus on a realistic picture of what participation in any of these "opportunities" is really like. Just like Slibuy auctions . . . read the fine print, do your homework, and be prepared to be pleasantly surprised or rudely disappointed.

Potential affiliates can sell nutritional products, knives, kitchen accessories, greeting cards, storage containers, cosmetics, etc. There are so many different products and services to choose from that many of the sellers of these various products get involved with more than one direct selling company. This allows them to offer a wide variety of products and services to their Customers. Remember, it costs about 90% more to attract a new Customer than to retain an existing Customer. So why not add products that you can sell to your established Customer base?

With commissions between 25% and 50%, little or no inventory to maintain, a back office support system and brand recognition—

the only thing really needed is your willingness and ability to sell. Direct selling companies don't provide Customers or leads—that is up to you. What they do provide is the product or service, name recognition, sales materials and other sales tools, then they leave the "selling" to you and your business network.

You can succeed at direct selling only if you commit to the product or service. At the minimum, you should have personally used the product or have a passion for it. I have been personally involved with several direct selling companies, including Isagenix. Isagenix is a nutritional product company that I personally use to keep my weight stabilized. My website is: jimfeldman.isagenix.com.

Let's face it, there are a lot of companies out there promising big money to work from home and many are not reputable or are scams. First of all, you must steer clear from those fraudulent claims. Here are some helpful hints to find a reputable direct selling company:

- Don't purchase an initial start up kit for over $150.
- A startup kit should contain all that you need to get started in selling the product or service. The best products are those you can personally use and demonstrate. If you don't like the product, how can you sell it?
- Maybe the most important advice is to look for Direct Selling Association (DSA) membership and to check out the company with the Better Business Bureau (BBB). If they are not members of DSA, it may mean they do not live up to DSA's strict standards.
- Review how you receive payment and when. Direct selling is a cash business and the money needs to flow back to you quickly. If you remit to the company and then wait for them to reimburse you, make sure

that you understand the turn around time for your reimbursement. Is it immediate? 30 days? 90 days?
- If the company requires you build a "down line" to get better prices or higher commission—this could be a red flag—research them carefully before you sign up or send any money. Legitimate direct selling companies offer bonus plans for building and recruiting, but don't require it. As long as it's an option that's ok. If it's a requirement, you may want to consider another company.

Remember, there are lots of direct selling companies and even more direct salespeople. It is not easy but it can be lucrative. Those who do well have the right personality, feel comfortable "cold calling," and "knocking on doors," are self-motivated and self-disciplined. Direct selling can be one way that Shift Happens. Do your homework!

According to Jim

- Recognize and understand, and most importantly ACCEPT, the real issue.
- You have to be honest with yourself.
- Look at the situation objectively—if you need to talk to a trusted friend to help you generate a pros and cons list, do it! Do whatever it takes to be objective.
- REALLY consider what the shift means to you and your future emotionally, physically, financially and socially. Can you accept the consequences of this shift?
- DO something! Create an action plan that will help you achieve the results you want and execute it! After let-

ting it sink into your daily life, evaluate the success—or failure—of your decision and action plan.

💡 Evaluate what the shift has meant to you.

💡 Ask yourself, "What problems might I produce with the solutions I created?"

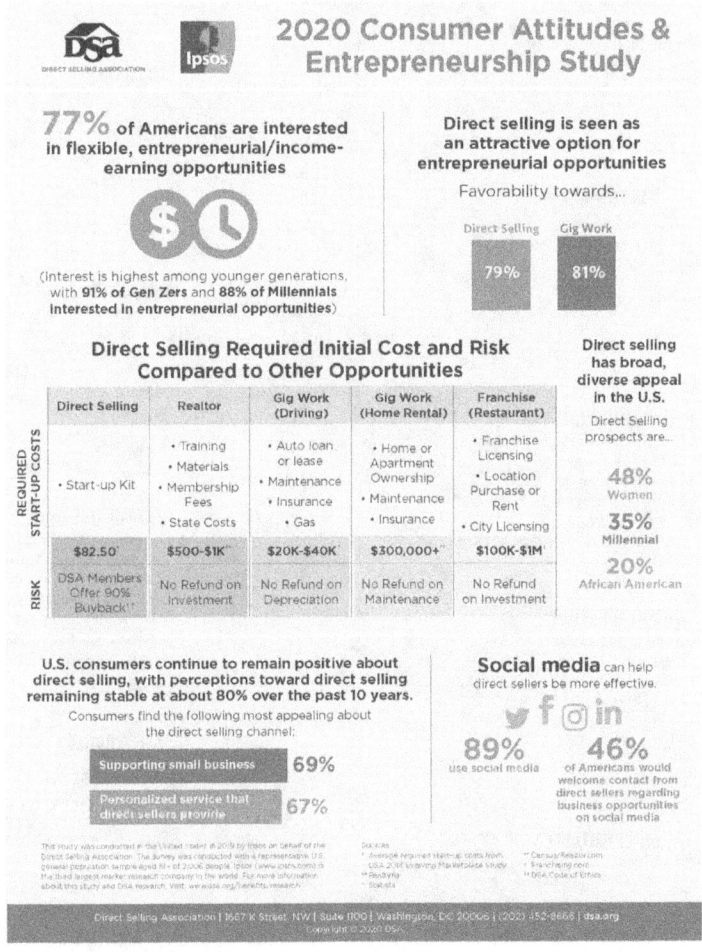

This chart is produced by the Direct Selling Association. Before considering ANY multilevel marketing company, do your homework. www.jfa.tips/MLM

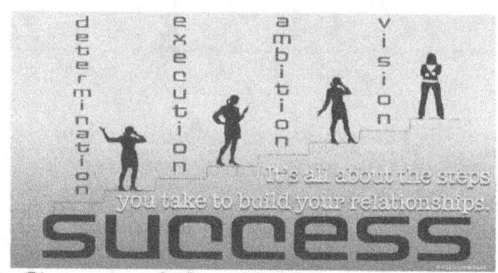

10 Competitive Differentiations

DISTINCTIVE
Is your business unique or offered in a distinctive way?
Do you answer WIIFM?*

1.

2.

VALUABLE
Does your perceived benefit(s) exceed the cost? Save Time or Money? Both? *Do you under promise and over deliver?*

IMPORTANT
Do you deliver a benefit that is critical to your Customers' success? *Do they acknowledge it?*

3.

4.

SUPERIOR
Are you a better problem solver? Offer better technology? Faster? More efficient? Measurable ROI? *Are you the missing piece for their puzzle?*

EMOTIONAL
Facts tell. Emotions sell. What do they love, hate, desire when they wake up in the morning? *Do you help them sleep better?*

5.

6.

PREEMPTIVE
Can you easily be copied? Do you have protected proposals and ideas? Are you the only one that does what you do? Are you the best at what you do? *Then charge for what you are.*

COMMUNICATION
Are you a persuasive presenter? Do you communicate effectively? *Do you upsell?*

7.

8.

AFFORDABLE
Price is NOT the differentiation. Customers will pay the higher price if the WIIFM shows a increase in ROI. *Do they get the 'red carpet' treatment they expect?*

PROFITABLE
Growing a business is not about gross sales but net profits. Contribution should exceed the cost difference. *(Margins x Volume)*

9.

10.

SHOWMANSHIP
Your PowerPoint must use high resolution images. Spell and grammar check. Readable but unique fonts Minimum 32 point Be entertaining, informative. WIIFM*

* What's In It For Me? (WIIFM)

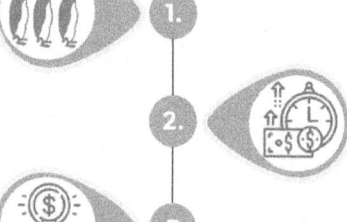
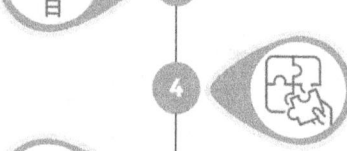

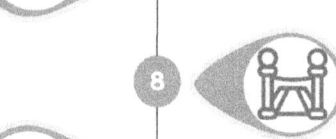

When Shift Happens, Where Does the Loyalty Go?

Employer–Employee relationships are not what they used to be. The loyalty of the past may be just that—a thing of the past.

The United States Department of Labor reports that people are expected to experience an average of 3-5 career shifts during their working lives. **That is career shifts, not job shifts.** And why is that? Because few people in the workforce actually work in fields directly related to their degrees. Who knew? But what we do know is that employees and employers alike are willing to sever ties faster than ever before.

People are now taught to value what they have to offer a company, and if their company does not value their contribution, then find one that does!

Just because you have a job, it doesn't mean that you should stop looking for a better one. If your employer finds someone who can do your job better, faster or cheaper than you can; you had better believe that you'd be shown the door. It is a harsh reality, but it is a reality. Recognize it. Your employer will not hesitate to advance their company, even if it is at the sake of your livelihood. So why wouldn't you have a back-up plan?

People without jobs are not the only ones looking for work these days. People are scared of losing their jobs and are trying desperately to hold onto them. In the event that your job doesn't work out, wouldn't you like to have another option? It makes sense to, yet, many people don't.

Have a Plan B that can become your Plan A. Shift Happens and whether you react to it or create it, shift is here to stay.

The pandemic shined a light on a future we can design. Sure much of the shift is not under our control, and uncertainty may bring undesired outcomes, but it will eventually bring us all together. Our wisdom is to approach uncertain times not just as a problem, but a grace period when we reflect, refine, and resolve these issues using 3D Thinking.

> *"Goals that are not written down are just wishes."*
> **—Unknown**

People who lived through the World War II era have a certain kind of loyalty to American products not held by younger generations. For older citizens, "buying American" is more than just a way to support the local economy; it is a way to proclaim the strength of the nation.

Younger generations consider the value of the products they buy. They look for products that will do what they promise and last as long as they are supposed to last. They will pay for value and buy what they think is the best deal—American or not.

Most of us don't look to our purchases to flex our patriotic muscles. We look to them to get the job done. After all, haven't the majority of American companies moved some part of their organizations offshore? Where is the loyalty in that?

Jonathan S. recently moved his family half way across the country for a new job opportunity. Immediately after moving, he began applying for positions at other companies. He has only been in this new state for a few months, but is already considering leaving the original opportunity for a new position. It's not that his current job isn't paying him well; it is just that the opportunities at the other company are greater.

> Shift is here to stay

Where does Jonathan's loyalty lie? His loyalty is to himself and his family. Not with his employer, that's for sure. And why not? Would his company consider his family if they decide to replace him? Not a chance. Personal loyalty has taken the place of corporate loyalty.

According to Jim

- 💡 Look out for yourself first. Ask "What's in it for me?"

- 💡 Times have changed and loyalty is not what it used to be.

- 💡 Your company owes you just as much as you owe them.

- 💡 Be remarkable.

9 IDEAS FOR AN IN-DEPTH LOOK 'INSIDE THE BOX'

1. This is the Situation.
Accurate identification of the problem is key to finding the real solution.

2. This is what I am doing about it.
Do you see a solution to the problem? Easy to implement? Can you monetize it?

3. What do I need?
Identify the components that make up the problem. Reorder them. Do the math. + x / -

4. Listen to others.
Collaborate. Get advice. Be willing to share the success with your collaborators. ALWAYS share your vision before you monetize it.

5. Remember your values & competencies.
Stay in your lane. Now is not the time to experiment with what you don't know.

6. Trust yourself and others.
Trust is the key. Build a network that can provide honest feedback. Solicit feedback often. Trust their opinions. Reciprocate.

7. Accept Failures and learn from them.
Learn from failures. Most successful person failed at something. T

8. See a need. Fill a need.
What's In It For Me? WIIFM is the key metric for any solution. Does your solution *really* solve their problem.

9. Celebrate
Make money? Save Money or Time? Would you buy what you are selling?

Shift to High Stakes, High Emotions: Where Are the Jobs?

High stakes, high emotions—you have no job and no money, but you need to feed your family and provide for them. How do you tell your 5th grader that she will not be getting those brand new UGG boots for Christmas this year like all of her classmates because daddy/mommy needs to pay the gas bill? Or how do you tell your other children that they have to give up karate or tennis lessons because you can't afford that and the mortgage?

One of the hardest things for a parent to do is to look their pleading and innocent child in the eyes and say, "*I can't.*" How are you supposed to tell your child that? You are their parent, their guardian and their provider. How do you tell her it's your fault they don't have everything they want because you won't swallow your pride and take just any job to pay the bills versus sitting around waiting on the "right" position?

When stakes are high and emotions are higher, you sometimes have to do whatever it takes to get the job done. Sometimes you must take the lesser job to make ends meet until you can find the right opportunity. So what if you do not add the "lesser" job to your resume? Is a future employer or interviewer going to turn you away because of it? Probably not.

You can bet that they will ask you what you have been doing since leaving your last job, but when you answer them honestly, they will find it admirable that you decided to do what you had to do in order to continue to provide for yourself and your family. So you took a huge pay cut—big deal. Even with that pay cut, you are probably making more than you would have collecting unemployment. And did you learn anything from that "lesser" position? Sure you did.

Apply what you learned to your new positions. Lillian Y. has her MBA, yet she has learned useful things from past positions, such as gift-wrapping at Macy's during the holidays. Sometimes, you just need to swallow your pride. You will often be glad you did.

Ask yourself: Where are the jobs? What are my skill sets? What have I learned throughout my personal and professional life that I can translate into job opportunities? What can I do better than anyone else that I know? Can I start my own company or business?

> Nobody cares more about your future than you

Today is the "perfect storm." It is the result of market dynamics, technological innovation and concerns for the pandemic. It is the result of dual career income families and pop culture. We are living at a time where social media, a growing sense of isolation, an increased desire for escape and a failing economy offer more opportunities than ever in our history.

Garrett Camp sold StumbleUpon, his one-year old company that he started in college, for $75 million dollars to eBay. StumbleUpon is a recommendation search engine that "learns what you like, so you only see what is interesting to you from across the web." He bought back the company for less than what he sold it for. The company doubled its revenue and increased market penetration. This is a perfect example of how to sell something, buy it back for less than you sold it for, and resell it again.

Don't have a company to sell? Sell advice. The same advice can be recycled again and again. And each time you sell it you get paid for the advice.

> What can I do better than anyone else?

The industrial revolution, the last depression, the fall of the real estate and financial markets, latchkey kids, multi-pet families and time constraints have "shifted" the needs and wants of our potential Customers.

Age does not affect the running of any business. Some started from college dorm rooms and some were built by years of experience and market research. You are not restrained by your environment or experience level.

Nobody cares more about your future than you. If you don't care enough to do something about your future then why would anyone else? This may sound harsh. Your friends may expect you to help them reach their goals, but often can't help you reach yours. It's time to be selfish because you can't help others if you can't help yourself.

As a reminder of the process of self-help, listen to the pre-flight instructions on an airplane. If you have not flown lately let me remind you about the use of the oxygen mask. "Put the mask on yourself first and then assist others." It's all about planning.

Always plan ahead. It wasn't raining yet when Noah built the ark.

According to Jim

💡 Sometimes you just have to swallow your pride.

💡 Go for it.

💡 When you are desperate for a job (because a job means shelter and food for you and your family), you will do whatever it takes to feed your family.

💡 You will get creative.

💡 You will find that drive.

💡 Consider all of the things that make you valuable to an organization, and remarket yourself. If your current approach is not working, come up with a new one.

💡 Listen. You will never listen yourself out of a job.

💡 The only limitation is yourself.

Creativity vs. Innovation

Creativity is the process of developing new or interesting ideas.
Innovation is the process of transforming creative ideas into valuable or profitable solutions.

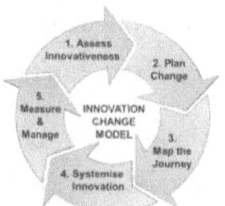

Volunteer a Shift

Even if you have No Job and No Money, the one thing you have is time. You can't spend 24/7 looking for a job or worrying about your finances. Use your free time to get involved in a local charity. Find a charity you believe in and donate some of your energy and time. Hundreds of local, nonprofit organizations are in need of volunteers, so your efforts are sure to be rewarded and appreciated at the same time. They may need your specific skills or just "warm bodies." Either way, it's a change of pace that may lead to other opportunities or just a chance to feel good about yourself.

Let's talk about the rewards. There are many reasons to consider sharing your time and talents with individuals or organizations that are in need of assistance. There are many diverse causes that need volunteers in every community. If you don't already know where you'd like to donate service hours, spend some time thinking about the type of cause you're interested in and look for relatable local opportunities.

You are probably asking yourself, "How can I donate my time when I have no job, no money, and am worried about what to do to 'shift' my own situation?"

Some of the most common reasons that people decide to do volunteer work include:

- **Supporting a worthwhile cause.** This is a feel good moment. By becoming involved in a charity's goal you are focusing on something other than yourself. This may provide the breathing room you need to "step outside" your own box or, even better, get "inside the box" to discover how to find a way to solve your own problems.
- **Gaining valuable skills and experience.** The choice of charities is up to you. As a volunteer you will learn something, meet others and obtain new experiences. You may also learn new job skills. Tell the volunteer coordinator what you'd like to help with and they usually pave the way with a bit of training.
- **Offering assistance to those less fortunate than you.** No matter how miserable you may feel about your own situation, someone is more despondent that you. Finding how they cope with their situation can be uplifting to you. You may become inspired to "stop shoulding" and start doing something to create your own shift.
- **Enjoying an opportunity to work with like-minded people.** Here is another benefit; charities have "glue" that bonds volunteers together. Whether it's fundraising for the zoo, the aquarium, a museum, a hospital, research, or the environment, other volunteers share a similar passion. It gives you a mutual interest that opens up discussion, builds friendships, increases business connections and often results in new opportunities. Conversations with like-minded people often enhance a positive attitude.
- **Repaying assistance received in the past.** Payback is also paying it forward. Donating your time will have dividends that may open doors, stimulate discussion and often find a solution. People involved in charities are

"giving back" and they may be able to give to you more than you realize.

- **Raising money for an illness, animal shelter, the environment, homeless, etc.** When people are focused on raising money, the discussion about your job, your business and your interests all become natural talking points. Find a passion, offer your hard work, knowledge, prior experience and wisdom and you will be amazed at what you get in return.
- **Volunteering looks great on your resume.** If you do not have a lot of work experience, you are unemployed or if you are changing career paths, then adding volunteer work can help round out your resume. The work does not necessarily need to relate to your job experience. Volunteering can also build self-confidence, show employers you are making a change, sharpen skills, create additional references or simply show employers you are a well-rounded potential employee. According to many experts, you may put unpaid or pro bono positions in chronological order in the job section of your resume or call it out in a separate volunteer section. If you are unemployed for a significant amount of time, this will help fill the gap in your work experience.
- **Creating a network of people that can help you find a new job or offer suggestions to making money.** Every charity that I have been involved with gave me opportunities and contacts that I would have never found without my involvement.

Many volunteers are successful professionals or are connected to other successful business people that get involved in charities for "personal" reasons. For instance, it is unlikely that someone will get involved in a serious illness–related charity unless they have a family member or friend that has been affected by that illness.

> Conversations with like-minded people often enhance a positive attitude

The main focus of volunteers for charities is fundraising. It's all about money or "in kind" services that are donated for the charity. Every time you attend a meeting it's about money. And if you have no job and no money you will get all kinds of ideas and contacts that have a similar focus . . . raising money.

Raising money comes in many forms. You might work the phone lines for a fundraiser, become involved in a social event like a dance or walk/run marathon, or solicit donations for an auction, etc.

Here's how to get started:

- Examine your schedule.
- Look at blocks of time where you can donate a minimum of three hours to a charitable organization. If you have no job you have lots of time so this should not be a problem. (As an added bonus, you may find that, particularly if too much time at home has you overthinking everything, volunteering may be good for your mental health.)
- Go to charitywatch.org. The American Institute of Philanthropy grades each charity on a comprehensive scale based on their finances and organization. There is a list of all charities in America, both national and international, and links to each organization. Your focus should be to research charities to which you have a genuine interest.

- 💡 Visit the website of charities where you would like to donate your time. Make a list of the ones that accept volunteers and write down the contact information.
- 💡 Contact each charity and confirm that they are still accepting volunteers. Sometimes they have so many volunteers, there is a waiting list. This happens often with zoos, museums, orchestras, aquariums, etc. Arrange a meeting or a convenient time for you to visit and have an informal chat with the individual who can explain the opportunities for your involvement. Let the volunteer coordinator know what your skill set is and your other interests.
- 💡 Evaluate the work that is being done by the volunteers and see where you might fit in.

At this point you might be saying, "Come on, Jim, how can donating my time have any benefit to finding a job?"

I have been involved in raising millions of dollars for several charities. I was instrumental, with many others, to create a Mother's Day March on Washington. It's purpose was to raise awareness and get signatures to present to Congress, in order to reallocate money from building Stealth Bombers to funding Breast Cancer Research. Our efforts convinced the appropriations committee to "shift" over $450 million.

After that success, I was explaining the Mothers' Day March and my involvement with the Y-ME National Breast Cancer Organization to one of my clients, Boston Market. At the time, Boston Market was moving their office to a newer, larger building. The new office's previous tenant had Voice Over Internet Protocol (VOIP) telephone systems (phone calls that are carried via the Internet, rather than the standard telephone lines); therefore Boston Mar-

> Volunteering can also build self-confidence, show employers you are making a change, sharpen skills, create additional references or simply show employers you are a well-rounded potential employee

ket did not plan to move their existing standard phone equipment. I suggested to my client that they donate the phone system to a charity. Boston Market was so interested in Y-ME and not only did they donate the equipment, they created a Mother's Day promotion that raised awareness and millions of dollars. The end result had many positive outcomes: Boston Market hired my company for the promotion, Y-ME received the phone equipment, the promotion focused on women's health issues and raised a great deal of money, and together we changed history.

While working with Y-ME, I met Margaret Harte, a cancer survivor, and at the time President of the volunteer board. She and I were discussing the popularity of the Chicago Marathon; it was once a struggling road race of 4,200 runners in 1977 and by 1990 it had grown considerably. Today over 45,000 registered participants make this one of the biggest marathons in the world. We asked ourselves, why couldn't our charity, Y-ME, have its own race? So in 1990, Margaret and I convinced the Board of Directors to let us create the Y-ME Race, which is now called *Y-ME Race At Your Pace 5K Run and 3 and 1 mile walks*. Y-ME celebrated its 20th anniversary of Chicago's largest cause-related event. Margaret and I remain friends and business associates. We leave a legacy and have given back to a worthy cause which, to date, has raised over $40,000,000. Clearly we made Shift Happen.

Unfortunately, Y-ME went bankrupt due to its rapid expansion and loss of oversight. There is a business lesson here. Not-for-profit is a tax status, not a business model. Y-ME expanded too quickly, escalated expenses, and did not increase contributions to offset those costs. Not-for-profit does not mean you shouldn't make a profit.

> Not-for-profit is a tax status, not a business model.

The US Chamber of Commerce offers these key differences between a nonprofit and not-for-profit:

- 💡 Nonprofits are formed explicitly to benefit the public good; not-for-profits exist to fulfill an owner's organizational objectives.
- 💡 Nonprofits can have a separate legal entity; not-for-profits cannot have a separate legal entity.
- 💡 Nonprofits run like a business and try to earn a profit, which does not support any single member; not-for-profits are considered 'recreational organizations' that do not operate with the business goal of earning revenue.
- 💡 Nonprofits may have employees who are paid, but their paychecks do not come through fundraising; not-for-profits are run by volunteers.

I have served on the advisory board of several charities and offered 3D Thinking to fundraising and building awareness. I have been the keynote speaker for March of Dimes, Association of Fundraising Professionals and other non-profits. I secured a donation from my client, Toyota, to help a no-kill pet shelter in Chicago called PAWS. I have already helped PAWS raise both awareness and donations while reducing the number of euthanized dogs and cats in Chicago by over 50%.

Charities often confuse non-profit as a business model and not a tax status. Charities often are filled with resistors, and to a large extent it becomes a distraction. You must be willing to listen to the "squeaky wheels" but don't focus on turning these people around. Focus on results. Save your grease for the quieter wheels that actually benefit the charity and YES could benefit you.

> *"Saving the life of one animal may not change the world but the world will change for that one animal."*
> **—Unknown**

Charities may not be receiving donations due to the current COVID-19 economics. It's time for them to seek out innovative problem-solvers. They have to see beyond what's happening today and focus on seeing beyond one possible solution.

It's time to apply that same thinking to look beyond obvious and explore the edges. Conventional alternatives aren't going to make you a millionaire. Start to think like a child. Improve your basic skills and focus on performance improvement.

Look beyond what first comes to mind. Look to the end results and then create the path to get there. Write down your ideas.

Problem-solving is not a straight-line sequence. Branches should be explored.

- Set Goals & Priorities
- Develop Strategies & Tactics
- Implement Flawlessly & Repeat

Can you look in the mirror, right now, and say you have given back? If not, start today. You never know—someone may give back to you as well.

According to Jim

- Donating your time to charity is a valuable way that you can give back to society and to those less privileged than yourself.

- No matter whether your interest is in people, illness, animals, or the planet, once you make a commitment to working as a volunteer, you'll likely find that the rewards you enjoy, as a result of your participation, are much greater than what you give up by sharing your time.

- The sooner you get started, the faster your efforts can begin to shift for you as well as the organization.

- Focus on a lifetime of value by giving back to others.

- Work to inspire not perspire.

- Simply ask yourself, "What am I going to do tomorrow that will benefit a charity more than yesterday?"

- Follow through on what you promise.

Shift Happens!®

6 Differentiations

Differentiation is the process setting yourself apart from others

Most companies find it difficult to grow at all, much less rapidly, without a constant stream of new products and service that meet customer needs.

How can yours be different?

Although you are under increasing pressure to lower your prices and that's the last thing to do.

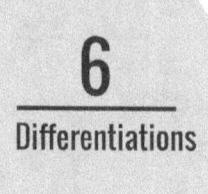

Product

Decide to take action no matter what
Features | Performance | Efficacy | Conformance
Durability | Reliability | Warranty

Service

Get organized
Ordering Ease | Delivery | Installation
Customer Training | Customer Consulting
Other misscellaneous services.

Channel

Stop & Go opportunity indicators
Coverage | Expertise | Performance
Look for under satisfied needs and wants. If you service 100% of a niche it could be more profitable than serving 2% of a huge market. Bottom line focus is more important than market share.

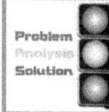

Relationship

Take fast action on your ideas
Competence | Courtesy | Credibility | Reliability | Responsiveness | Communication

Reputation/Image

Get active on social media
Perception | Communication | Advertising

Price

Get out and meet people
By Customer | By Quantity | By Segment
Lower prices lowers margins and bottom line contributions. Work on the five suggestions above before any price reductions. *Buyers don't default up!*

www.jfa.tips/Differentiation

Shifts
to Create New Opportunities

Human beings are creatures of habit. And creatures of habit tend to resist shift—regardless of what that shift is. The shift could be big or small and could even make people's lives a thousand times easier and we, as creatures of habit, will instinctively resist that shift. Shift = Work! That's why it is important to understand that all shifts require management. Regardless of the size or impact that your shift has on your personal and professional life, you have to treat all shift equal. Don't overlook something because you don't think that its impact will be great—give each shift its due diligence and you may find a surprising opportunity where you least expect it. A good strategy relies on a good insight. Not all shifts need to be huge in order to be significant—but they all need managing.

Shift brings about opportunities—opportunities that you may not have recognized or even considered before. So don't dwell on the shift—accept it! Once you do, you can then redirect your efforts from worrying to finding new opportunities and planning for success.

It is important to recognize that small and simple shifts can lead to large and great opportunities. The key is learning how to capitalize on those opportunities. It is not enough simply to accept that Shift Happened. This is the time to get through the "What?" phase and start moving into the *"So What?"* and *"Now What?"* phases. What opportunities have been created or can you create from this shift? What is your "golden egg"? What is your "AH-HA!" moment? Shift Happened! *So What?* So find your opportunities and hit the ground running!

> **Shift = Work!**

Priscilla Claman, president of Career Strategies, Inc., a Boston-based firm offering career coaching to individuals and career management services to organizations, is the author of *ASK: How to Get What You Want and Need at Work*. She says that traditional one-on-one mentoring relationships have gone the way of the cassette player. Today you need a Personal Board of Directors (PBOD)—a group of associates you consult regularly to get advice and feedback. Monthly board meetings may be impossible for everyone's schedules, but you can keep in touch through email, social media, text, etc. Once you establish the PBOD and a way to communicate, you can reach out when you need their collective counsel. The PBOD should be a diverse group of people who can each individually contribute to your problem-solving.

The key to the PBOD is to invite people who know more than you about a given topic or area of "wisdom." Perhaps you can use their expertise as a soundboard for your ideas and they can use your expertise in return.

> **Continue to shift upward and the changes will be positive**

My friend Randy Gage, speaker, consultant and author of *Why You're DUMB, SICK & BROKE . . . And How to Get SMART, HEALTHY & RICH*, says that if you look at the five most successful people you associate with, you will find that your income is about the average of those around you.

When you create your PBOD you want people that are smarter, richer and healthier. People who will make you stretch.

Let's talk about a small shift that can lead to new opportunities. A shift in job title can move you in one of two directions: up or down. A shift upwards makes you feel valued, noticed and rewarded. When you feel that way, it almost makes you feel like you just got a new job. You want to dress better, act better and take on a different kind of pride in your work. You take yourself more seriously. In addition, you may even feel a little more committed to your company. Essentially, you do your job better. Companies realize the benefit for themselves in rewarding an employee with a pay raise and a title.

> A good strategy relies on a good insight. Not all shifts need to be huge in order to be significant—but they all need managing.

A shift downward may be very humbling and can even motivate you to look to other avenues. It sometimes makes you want to work a little harder at your current job, so that they realize what they are losing when you leave. Or it could create indifference to the company and/or projects and your quality of work could slide further. Find the opportunity.

Depending on your financial situation—and if you don't care about the title—it can also relieve some pressure and responsibility. It may open up your personal life to other opportunities you may have been wanting to pursue. Maybe you choose to go back to school. Now, you can take the classes you have been putting off and don't even have to compromise your workload. You can take on

> **Find the opportunity**

fewer responsibilities while still working to better yourself in other ways. Adjust your attitude.

On a plane, there is a small lever called a "trim tab." Minor adjustments to the trim tab help keep the plane level. When I was learning to fly, this lever was constantly requiring adjustment. As I got more experienced, I learned to make smaller corrections more frequently, rather than larger, more radical adjustments because I waited too long to "adjust." Small, frequent adjustments are easier to accept. They provide an ongoing "touch point" that focuses you on "staying level" and flying straight.

Howard Putnam, former CEO of Southwest and Braniff airlines, motivational and business speaker and author of *The Winds of Turbulence: A CEO's Reflections on Surviving and Thriving on the Cutting Edge of Corporate Crisis,* made these "trim" adjustments to make flying fun. Howard helped create Southwest's "low-cost" business model. He reasoned that by not offering a First Class cabin, airport lounges, reserved seat assignments and video/audio programming Southwest could offer lower fares and produce a higher return on invested capital than other airlines. They created value for the Customer by offering a no haggle price and created a company culture built on Customer service and "on time" arrivals and departures.

We can't all be CEO of an airline, but we can apply the same thinking that Howard used to take a commodity product and make it unique. There are opportunities to solve problems if you only look around.

A small shift of your daily routine can lead to new opportunities. A shift in your diet can lead to several things: a new outlook, new-found confidence, health benefits and so much more!

These tiny little shifts in your life can make a world of difference, opening up new opportunities. Join a new social group, take the train to work instead of driving or sign up for any kind of class.

> Find your opportunities and hit the ground running!

Exposing yourself to new surroundings not only allows you to meet new people, but you can also develop your networks at the same time.

You never know who you'll meet next, so put yourself out there. Go on that blind date that your friends keep pestering you about. You probably won't end up marrying the person, but you might be able to learn something new. If you take a class at a school, you may realize that you have a genuine interest in a new or different field.

There are tons of networking events out there that are free or low cost. Ask your friends and colleagues or look online. You could end up meeting great people and finding new opportunities. Remind yourself to always go to a meeting or event with a note pad or write on the back of business cards and always follow up. Keep notes or voice notes on your cell phone if you don't have paper and pen. And don't forget your business cards. It looks incredibly unprofessional to show up to a tradeshow or networking event without business cards. Even if you're out of work, go online and have some printed with just your name, email address and phone number. Sites like Vistaprint have low-cost business cards. Don't forget to also follow those contacts on Facebook, Twitter and LinkedIn, to take full advantage of your connections.

> Adjust your attitude

"The world is changing so rapidly that we're all just trying to keep up."
—Sam Neil, actor, *Jurassic Park*

Small shifts can create new opportunities. Today, as you read this book, make some small shifts in your life. Start slowly. Pick an area of "shift" and start to make positive adjustments. The more that you accomplish the more you "raise the bar." Continue to shift upward and the changes will be positive.

Don't confine your shifts to one thing or one area. Look at yourself as if you were creating a "body scan" of your life. Find those areas that need some improvement and start to make changes that you control. Keep a record of your results. Over a period of time, if you stick to it you will discover that you are in control of your shift.

> A small shift in your daily routine can lead to new opportunities

I was once a partner in a single wine varietal. When we started to sell cases, breakage of one of a dozen bottles was a frequent occurrence. We investigated a double-walled box but it cost too much. We looked at packing a box inside a box but the additional freight and boxing costs were prohibitive. Going "inside the box" I found that 98% of all complaints revealed one bottle arrived broken.

Solution? I kept the case price the same but changed the description to eleven bottles per box. If all twelve arrived in tact the buyer perceived a bonus. If one arrived broken, no one complained since they had purchased eleven and received eleven. Complaints dropped and profits increased. Shift Happens!

Shifts to Create New Opportunities

- 💡 We have already established that there has been a shift. Now, it is time to look at the "so what?" question. Take the shift to the next level.

According to Jim

- 💡 What does that mean for me?
- 💡 What can I learn? Can I gain experience?
- 💡 What is in it for me?
- 💡 Figure out the answers to those questions and capitalize on the new opportunities!
- 💡 If you are meeting new people—make connections!
- 💡 Look outside your profession for ideas, contacts and opportunities.
- 💡 If you are cutting back on spending—SEE how much money you save and actually do something you *want* to do with that money!

What Drives Innovation?

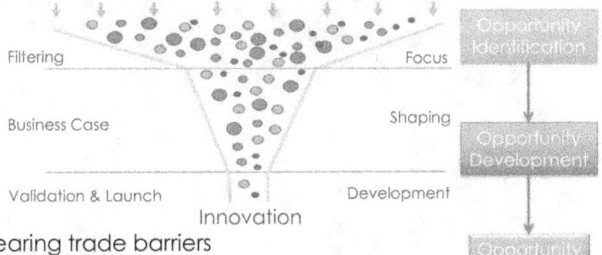

- Disappearing trade barriers
- Increasing rate of "shifts"
- Increasing customer expectancies
- Increasing amount & access to data/information
- Decreasing cost of entry

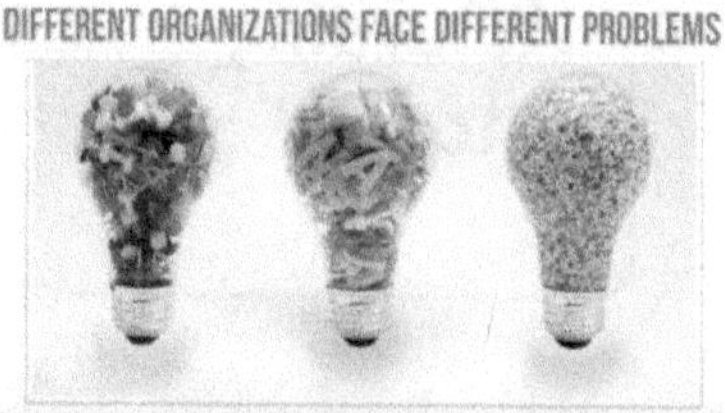

DIFFERENT ORGANIZATIONS FACE DIFFERENT PROBLEMS

Business Transformation

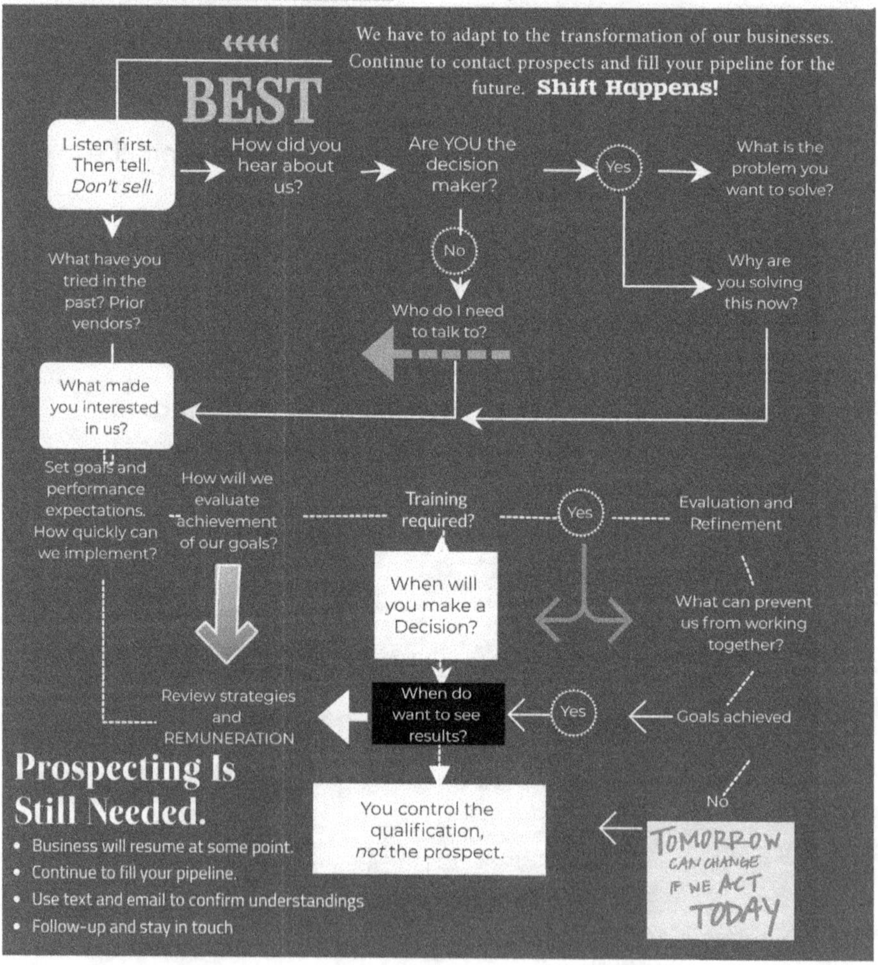

We have to adapt to the transformation of our businesses. Continue to contact prospects and fill your pipeline for the future. **Shift Happens!**

BEST

- Listen first. Then tell. *Don't sell.*
- How did you hear about us?
- Are YOU the decision maker?
  - Yes → What is the problem you want to solve? → Why are you solving this now?
  - No → Who do I need to talk to?
- What have you tried in the past? Prior vendors?
- What made you interested in us?
- Set goals and performance expectations. How quickly can we implement?
- How will we evaluate achievement of our goals?
- Training required?
  - Yes → Evaluation and Refinement → What can prevent us from working together? → Goals achieved
    - Yes → When do want to see results?
    - No → TOMORROW CAN CHANGE IF WE ACT TODAY
- When will you make a Decision?
- You control the qualification, *not* the prospect.
- Review strategies and REMUNERATION

Prospecting Is Still Needed.

- Business will resume at some point.
- Continue to fill your pipeline.
- Use text and email to confirm understandings
- Follow-up and stay in touch

Shift

What Others Know About You

One of the best benefits of LinkedIn is the ability to ask for referrals or recommendations. When I asked my clients, I was amazed at the similar comments that were provided. What we all forget is what we know, or more importantly, what others think we know. Ask others what you have that they want or desire. It's not about material things—it's about intellectual capital.

It's time to reinvent yourself. It's time to be creative. Creativity is a release from perceived boundaries. Creativity opens up possibilities and removes restrictions. Remember, creative solutions aren't necessarily expensive or unattainable. View your decisions from the viewpoint of the Customer by asking the questions, "Would I use this if it were free?" and "Would I use it if I were charged for it?"

What is the economic or emotional value of what I provide? At this point I want to remind you of some of the "shifts" that you can create for yourself in order to achieve your goals.

> Create a plan that you can stick to so that you don't fail

Shift #1 Get Happy

Most people don't have fun at work. The fun factor is what makes a good company great and a great company exceptional. Do your homework. Check out Groupon and you will find that many of their staff members are improv comedians. Review Apple's history and you will see that they offer casual work dress codes, free food, concerts and daycare.

Shift #2 Be Specific, Be Reasonable

You wouldn't intentionally take a loan from your bank without a repayment plan and completion date. Don't do it to yourself. Pay yourself first. Create a plan that you can stick to so that you don't fail. If you have doubts then reduce the expectation, but don't give yourself more time. Specific goals and deadlines should be reasonable. Create a deadline that is 90 days away, not a year.

> Reward yourself with something, but a treat doesn't mean you need to break the bank

Certainly some things can't be totally accomplished in 90 days, so break it down to manageable shifts. Most of us can't pay off a mortgage or our credit card balances with one check. Instead you make payments, stop charging and reduce your obligations a little at a time. Once you accomplish that goal, focus on another credit card or other financial obligation. You will find that you can reach each subsequent goal even faster than before.

Shift #3 Tell Me Why?

Do something everyday to reach your goal. For example, if I were building muscle mass I might not lose weight, right? Give yourself a break. Shifts take place in many forms. Why not record all changes so that your progress becomes your incentive to keep shifts occurring? If you're trying to lose weight, record measurements, not just weight. If you're trying to find a job, record how many resumes you've sent out and not just the responses.

Shift #4 Tell Others

When you share your goals with others you make a more formal commitment to yourself. Ask your friends, family and significant others to "co-sign" your I OWE ME. Not only does it formalize the agreement, but you now have someone interested in assisting you in your journey. This may cause them to ask about your progress, motivate, offer advice and become your "conscience."

Most of us can't do it alone. Partner with someone that you know will encourage you to reach your goals and you do the same for them.

Shift #5 Discuss Obstacles

Obstacles are often part of your mindset. By partnering with someone who believes in you and your goals, they can become your cheerleader and help you achieve success.

> When you share your goals with others, you make a more formal commitment to yourself.

Shift #6 Visualize Your Goal

"Traditional thinking is all about 'what is.' Future thinking will also need to be about what can be."
—**Edward de Bono author,** *Six Thinking Hats*

As we emerge from the gloom and pessimism of the past few years we can all create goals. No one woke up "needing" a $4 cup of coffee but Howard Schulz, founder of Starbucks, started a billion dollar company that created a demand or "need." Schulz says, *"Life is a series of near misses . . . it's seizing the day and accepting responsibility for our future. Pour your heart into your work and you can achieve dreams others may think impossible."*

You have to see your goals before you can achieve them. How? Create a vision board by making a sign and taking a picture. Now cut and paste your face onto a picture of a movie star, an athlete and/or a businessperson—anyone you admire. Put it up in your closet or on your bathroom mirror. Use it to focus on your goals. Put up a picture of a Visa statement with a zero balance or a photo of you in your new office at your job, etc. Just as you would form a mental visualization, also create this physical visualization to hang it in a place where you can see it every day. Use it as a physical reminder and motivational tool.

Have some fun with your "visualization." Close your eyes and imagine yourself after you accomplish your goal. Can you see yourself? Now snap a photo and make a picture in your mind of what you want. Open your eyes and write down what you saw. Now recreate that image into something you can create into a physical reminder. Find a photo, make a sign, create a sales chart, find pictures of people signing deals or receiving an award. Whatever you want to achieve, visualize the achievement of your goal and chart a course to complete it.

Now you have:
- Clarified your goal(s)
- Written it down
- Shared it with others
- Created a visual reminder
- Begun your journey

Shift #7 Reward Yourself

When we arrive at the "new normal," reward yourself with something, but a treat doesn't mean you need to break the bank. If you have no job, it's not a new car. Reward yourself with something you really enjoy. A nice bottle of Prosecco? A new article of clothing? Chocolates? The perfect cappuccino? A fruit smoothie? A drive in an exotic sports car? Make sure your reward is not too expensive or puts a strain on your pocketbook. Think of this process as a treasure map. You wouldn't spend all the money in the treasure chest until you knew what other costs might lurk. Take time to spend reflecting on your success and give yourself something for achieving your goals . . . and don't forget to include your support group.

Now that you've received that reward, create a new goal with a new reward level. Keep the motivation flowing.

> Obstacles are often in your mind

Dream BIG! Shift Happens!

Toyota, my biggest client at the time, wanted a recognition and incentive for used car salespersons. A survey revealed that a Rolex Submariner was the most wanted reward. It was a universally accepted recognition for achievement amongst salespeople.

The MSRP for that watch was $8,750. With the budget provided, we couldn't buy enough watches to fulfill the anticipated winners.

SOLUTION? I sourced used Rolexes. After all, once the watch is worn it's used. And used car salespersons found it more intriguing. I went to watch shows, shopped online, and visited pawn shops. I was able to offer used Rolexes to Toyota at 50% MSRP.

The promotion was so successful that Toyota outsold their competition and created a recognition program for the dealers used car sales staff. SHIFT HAPPENS!

What do you want to accomplish?

According to Jim

- 💡 Set small, measurable, attainable, steps.
- 💡 Imagine achieving that goal.
- 💡 Write, talk, and visualize your goal.
- 💡 Get people to share your goal. Ask them to support your efforts.
- 💡 If you can't see tomorrow, it will be the same as today or yesterday.

Shift
to Thinking Like An Entrepreneur

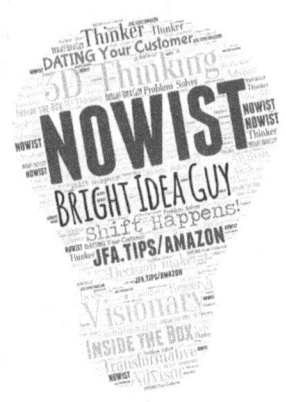

10 Powerful Tools To Leverage Technology
Save Time & Be More Productive

01 — http://jfa.tips/FreeEmailManager
Mailstrom automates the sorting and filing of emails into folders for immediate notification or moves to trash with one simple 'rule' you create.

02 — http://jfa.tips/Reviews — Online reviews
SoTell Us allows your Customers to upload powerful video and audio immediately and directly to your designated website.

03 — http://jfa.tips/Zoom — Video Conferencing
Zoom offers so many tools that video conferences will never be the same. Recording, share the screen, toll-free phone numbers, up to 100 participants on the free plan. Pro plan worth the upgrade.

04 — http://jfa.tips/YouMail — Customized Voice Mail
- Voicemail greeting can be created for each Customer
- Convert voicemails to emails or TXTs
- Privacy GuardCaller ID to unmask unknown callers
- Virtually Unlimited Voicemail-To-TextRead your voicemails.

05 — http://jfa.tips/ClubCalendar — 200+ meetings
How do you find meetings that need your services? This calendar is offered on a monthly basis. Free trial. Loaded with contacts, websites, dates, and even content requirements. Well worth the monthly fee.

06 — http://jfa.tips/FreeFlipbook — PDF>Brochure
Explain how your ideas will create a competitive differentiation without breaking the bank by using flipbooks. Learn from Starbucks, Apple, Rolex, Zappos how to add AHAs to your presentation by looking like an animated brochure.

07 — http://jfa.tips/TinyURLs — Shorten URLs
Tiny.cc lets you shorten, track and manage URLs. Generate QR codes or create custom URL slugs using a keyword. Free plan or a variety of paid plans with tons of upgraded features.

08 — http://jfa.tips/Chocolate — 10 pound bar
This is an attention getter. Over 1" thick x 19" long. Too much is better than too little. Chocolate is always a 'WOW' gift for any occasion or meeting.

09 — http://jfa.tips/WebMessaging — Live Chat
Monitor and chat with visitors on your website, mobile app or from a free customizable page. Load on all your websites, for free and start live conversations.

10 — http://jfa.tips/WhatFont — Font identification instantly.
Drop an image-PNG or JPEG-and this site searches 133,000 font styles. Then go to https://www.fontsquirrel.com to download the actual font file. No more boring type styles. Easy and fun addition to any presentation.

www.jfa.tips/2020Tools

Shift
Your Flight Plan for Growth

When we deliver unique, true and compelling value that matches the opportunities where buyers will pay for that value, we fuel our growth. Consider the value of your KSAs—Knowledge, Skills and Abilities. You do that already, you say? Well, maybe you *think* you do. But what if your mind has you thinking you know your best markets and value—and you're wrong? What if you're stuck in a downdraft and don't even know it yet?

We tend to create a business flight plan and then follow it. Most companies make course corrections at annual planning meetings, but often those shifts are too late due to the velocity of today's changing marketplace. To grow, we have to be ready to be dynamic—prepared for continuous and constant shift. I'm not saying we run around like chickens with our heads cut off—changing our plans every day. That would be silly. But we certainly need to adjust our perspectives and be ready to shift with the winds of our markets. Either that, or we crash and burn.

Reevaluate your KSAs to make sure that the pandemic hasn't gotten a hold of you. Are you trying to operate within the right markets? Where are your opportunities?

> Create a business flight plan and then follow it

Companies who fly with the market winds, who are willing to focus forward, spin on a dime and consciously evolve their value to be in sync with their market lift—wherever it may be—are the companies which defy gravity and grow.

The rest, those who choose to continue with the way they've always done it, staying stuck in gravity—well, they sink out and are often never heard from again. Which are you?

Here's a simple "flight plan" checklist:

1. Assess your options.
2. Find someone that can advise you and that you trust.
3. Do not cash out your IRA.
4. Make a shift for your lifestyle changes.

How many housewives do you know with a CPA (certified public accountant)? Not too many, right? Well, let me tell you a little story about Janet P. who married a man who was a senior vice president of regional sales for a technology company.

Now, given his title, it is safe to assume that Janet's husband was making their lives comfortable. The housewife had earned her CPA, yes, but due to her husband's generous annual income, was able to stay home and raise their children and was not obligated to work outside the home. She stayed at home for seven years and took care of the house, the kids, the shopping—everything. For seven years, she did nothing with accounting except prepare her family's taxes and continue her education in order to keep her certification current.

Unfortunately, due to the 2009 downturn in the American economy, Janet's husband lost his job because he fell into the category of "highly paid middle-management."

So let's recap: we have an out of work, middle-aged middle manager and a CPA who has been out of practice for nearly a decade. What will this couple do? Well, the husband will spend his time trying to find another job, but, due to the downsizing of many large corporations, there will be little opportunity in the near future.

Because of her accounting background, Janet calculated that the cost of her husband sitting without work for an undefined period of time would not allow them to maintain their standard of living. It would also lead to falling behind in other aspects of their financial lives.

Janet decided to take matters into her own hands. She ended up meeting a gentleman who was shopping for his wife and owned a local accounting firm. He was willing to hire her to allow her regain experience in the field while paying for her continuing education for her certification.

Families are not the only people who need to manage their debt. In 2010, one student took her financial matters into her own hands.

Completing her work-study requirements in the financial aid office at her university, Sara J., a college sophomore decided to start her financial future out right. Sara considered the amount of loans that she had already taken out for the first two years of her education and realized that that number would only double by the time she graduated.

To combat the stress that she was seeing her graduating friends endure upon realizing the amount of debt in which they started out their post-college lives, she decided to save some money. She opened a savings account, linked it to her checking account where her work-study paychecks were direct-deposited, and set up an automatic transfer of $200 on the 15th of every month. She figured that, by continuing this process, she would be able to save over $7,000 by graduation.

Foresight allowed her to find the opportunities she needed to help her.

Had Sara started this process her freshman year, she would have been closer to $10,000 by the time she graduated, but she wasn't too upset about that. How many recent college graduates do you know who have over $7,000 in their bank accounts? Not many.

Sara may not have the money to pay off *all* of her loans right away, but she certainly has a healthy cushion of support while she searches for work. What is the best part about her plan? She is still in school and has not even begun accruing interest on these loans, yet! This money is going to go directly to the principle and knock years off of her repayment schedule. Good thinking!

Who hasn't been short on cash at some point in their lives? When you are making life decisions at the gas pump—am I going to eat today or am I going to drive to work?—the phrase living "paycheck-to-paycheck" rings very true. Making minimum payments on maxed out credit cards and getting angry when people unintentionally run up your utility bills constantly reminds you that you're barely making ends meet.

Everything stresses you out. Your constant worry about whether or not the bills will get paid on time or if your heat will get turned off in the middle of winter contribute to that stress. Everything in your life seems as though it has to do with money and your paycheck is simply not enough. Well, you have to *make* it enough.

It is time to create shift. Get another job, reallocate funds *and plan* how you are going to use your money. Take control and start valuing the opportunities that you have. Get creative with what you have and what you have to do. Take grocery shopping from a panic attack to brain teaser—see how far you can stretch your dollars and actively look for the best deals! Shift your attitude and you, and those around you, will be able to live harmoniously and happily while alleviating some of the stress.

> What can you do tomorrow to better your situation from yesterday?

FritoLay hired me to create a travel incentive for their route drivers. I polled the drivers about their desire to attend the USBC Open Championships. There was no interest in seeing any shows by the drivers, but the FL management team wanted to see a sold out show. The tickets were ridiculously expensive. I went to the Caesar's show room director.

He seemed distant as he told me he could get me tickets for $1,000 each. For my group that would have been $30,000. While I was talking to him I saw a photo of a lot of youngsters on his desk. When I asked, his demeanor changed as he bragged about his 22 grandchildren.

I asked if they liked Cheetos, Doritos, Lays, Fritos, etc. "LOVE THEM!" Can't get enough of them, but they are too expensive so they don't purchase them often.

SOLUTION: I went to my client and asked if they would donate the items they picked up from the convenience stores. These are products that are rotated off those shelves so that the freshness date is current.

I went back to the room director with an offer. He was to provide me with 30 VIP tickets and I would deliver a 40' trailer filled with FL product. His children, grand children, and great grandchildren could also invite friends and neighbors. SHIFT HAPPENS!

According to Jim

💡 When you owe money, whether it's credit cards, student loans or personal loans, the thought of your debt can consume your entire being, your thoughts and even add to the proverbial "weight on your shoulders."

💡 Create a game plan to make your debt manageable.

💡 No one likes to be in debt, but with layoffs and unemployment where they are, staying out of debt is not most people's priority, its learning how to manage it.

One-On-One Coaching Registration
(Proof of hard cover book purchase will be required)

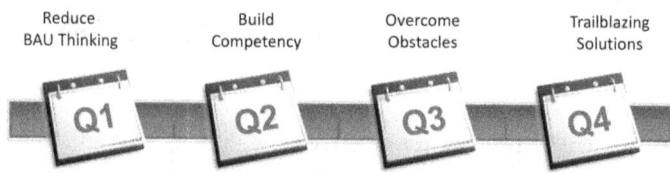

Reinvent Yourself
Our team will support your efforts to create and sustain your 3D Thinking™ with our One-On-One complimentary coaching.

jfa.tips/BookRegistration

Shifting
to a New Business

Starting a new business can be exhilarating and scary at the same time. First and foremost is your level of commitment. Many of you reading this book come from corporations. If that is the case, the pandemic probably forced you to "stop" and think about why you want to start your own business. You must consider the services and support your company offered that may have been taken for granted: utilities, technology, financial, fulfillment, legal, etc. You don't have all those resources when you start a new business. Make a list of friends or associates that can provide support during your start-up. Before you start any self-employment venture, consider what you need to run the business on a day-to-day basis.

I am a risk taker, are you? I swing for the fences, do you? I have risked it all and lost. Can you really do that today? Think! Do you think the "grass is greener" because you can't get fired? You want to be your own boss? Well neither is true. The grass is not greener and working for yourself is not all that you may think it will be. Running a small business requires commitment. First of all, the owner is normally the last one to be paid. Start with the idea that you are an employee and you need to be paid just like anyone else. If you stop paying yourself it will have a negative effect on your ability to continue during the rough times. You would not work for free for someone else, don't work for free for yourself.

Starting a business with a minimal amount of cash is not difficult. It's called "bootstrapping" and those types of businesses often serve a niche. If you can produce the right product or service, at the right price, it could thrive in any economic climate. Hewlett-Packard, Walt Disney, Facebook, Playboy and United Parcel Service all began as bootstrap enterprises that became global successes.

There are some basic decisions you must consider when you get started, and now may be the best time to do your homework.

Purchase an existing business or franchise. The upfront investment is higher but you often get a business that has a proven track record and a well-defined brand. The bigger problem is that you might be purchasing a business where you have little or no experience. If you are looking for a proven business with little start-up costs I suggest you consider direct selling companies, also called network marketing. (See page 151.) The advantage of a direct selling company is that they have the products, the literature and often the accounting, to help support your direct sales efforts. There are so many direct selling companies that I am confident you can find a product or service that interests you and supports your prior work experience. But you absolutely still need to do your homework. Don't be fooled by the success stories without finding out what an "average" person earns or loses.

I have dozens of stories of corporate business associates who left large companies with the goal of becoming an entrepreneur. Bottom line: most people who have been in corporate America for the majority of their careers should find a niche that services those type of companies. Venturing into a new business without any experience is a quick way to lose whatever savings you may have remaining. I wouldn't recommend it.

Some of the YES BUT stories are from entrepreneurs that did the "dumb" thing and quit their job, which resulted in success.

Terra Chips were born as an appetizer to serve at a bar, and the fried vegetable roots quickly exploded into a startup of its own. Once Dana Sinkler and Alex Dzieduszycki packaged and started selling them in stores, it only took a few years before success had them making $23 million a year in sales. And they sold their company for $80 million to Hain Celestial.

Steve Jobs was fired from the company he created. He was rehired and his second act was better than his first.

Oprah was fired because she was "unfit for television news."

J.K. Rowling was fired because she was writing fiction stories on the job.

Walt Disney and Charles Schultz were fired for not being creative enough.

Mark Cuban was a lousy computer salesman and was fired.

> "I was so confronted by this lack of opportunity that I decided to take it upon myself and start The Dream Collective. There were a lot of women specific programs targeted at senior level executives, but I believed if we wanted to see the dial switch, we needed to look at the start of the pipeline."
>
> **—Sarah Liu, The Dream Collective**

A friend of mine, Steve S., was the CEO of a large marketing and promotion company. When the company was sold he walked away with a significant amount of cash. Bored, he purchased a food franchise and planned to expand into several locations.

Steve had no experience with restaurants, consumer's taste preferences, restaurant suppliers, or employees. Within a short period of time he had invested most of his surplus cash and was tapping into his retirement money. He violated a rule of most successful businesses, he didn't stick to what he knew.

Stick to what you know not what you think you will learn. Find something that is needed, is wanted and you can deliver. As a start-up business your costs should be less than some of your competition so you can profit where your competition can't compete due to their overhead.

> Find a need.
> Fill a need.
> Charge for it.

No matter what your new business venture, keep costs under control. If possible find a partner. Start with as little of your own money as possible. Giving up a fair share of the profits to your investor is less of a problem than losing all of your savings. If you want to take that kind of risk go to Vegas, bet it all on red and pray. Sounds silly doesn't it? Then why would you risk what ever you have left on a business venture knowing that most new businesses fail in the first few years? Don't borrow money. Find someone that has money and believes in the product or service you have created for the niche and make them an investor and/or partner.

> Keep costs under control

Try to keep your start-up costs to under $1,000. I assume you have a home or apartment and a computer. Corporate identity can make your company look much bigger than it is. Create an identity for your business. A logo is important if you want to appear to be more than a simple, home based business. Freelogoservices.com will provide you with a logo for little or no costs.

Before investing in business cards or other printed materials, consider if they're necessary. With most correspondence handled online, there is no need for stationary or envelopes except for "snail mail" invoicing, if required. Use your logo on all promotional material, websites, etc. You need to brand yourself.

Websites can be simple or costly. Keep your costs down. A website is a sales tool and too many businesses spend more than they can afford in the hopes that the website will create business for them, it doesn't. Here are a couple of resources for low cost website design.

- WordPress.com
- Strikingly.com
- One.com
- Weebly
- Ucraft
- Webnode
- Wix
- Jimdo
- TemplateToaster
- Gator
- DreamHost's Website Builder for WordPress
- Shopify

The legal ramifications for starting a business vary from state to state, but there are a few points I want to highlight. Always get your legal "ducks in a row."

First of all, make sure the business name you want to use is not being used. You can start with a search through Google or another search engine. Next, check with your county clerk's office. Then check the US Patent and Trademark Office database (USPTO) to ensure it is not trademarked. You should also check your state's trademark database. These are just a few ways to ensure your business name will really be your business name before you start promoting. However, the most reliable way is to hire a lawyer or service. Also, make sure a domain is available at sites like GoDaddy.com.

The next most important order of business is to incorporate or form an LLC. No matter what you decide to create, don't leave your personal assets legally exposed. Sole proprietorships do not shield your personal assets against claims that may arise from your business.

Invest in a dependable accounting application to keep track of your finances. There are many small business accounting software packages that permit a start-up business to track purchase orders, payroll, invoices, inventory, etc.

> Invest in a dependable accounting application to keep track of your finances

One of the most popular accounting systems is Quickbooks by Intuit. It's simple, inexpensive, and constantly offers upgrades.

According to Outright, now GoDaddy Bookkeeping, 75 percent of the 20 million small businesses in the U.S. have no employees. "Outright is for people who don't want to record expenses—or miss deductions, deal with bookkeeping or think about what to send the IRS but do want to be instantly organized and ready for tax time, have an up-to-the-minute snapshot of how business is going and use a simple and free accounting solution."

Outright is a solution that handles the basic requirements of a small, simple business. It does not have the accounting features of QuickBooks, but not everyone needs all that horsepower when they start a business. Start with the basic accounting package that Outright offers for free and focus on making a profit. Once you make money you can always upgrade to a more powerful software.

> Set a timeline

Make a profit. This sounds like basic advice but it isn't. Think about your friends in non-profit companies. They ask people to contribute to their cause but sometimes they forget that they are running a business. Don't start a business just to fill your spare time. Ensure that you have done your homework and want to start a business that has potential of making money. Set a timeline. Two years or less. No more. If the business can't turn a profit in two years then the potential versus the risk is not worth your consideration.

Get some attention. Focus on what your business does and why someone will pay you for the product or service. Satisfied Customers sometimes tell others, while dissatisfied Customers almost **always** tell everyone. Customers have choices for almost everything. You must be the better choice. Try to be easier, faster, more convenient and more productive.

Don't, and I repeat, don't focus on price. Every competitor can meet your price if they want to compete. Price wars only benefit the consumer. And if the consumer is only purchasing from you because you have the lowest price then next week they will find someone with a lower price. For this reason, I don't fill out RFPs

(Request for Proposals) that are sent out to find the lowest bidder. Why would anyone compete to be the lowest cost provider? It means you make less profit for the same product that someone else thought was worth more money. If you try to compete on price you lose profit. If you lose profit you will go out of business.

> Compete on service, quality and reliability

Do the math. Do you want to spend time and resources filling out RFPs to win low-margin business?

I repeat, don't try to compete on price. Compete on service, quality and reliability. Compete on value not price. All Customers are not equal. If you compete on price the Customers will vacillate from one low price to another. The problem is: Customers are not loyal. They don't even adhere to the "low price" supplier. One day they shop at Wal-Mart and the next day they shop at a gourmet food store. **Discover why your Customers do business with you** and focus on providing that competitive differentiation. And don't charge by the hour. Project-based fees guarantee your income and reduce resistance from the client becoming upset at the hours and hourly rate. That's why we avoid attorneys and accountants. We want to pay for results not the number of hours expended.

> Don't, and I repeat, don't focus on price

Thomas Winninger, a fabulous speaker and good friend, is a business expert that has written a book called *Full Price*. He identifies five ways to make your business unique.

1. Response. "How soon do you respond to a Customer's inquiry or request?"
2. Knowledge. "What information do you possess that is important to your Customer?"
3. Quality of your product or service. "What is the application of your product to its highest need?"
4. & 5. are discretionary for you to discover from your own Customers. "How do you find out what your Customers think? Ask them."

Tom says that *"the challenge for us is to make what we do tangible: to turn the perception into the highest possible reality—to do one thing."*

Get some free advice. You need a business plan. You need operating capital. You need a product or service that people will purchase. Turn to the Small Business Administration (www.sba.gov) where you will find information and resources at no cost.

You can even file online for free at www.taxactonline.com.

Don't rush into a new business without a plan. Don't expect to make money immediately. There is a learning curve that will require you to learn about your Customers, the competition and the resources needed to succeed.

Take the time to analyze your niche and find the need.

Instead of reducing your price, increase it. People equate price and value. If you only needed transportation then Mercedes, BMW, Rolls, and Lamborgini would have no Customers. Cartier, Jimmy

Choo, and Joy Perfume don't compete on price but heightened perception.

I get hired because I deliver results. I am not the low-cost provider. I don't fill out RFPs. I don't write up complimentary proposals. If you want to hire me you know what I can do because of what I have done. 100% of my clients will give me glowing recommendations because I under-promise and over-deliver. It's not about my ego. It's about how I used creative innovative problem-solving that delivers a great ROI (Return On Ideas).

Our recanted slogan is "Consultants write reports. We deliver results."®

> "Everyone told me I was an idiot for quitting my job and then my first business failed and everyone expected me to just fail again. You just have to back yourself.
>
> "Yes you could fail but you could also be stuck in a job that you don't like. My main motivation was not to go back to my job. [Lu worked for accounting firm Ernst & Young]. Having a business degree is meant to help, but if anything, university gives you life skills. There's nothing directly applicable from my commerce degree to what I'm doing."
>
> —Jane Lu, Showpo

- Think about starting a business with little or no initial cost.
- Think about what your skills or knowledge base is and use it.
- Find a need. Fill a need. Charge for it.
- Upselling increases the size of the transaction. Upserving increases the amount of satisfaction.
- Don't forget to cover all your bases legally. Make sure your business name is not trademarked or being used and incorporate or become an LLC.

According to Jim

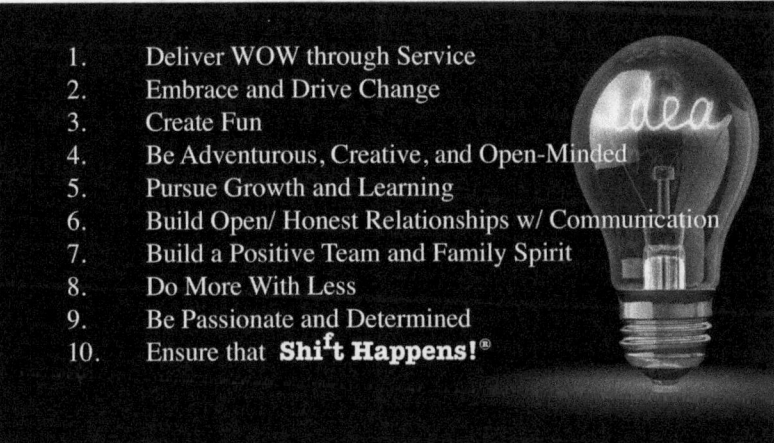

1. Deliver WOW through Service
2. Embrace and Drive Change
3. Create Fun
4. Be Adventurous, Creative, and Open-Minded
5. Pursue Growth and Learning
6. Build Open/ Honest Relationships w/ Communication
7. Build a Positive Team and Family Spirit
8. Do More With Less
9. Be Passionate and Determined
10. Ensure that **Shi^ft Happens!**®

Transformational Sales Questionaire For Post Covid-19

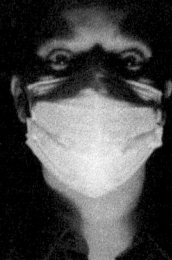

WHAT DO YOU WANT TO DO DIFFERENTLY TOMORROW THAT WILL BE BETTER THAN WHAT YOU ACCOMPLISHED YESTERDAY DURING COVID-19?

DEFINE
What specific "take away" goals do you have for you to revamp your business after Covid-19? How can we help deliver a transformational WOW?

MEASURE
How do you define the transformational sales process results and how will they be measured after Covid-19? Save Time? Save Money? Make Money? Return to normal?

ANALYZE
What are the most important causes of these issues that you can control? What would create your major upward trajectory after Covid-19?

IMPROVE
What is the most important area(s) that needs improvement to grow your business after Covid-19?

IMPLEMENT
What challenges do you have for implementation in your organization? Resources? Time? Money? Talent?

Shift
to Business as Unusual

After COVID-19 everything will be different. The marketplace is global. Technology is out of this world. And you can make a living doing just about *anything*.

Between the 18th and 19th century, the United States Industrial Revolution created a rapid increase in farm technology, manufacturing and transportation.

Like previous economic revolutions, the current Technology Revolution is marked most noticeably by a series of developments in electronics and computer technologies, along with dramatic changes in telecommunications.

Not only did technology create the basis for shifts, but it also created the fast pace of technological development and breakthroughs, which makes foresight difficult. Shift is happening at a rapid pace for various ethical, economic, legal, environmental, safety, and social concerns. Singer-songwriter Bob Dylan's prophetic song reminds us . . .

> *"Come mothers and fathers throughout the land*
> *And don't criticize what you can't understand*
> *Your sons and your daughters are beyond your command*

Your old road is rapidly agin'
Please get out of the new one if you can't lend your hand
For the times they are a-changin'"

As of the writing of this book, the highest paying jobs are mostly held by entrepreneurs, some who created apps, websites and online markets/communities. They are not doctors or lawyers, and they do not work in the medical or medical services field. However, I see it differently. Post–COVID-19 will shift job growth.

One of the greatest areas of true growth in medical providers seems to be in "pet care." Many people will pay more out of pocket for the care and feeding of their pets than that of their own families. The government does not regulate pet care. The cost of a pet care exam or procedure is often three to five times greater than the same medical treatment for a human. Pet specialists can charge what they want and the pet insurance, unlike human insurance, does not negotiate a "fixed" or "discounted" rate. The insurance coverage simply pays a portion and the pet owner is responsible for the balance.

Here are a few examples for comparison: Chicken breast for humans is priced around $2 per pound. Dried chicken breast dog treats are priced at around $6 per pound. An eye exam is approximately $40-$70 for humans (without coupons or specials) and $250-$300 for cats and dogs. The costs of owning a dog or cat can run as high as $700-$3000 per year and that is without extraordinary medical treatments.

> **Pet care is one of the fastest growing medical provider segments.**

Type of Expense	Yearly Expense
Food and Treats	$250 – $ 700
Toys	$ 25 – $ 150
Beds	$ 50 – $ 200
Leashes and Collars	$ 20 – $ 50
Grooming	$ 30 – $ 500
Routine Veterinary Care	$100 – $ 300
Preventive Medications and Supplements	$100 – $ 300
Training Classes or Resources	$ 25 – $ 300
Pet sitters or Boarding	$100 – $ 300
Yearly Total	$700 – $2800
Approximate Monthly Cost of Owning a Dog	$ 60 – $ 235

Can you see some opportunity here? Perhaps dog training, grooming or walking? It costs me $120 to have my two dogs receive a shampoo and haircut, while I go to Supercuts and get the senior discount for $11.95. The possibilities are endless for pet products. What about a pet clothes rack which sells for $54.95 or a Super Pet Rabbit Hay Manger Feeder with Salt Hanger for $14.95? Let's not forget collars, carriers, blankets, bowls, furniture, sunglasses, shoes, toys . . . and the list goes on. You don't have to have a medical degree to make money by creating a pet car seat, stroller, playpen or backpack.

We all know about the jobs lost as spending and program budgets were cut in various industries. If you have the skills to work in on technical infrastructure and information technology, the future seems bright. But if you have those skills, you probably aren't reading this book because your clients have kept you busy updating and revitalizing their technology.

No matter what you have, in the way of skills, you need to find a market that will pay you. So look around at the trends in the

> "Starbucks is in the business of selling dreams not coffee"

marketplace. Do some homework and find a niche that you can fulfill. You can't be all things to all people, so find a marketplace of Customers whose needs for specific services or products are going unmet.

In an interview, Howard Schultz, founder of Starbucks, said, "We're not in the coffee business. It is what we sell as a product, but it's not what we stand for. Starbucks is in the business of selling dreams not coffee."

Once you identify what Customers really want you can create a solution. Charles Revson, CEO of Revlon, said, "We manufacture cosmetics. We sell hope!"

Ask yourself: "What new product or service can I develop that is unique, deliverable, and profitable? How do I create the next big thing?"

Think of a bull's-eye target. Most companies focus on the center of the target and leave the outer edges, or fringes, unsatisfied. Look to those outer edges and find those unsatisfied needs and then fill them.

In Chicago, there were hundreds of restaurants that did not offer delivery services. Caviar, Grubhub, UberEats, and others provide a delivery service by taking orders online or by phone or text. To be unique, one company permits the Customer to order from different restaurants and consolidate the order into one delivery; appetizer from one restaurant, main course from another and dessert from a third.

Delivery services will grow. Can you deliver something that customers would desire? What other products could use a delivery service? Redbox? Cleaning supplies, groceries, toiletries? Mobile pet grooming? Haircuts? Some of these exist already (grocery & household delivery and pickup from stores like Target and Whole Foods; digital movie rentals, albeit more expensive than their DVD counterparts from Redbox; retail/grocery shoppers via Instacart or Shipt; local stores offering delivery or pickup), but many systems are strained under the current usage and could use improvements.

In Chicago, a very successful restaurant, America's Dog & Burger, sells hot dogs. What makes them unique? The two founders took a road trip across the United States and sampled various cities' "local" hot dogs-Atlanta to San Francisco and New Orleans to Los Angeles. They brought their favorites back to Chicago and now offer 21 different "city" dogs. After adding fried Twinkies, slim burgers and buffalo popcorn chicken this restaurant chain created a unique menu that has long lines during the lunch hours. The menu is so good and varied that the City of Chicago Courts offer America's hot dogs to the jury members.

> Find out if markets outside of their normal trading area for a business will provide new opportunities for local products

- 💡 Generate ideas by examining your own interests or skills.
- 💡 Talk, blog and use social networks to keep up with local and current trends to consider business opportunities.
- 💡 Take an existing product or service and add value to it. For example, the delivery service takes a restaurant that offers great food without delivery and provides delivery, thereby increasing the value to the Customer by providing convenience and variety. Consider taking local

products outside of their normal marketplace. Vienna Red Hots are made in Chicago, New York is known for its cheesecake, Philadelphia is recognized for the Philly cheese steak, BBQ from Texas, etc. Think about what you have locally that could possibly be offered in other locations. Find something that is not being delivered outside their normal trading area.

- Partner with a company to improve their products or services. Every product can be improved in some manner. I worked with a winery to improve their sales. They had the capacity to produce much more wine than they were currently producing. I suggested creating personalized wine labels with corporate logos, special messages, etc. and marketing it to the incentive and promotion industry. By personalizing the label for special events or corporations, I helped them find an entirely new market, which was not as price sensitive and had less competition. They now create personalized wine labels and bottle etched labels that are available for corporate promotions, engagements, weddings, birthday gifts and much more. This has become their niche and has expanded their business reach considerably.
- One of the latest trends is green technology. Some of the companies need local reps or additional distribution channels. Investigate becoming a rep and earn a commission for the introductions or sales.
- Get involved in goods and services for the ever-growing senior citizen segment of the population. There are opportunities in: home services, renovations, hospice, home deliveries, personal visits, pet care, etc.
- Consult or teach specialized skills. Home based businesses don't have IT departments, marketing, human

resources, SEO, web design, public relations, etc. With growing home-based businesses, there are emerging opportunities to provide services for those looking for assistance.

💡 If you understand social media, you could become a "ghost" writer, editor, tweeter and/or blogger for individuals who don't understand, don't have time, or don't have the skills to create social media campaigns.

> The secret to earning a lot of money is to multiply your time by setting up multiple sources of income

Do your homework. Find something that does not cost you a lot to start up. If you don't have your own "burning vision," consider franchises, and look for mentors, partners, and startups. "Find a need. Fill a need." Research your field. Create a financial business plan. DO NOT QUIT YOUR JOB. Once you get some cash, pay off some bills and learn how to run a business.

> Remember Tarzan's Rule of the Jungle: "Never let go of vine A until you have a firm grasp on vine B.

Take the time to investigate new trends, especially if you don't want to start your own business. If you are set on finding a new job, look around for who is hiring and create a resume or cover letter for each company. Be specific. Read each job description carefully and make sure to highlight the job qualifications that you meet in either your cover letter or resume.

So what can you do? Become self-employed? Yes, that's right. More millionaires are self-employed than are working in any other industry.

> "I realized that the secret to earning a lot of money is to have multiple sources of income. You don't trade time for money. That's the worst way to earn money! And that's what the masses do. That's what school teaches. 96% of our population trade time for money. It's a fool's game, because it's got an inherent problem. It's called saturation. You run out of time. So I started to learn things about money that school doesn't teach you. The secret to earning a lot of money is to multiply your time by setting up multiple sources of income."
>
> **—Bob Proctor, *The Secret***

I have given you a great deal of information to digest.

- Read this chapter again.
- Make notes.
- Be honest with yourself.
- Do you have the discipline and the persistence to be your own boss?
- If you can't sell yourself on your idea, you can't sell it to anyone else.

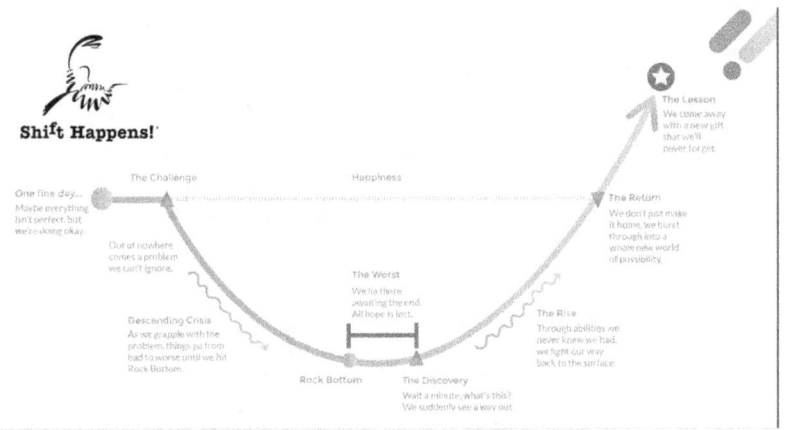

TRIGGERS
10 — Getting to YES
Motivate · Influence · Persuade

01 — Determine Who You Are
Your sales funnel is your lead filter. Aim for visibility and relevance.

02 — Focus on Your Prospects WIIFM
Provide solutions that solve pressing issues. What's In It For Me (WIIFM)?

03 — Focus on a NICHE-Do one thing well
- Audience • Industry • Business Role
- Method • Topic • Media

04 — Use FaceTime and Text
Emails get lost or ignored. Face to Face or FT is best. Text is instant and doesn't get misplaced.

05 — One-handed tablet handle
Smartphones and tablets replaced computers. Make it easier, faster, productive, simple and in line with your prospects needs.

06 — Create Experiences
You must strive to be what no one else but you can be. Interact with your Customers often.

07 — USB Stick (schtick)
Printed materials are expensive and often discarded. Consider a USB for your documents, proposals, etc. Put your logo on it.

08 — Chocolate gift set is not for everyone
Create or source a **unique gift** that you can deliver to your prospect when they become a Customer. Add birthdays, anniversaries, etc.

09 — Coffee doesn't use a fork
Express the true advantage and emotion your solution has to offer and **motive the greatest number of people to buy it.**

10 — Bath Truffles
Combine what the Customer wants and upgrade to what they need. Price is not the issue if you create a competitive differentiation that solves their problem.

Shift
Your 2020 Vision

Do you ever lay in bed and think: *"I wish this coffee would brew itself"*? Yeah, well, so had thousands, if not millions, of other people around the world. But one innovative individual decided to do something about it. This forward thinker identified a popular need, based on a personal desire to stay in bed longer and have coffee ready upon waking, and capitalized on it with the invention of the programmable Mr. Coffee. More inventors have built on this concept, and now you can have beans ground and the coffee made without ever getting out of bed.

The formula to invention and innovation is simple: Think about something that you often find yourself repeating like, *"I wish there was a store that sold such-and-such"* or *"There has to be an easier way to do this."* Find something that addresses a need that you have, because chances are that other people have the same need. What stops you from capitalizing on the opportunity to make people's lives better? Nothing.

Share your idea. However to keep it confidential, ask them to sign a non-disclosure agreement (NDA). Sharing is probably the best way to give your dream the greatest chance for survival and success, but you don't want someone else to steal it. (www.jfa.tips/NDA)

Consider what it was that made you think it was a good idea. Why was it helpful to you? Maybe that's how you market the idea. If it works for you, why wouldn't it be transferable to others?

> Ideas come from the strangest places. Don't ignore them.

Think about what your inspiration was and how you felt once you realized that there was a way to fulfill your need. Then, use that to actualize the idea and share it with others. Fulfilling their needs translates into your success and longevity. As long as you can continue to address and fulfill needs, you can continue to grow your presence in the market.

Morgan Newman and his college friends had an idea. IdeaPaint turns virtually any surface into a dry-erase board. Within a short period of time the company expanded beyond the US and made their products available worldwide.

Here's how a man found the true inspiration behind his vision. A 29-year-old chef, Brian D., landed a position as head chef and partner-to-be at an upscale, popular Chicago bar. Excited about his new endeavor, he jumped in headfirst. He created and developed the food concept, as well as the menu for the bar. When Brian wasn't at the bar, he was entertaining his family and friends by cooking for them in their homes.

Unfortunately, after a few months of extreme dedication, Brian was not seeing the money that was promised to him and his partnership status was a topic the other partners routinely avoided. Essentially, he was forced out of the bar and left without another job to fall back on.

Not being at the bar gave Brian a lot more time to spend with his friends and family. As he was investigating new positions, his friends suggested that he become a personal chef. He could then continue doing what he loves, basically set his own hours and experiment with all types of cuisine.

He looked into it and began developing a network. Brian hosted dinner parties for his parents' friends and business acquaintances and eventually put together a full-fledged business plan. Brian's schedule is booked! He is making good money and great connections. Recognize opportunities to capitalize on your talents and abilities.

Understanding how to recognize your inspiration may require some assistance. I often go online to find new techniques, blogs, tweets or suggestions that force me to think about how to engage those techniques on my own "shifts."

> Don't follow the rules

I read lots of materials from outside of my industry to see how they solved a problem or created a new opportunity. By reading outside of my area of familiarity, I can find entirely new solutions to solve a problem or get inspired to reach for a higher goal.

I don't follow the rules. Years ago I found a small poster with a quote. It has become a benchmark for my inspiration:

> "When they hand you ruled paper, write the wrong way."

> **Recognize opportunities to capitalize on your talents and abilities**

So change things and don't follow the path that others have created. Pretend you are an outsider, an explorer, and you have to create your own path. You might get lost, but then again, you might discover a new world.

For my inspiration, I look at all kinds of problems. Sometimes it only requires a small shift, other times you need to turn to others for inspiration. Research some of the greatest thinkers: Edison, Leonardo da Vinci, Jules Verne, Einstein, Benjamin Franklin, Darwin, Vannevar Bush, Winston Churchill, Napoleon, Sun Zu, Copernicus, Elizabeth I, Gandhi, Plato, etc. Each of them faced challenges and developed revolutionary, and sometimes controversial, solutions. Each of these people saw or sensed something from a different inspiration.

Learn from the masters and apply their process to your own problems. Columbus shows you how to strengthen your vision and courage, Jefferson focused on the pursuit of happiness, Eisenstein unleashes your imagination, etc.

Visionaries like Steve Jobs, Bill Gates, Nelson Mandela, Sir Richard Branson, all share the same vision—"to go where no one has gone before." That quote is from another visionary, Gene Roddenbury. For those of you that live in a black hole—a region of space from which nothing, not even light, can escape—Gene is best known for creating *Star Trek*. Roddenberry's imaginary universe has spanned over four decades, produced 6 television series, 715 episodes and 13 films. With new television episodes airing on CBS Access and talks of *Star Trek* 4 for the summer of 2022, it appears this movie franchise will "live long and prosper." So learn from these visionaries . . . and prosper.

- Sometimes you look at the paper sideways, upside down, or behind it to see the solution.

According to Jim

- We are all born with potential. The only question is whether or not we can live up to that potential.

- In a world that often sinks to the lowest common denominator, force yourself to climb to the higher plateau.

- To know more you have to notice more.

- Look at the world through your own expertise. Expertise is insight not information.

- Knowledge you get from books. Wisdom you get from experience.

- Rethink everything you do.

- Play Fair. Tell the Truth.

- Examine the intent, not the letter, of the law.

"It's okay to change direction, but if you have a vision in place, you'll always end up at the same place—even though the path you thought you'd take to get there becomes different."

—Eraina Ferguson, founder of My Good Life Now, an online resource for parents of special needs kids

Shift Happens!

Stimulate Organizational Culture Shifts To Refocus On Outcomes

1: Create an Innovation Culture

 Identify a problem that needs an innovative solution that either saves money, saves time or introduces new profit. →  Determine how to monetize the solution and compare to the investment of time and money.

2: Incentivize Employee Engagement

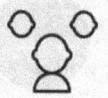 INTERVIEWS AND DISCUSSIONS TO DETERMINE THE WIIFM* 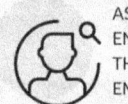 ASSESS NOT ONLY THE ENGAGEMENT BUT THE RETENTION OF EMPLOYEES

3: Collaborate/Evaluate

 SHARE A SET OF DOCUMENTATION AND OBTAIN EMPLOYEE BUY-IN →  BUILD A LIST OF DOCUMENTATION THAT SHOWS CREATIVITY SKILLS

4: Refine Current Innovation Process

 GAIN MOMENTUM TO BECOME PART OF CULTURE AND S.O.P. → 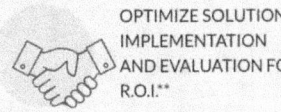 OPTIMIZE SOLUTION IMPLEMENTATION AND EVALUATION FOR R.O.I.**

5: Inspire, accelerate, & collect ideas

 DISCOVER WIIFM*
ALIGNING ENGAGEMENT
EVALUATE BENEFITS
MONETIZE RESULTS →  SHARE THE CREDIT!
REWARD ACHIEVEMENTS
REINVEST IN R.O.I.**
ENSURE THAT
SHIFT HAPPENS!

www.jfa.tips/Outcomes

Lessons From Marcus Lemonis "The Profit"

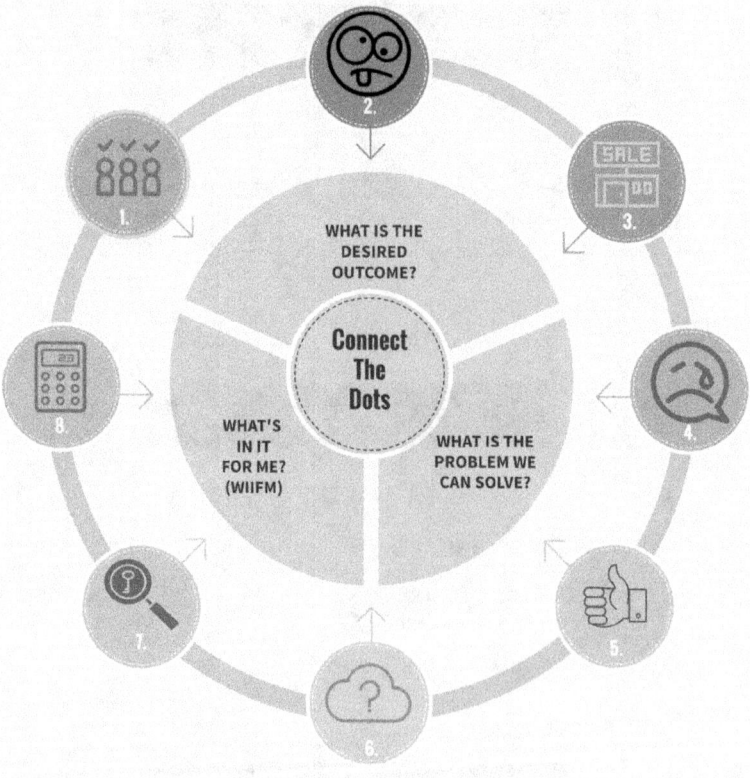

Connect The Dots
- WHAT IS THE DESIRED OUTCOME?
- WHAT IS THE PROBLEM WE CAN SOLVE?
- WHAT'S IN IT FOR ME? (WIIFM)

1. Make Your Employees #1
Unhappy employees can not be good evangelists for your organization

2. Accept The Crazy
Every day we discover 'crazy' ideas that receive *Yes, But* responses. Be open to crazy. It may be brilliant.

3. Be Authentic
Social media, buzz, PR, news feeds are easy to access. Ask yourself: What would my mother say or do?

4. Quit Whinning and Start Winning
No one wants to hear about *your* problems. They only want your solutions to *their* problems.

5. Follow Through
Stay in touch will your Customers and employees to ensure success.

6. Know What You Don't Know
You can't be an expert in everything. Surround yourself with smart people and share rewards.

7. Be Transparent
Check your ego at the door. Your credibility is your greatest resource.

8. Know Your Numbers.
Nothing is more important. Numbers don't lie. Rely on them. Embrace them.

Shifting
the Mind to the Marketplace

Ideas are great. And I encourage everyone to think, to brainstorm, to come up with whatever you can. Think all day long. Think on the bus, in the shower, on your way to work or during your lunch break. Look at the world through different lenses—gain new perspectives. Look at a situation from another point of view. And whatever you do, don't stop thinking!

Remember, creating an idea is only half the battle. The hardest part—the part at which most people give up—is actualizing that idea.

You can sit and think all day every day about how miserable you are because of this factor or that factor, but until you actually *do something* about it, you will continue to be miserable.

As a consumer in this fast-paced, hectic world in which we live, if your idea is something that is going to make people's lives eas-

> You have to get past the hard part: take the steps to actualize your idea. Taking it from the **Mind** to the **Marketplace**. This is the time to make it happen!

ier, then it will have a higher likelihood of success! If you can make someone's life or job *easier,* you *will* find a niche.

Take your idea to the next level, no matter how scary it is. And it will be scary. For you to find that one person to tell you "yes," you will hear "no" a thousand times. But it only takes one "yes." Chances are, what you are scared of is failure. You don't want somebody to tell you that your idea is silly or that it won't work or isn't worth their time or your time—especially if you believe in it. Offer your advice and accept advice in return. Your perspective may be exactly what is needed to help someone else's idea blossom and theirs may be incredibly valuable to you.

> Get off of your pity porch! If you have an idea, bring it to life!

Eric Adler and Julien Chabbot hated waiting in lines. The roommates came up with the idea of using social media to relay various wait times in order to avoid them. They built a free iPhone app called Line Snob. It rewarded users with points for providing information on the lines they are standing in. Users can redeem their points for coupons. Line Snob makes money from diversified revenue streams:

1. After a free three-month trial, participating businesses pay a monthly fee.
2. Line Snob earns a commission with in-app promotions, which their clients use to make a purchase at the business venue.

Did I mention that the app was developed while they were still in college, with No Job and No Money? Did I mention they are now out of business? Did I mention that it may still be a good idea? Or is it? Learn from others' failures. It may be timing. It may be bad management. What I am suggesting is "learn from it."

Go out and buy an edition of Entrepreneur Magazine. Each issue is loaded with suggestions, concepts, success stories, franchise information and "wacky ideas." I have been a reader for many years but nothing has struck me as "wackier" than this money-making idea:

Ruth Haldeman is an analytical chemist that makes . . . get ready for this one . . . Chicken Diapers in Hot Springs, Arkansas.

> The hardest part is actualizing that idea

According to BackYardChickens.com, there are about 60,000 pet chicken owners. Ruth reasoned that diapers let owners spend more quality time with their chickens instead of dealing with poop. That means Ruth discovered that "Shift Happens!" and now, she can't keep up with the back orders.

> Over the last decade, raising chickens—once the domain of rural farmers who would house flocks of hundreds of chickens on their property—has become an elite hobby. Nearly 1 percent of households in the country's biggest urban areas, like New York, Denver, and Los Angeles, keep chickens, according to a 2013 Department of Agriculture study. These urban and suburban hobby farmers are bringing their chickens into their homes, buying them speciality food, and taking them for walks with their dogs.
>
> In wealthy cities like San Francisco, chickens have even become an unlikely status symbol, with poultry owners going to unimaginable lengths to care for their pets. As The Washington Post reported in March, certain chicken owners have hired "chicken whisperers" to consult on their pets' comfort (to the tune of $225 per hour). These

nouveau livestock enthusiasts have also been known to invest in personal chefs for their birds, and some have even installed smartphone-enabled, motion-detecting coops that control ventilation, temperature, lighting, and security from afar (ballpark cost: $20,000).

www.jfa.tips/ChickenDiapers

By thinking "inside the box" and observing human nature you may find the next booming business.

OK, Chicken Diapers are not for every pet owner, so perhaps you can create something for a broader audience?

> You never know until you take that leap

In response to the coronavirus outbreak, some companies are moving quickly to integrate or advertise their existing thermal imaging capabilities. The technology scans a person from afar and estimates what their temperature is, so some think these systems could spot fevers and ultimately infected persons.

ThirdEye claims its augmented reality glasses can be fitted with thermal imaging to make this process more seamless. The company says it has received about 2,000 orders since the coronavirus outbreak.

In the case of this current pandemic, Netflix will entertain people stuck at home, and video platforms like Zoom will power businesses whose work can be done remotely. Meanwhile, all sorts of disinfectant brands, like Clorox and Purell, will benefit from companies and Customers eager to stay clean and cut down on the spread of the virus.

But we must also keep in mind that people eager to protect themselves from the coronavirus will search for other products to help, regardless of whether or not those products are actually useful. Now more than ever, it's vital that we remember that some companies pushing these goods are just hoping to make a quick buck by exploiting people's fears. There is a balance. Remember: FIND A NEED. FILL A NEED.

> Take action! Don't just sit back and complain.

Aside from the growing number of gadgets being marketed during the coronavirus outbreak, there are also opportunities for low-tech products. On Amazon, for example, you'll find a slew of new listings for hats that come fitted with protective "screens" that are meant to block someone spitting or sneezing into your face. There are baseball hats with screens, sun hats with screens, and even visors with screens. The premise seems to be that the coronavirus, which can spread through droplets, will be blocked by the device. I found an "I Survived Coronavirus" cuff, merchandise tagged with "Don't Cough on Me," and a coronavirus-themed mug all available for purchase.

Do you ever wish there was an easier way to do something? A lot of us do. From mail merges to email blasts, if you are not familiar with the process, trying to get a project done can be a very stressful task. One administrative assistant at a sales office spent several frustrating hours manually entering each and every detail of every sales lead generated.

After several months of this tedious effort, she was finally fed up with wasting her time and decided to look up tutorials on how to export information automatically versus entering it all manually. Take action! Don't just sit back and complain. She learned how to expedite and automate the process. This allowed her to build a database quickly to easily and seamlessly organize information. More importantly, she freed up a lot more time to focus on completing other tasks.

> Failure is the second cousin to success

Here's a thought: For years, soda cans came in one size—12 ounces, while a typical drinking glass holds 8 ounces. People wanting to enjoy a soda had few options: drink the entire can, pour it into a glass and waste the rest or save the can, only to come back to flat soda. And what about mothers who didn't want their young children drinking an entire can of soda? What were they to do? How could they pack the drinks in their child's sack lunch and still make sure they weren't drinking too much sugary soda?

It wasn't until recently that the industry decided to take a leap and tap into that otherwise untouched market. They created a shift in their packaging size. They started to produce smaller cans. Who purchased this new product? A lot of people.

The smaller cans are easier to take on the go, store, drink, and pour without wasting any product. In addition, moms can more easily monitor the soda and sugar consumption of their children. What took them so long to realize this opportunity? Who knows? I'm sure they'd heard complaints for years, but continued with business as usual. It took a brave, smart and forward-thinking person to actualize the idea and take it from the *mind to the marketplace*.

Soft drinks have always been innovative. Some succeed, like Diet Coke, Red Bull, and Vitamin Water; and some fail, like the New Coke, Coors Water, Life Saver Soda, Pepsi AM, and Crystal Pepsi.

Colgate made the decision to use its name on a wide range of food products called Colgate's Kitchen Entrees. The products did not take off and never left U.S. marketplace. You never know until you take that leap.

Even a company like Apple has not always been successful. How about the Apple Newton? Apple debuted this PDA device in 1993, it never took off and the Newton faded away by 1998. However, it chartered the course for the Palm Pilot, BlackBerry and iPhone. Many companies make good decisions and succeed. Still, those same companies may crash and burn, but learn from their failures. Each of us must remember: **failure is the second cousin to success.**

We live in a world of 360 degrees of opportunity. Some are great, some are bad, some are emerging and some are waning. A great opportunity two years ago may be foundering now. Our best opportunity may have cropped up in the past six months.

We must be focused on seeking the right opportunities or we'll end up stuck in a waning opportunity, missing a better opportunity or limiting our growth by staying focused on an opportunity that is spiraling away from profitability. When we focus on the wrong markets for our success, we get stuck in gravity.

"Do not go where the path may lead, go instead where there is no path and leave a trail."

—Ralph Waldo Emerson

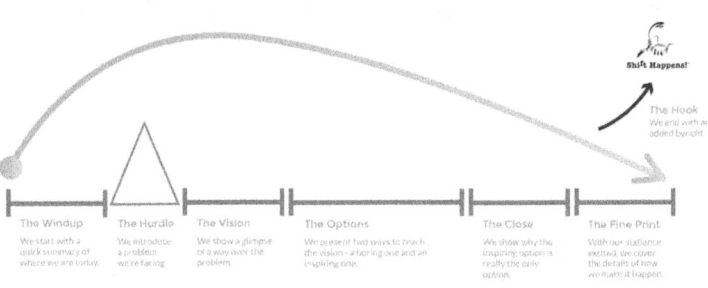

- It all started with the microwave. We were able to cook and reheat food faster than ever before and now we expect everything in our lives to be just as simple.

According to Jim

- Standing in lines??? No way! I've got an app for that.

- It seems as though, sometimes, we just like to complain. If something bothers you or you have an idea, don't just sit around and talk about it—do something about it!

- Take that next step to actualize your idea.

- Figure out how to take your idea from the mind to the marketplace.

- Create meaningful marketing.

- It's always about them and not about you.

- Make life easier, safer and more profitable for others and they will become advocates.

- Are you relevant? Unexpected? Dramatically Different?

- Inaction is worse than nonaction. ("The difference between nonaction and inaction is that *nonaction* is the absence of action; failure to act while *inaction* is want of action or activity; forbearance from labor; idleness; rest; inertness" [https://wikidiff.com/nonaction/inaction].)

Shifts
that Are Lost in Translation

There are forces that shift your world and there are shifts that force your world to shift.

A college student wanted to create a dating site and it became Facebook. Mark Zuckerberg was a billionaire at age of 26, had an Oscar-nominated movie based on his life, and was *Time* magazine's Man of the Year.

A couple of computer whiz kids built a friendly computer and launched their company in 1976. In 1985, one of the co-founders, Steve Jobs, was forced out of the company due to differences in opinion with the CEO about testing innovative new ideas. After his departure, stock prices dropped and the company struggled. After Apple rehired him in 1996, he not only launched a new product—the iPod—but also brought with him a new philosophy. He wanted to recreate a brand that had recognizable, unique products with intuitive designs and game changing new technology. Under Jobs, Apple was able to establish itself as a leader in the consumer electronics industry, and continues to release new products such as the iPhone and iPad. Today, Apple is the largest technology firm in the world and boasts annual revenues over $260 billion.

> "If we want to move forward and see Apple healthy and prospering again, we have to let go of a few things here. We have to let go of this notion that for Apple to win, Microsoft has to lose. We have to embrace a notion that for Apple to win, Apple has to do a really good job. And if others are going to help us that's great, because we need all the help we can get, and if we screw up and we don't do a good job, it's not somebody else's fault, it's our fault."
>
> —**Steve Jobs, Apple, 1997 MacWorld Expo**

Steve Jobs's comments are as relevant today as they were over two decades ago. Now, apply that same philosophy to your own shifts. It's time to let go. It's time to let go of the notion that for you to win someone else has to lose. Sidebar: your success is not a zero-sum game.

According to Jim

- Learn from the examples of others.
- You do not have to create the model, just follow the tried and true.
- Redefine what success means to you—it does not have to be a zero-sum approach; both or all parties can benefit.
- Never give up control without knowing what you are really giving up.
- Read what your client or boss is reading so you can speak in their language. Examples include *Forbes, Barrons, Investors Business Daily,* and *The Wall Street Journal.*

Take Your Shifts Investors to the Bank

Find something you like to do.

Find a solution to a problem that you can provide.

Find out how much people will pay for the solution.

Think about it from your earliest day of working. Did you shovel the walk or mow the yard for your neighbor? Did you sell lemonade? Did you walk the dog, rake leaves, wash the car or deliver newspapers? Then, you were self-employed. Forgot that, didn't you? See, it's not so hard.

> Make a profit

Evaluate Your Strengths And Weaknesses: Be honest with yourself. This is often the most difficult part because most people think that they have more strengths and fewer weaknesses than how others evaluate them. If you've been in a relationship for more than a few years, ask your significant other—they are a great resource for discovering your weaknesses. Once you know your weaknesses, recognize which ones you can change with training and/or hiring someone to fill that gap.

Gauge Self-Employment Resources: Your resources, to begin with, are usually time and interest. You need to know how much money you have to devote to the new career before you start . . . otherwise, you could deplete your remaining resources. Test, test, test the marketplace and your ability to deliver goods or services and make a profit.

Ideas For Self-Employment: The library and Internet are full of ideas. Get a few magazines like Fast Company, Entrepreneur, Inc., Smart Money, etc. Read about new ideas, franchises and start-ups that peak your interest. Look around to see how you can partner with existing businesses. See a need. Fill a need.

I know people who clean and organize other people's attics, basements and garages. There are lots of opportunities if you simply look at what skills and interests you have and then determine if there is a market willing to pay for those skills. Find the source of their pain and provide a solution. The greater the pain, and the closer you get to removing that pain, the more money you can earn.

Assess The Market: Stay away from any business that can't verify the success of others or that tells you that you can build a business with no experience and little money. Don't get caught up in business scams. Look at the market potential of everything you might want to do. The best businesses for self-employment are those where you can do things others are unwilling or unable to do for themselves.

This is the moneymaker! Evaluate what others in your market are earning and take note as to how they are earning it. If you don't have the "entrepreneurial" spirit yet, start by working with them. Who knows, you could end up being a partner and not having to start from scratch.

> **Find the pain.**
> **Cure the pain.**
> **Charge for the cure.**

Take Your ~~Shifts~~ to ~~the Bank~~ Investors

> Never, ever, give up control

Ding! Ding! Ding! Remember, people often pay others to do what they could, but don't want to, do for themselves. Peapod is a home delivery service that picks up food at a grocery store and delivers it to those that can't, won't or don't have the time to shop. Can you apply that same principle to picking up dry cleaning, laundry, pet supplies, prescriptions, etc.?

The Costs of Earning a M.B.A: I want you to stop worrying about not having a job and go get a M.B.A. That's right. Use other people's money while you earn your M.B.A.

Ok, perhaps your thinking, *"Jim's lost me. How can I find the time to get a M.B.A. while starting a business?"* Simple. I want you to get a different kind of M.B.A—a Massive Bank Account. Money is out there. Find it. Your grandparents or someone with a pension that is being depleted may be willing to invest. Find a partner with money. It's not the bank. They want their money back. Investors want a return on their money and often provide insights, resources and even Customers just to insure that return. Banks don't provide anything but "interest" in you paying them "interest."

> The greater the pain, and the closer you get to removing that pain, the more money you can earn

Don't fool yourself. More businesses fail because of under-capitalization than because of competition or a bad idea. Find an investor. Use their money. Earn your Massive Bank Account and then expand or buy out your investor. Always have a plan to get rid of them. Now, that's a nice way to operate! Never sign a deal in which the investor has more than 49% of the voting stock. Never, ever give up control.

Take your plan to the bank

A woman cut the feet off of her pantyhose and wore the control top stocking. She now owns a $150 million company—Spanx!

Make A Business Plan: Thousands of articles are out there on how to create a business plan: businessplanpro.com, planware.org, or TheBestBusinessPlan.com. Once you have a plan, take it to a bank to ask for a loan. "Why? Jim, you just said don't go to a bank for a loan."

> **Here's a well-kept secret:** banks will review the plan for free. Take your plan to the bank. They have lots of Customers that may have been successful in business, and the bank will offer their suggestions for free. Don't get the loan. Get the advice. It's the only time you will get something for free from the bank other than a paperclip or an envelope.

Banks will most likely turn down your loan, but they will also tell you the reasons. Those reasons could be potential problems with your business plan. This will give you insight into those potential problems so you can use that advice to refine your business plan. They will tell you the R.O.I. (return on investment) or capitalization or resources needed—and here's the best part—they will often tell you where to get additional contributions. If you ask, they may introduce you to one of their Customers who could become your mentor or partner. That is worth your time and it creates a huge R.O.I. for you. In this case R.O.I. means Return on your Ideas.

Growing up, we heard our parents and teachers tell us, "You can be anything you want to be!" And that is true. If you can visualize a way to make money and survive doing something, why not do it?

As I keep saying: make someone's life easier. Laid-back work environments, telecommuting, and a huge focus on technology will all be important moving forward. Starbucks coffee shops offer free Wi-Fi in all of their locations and have thus transformed themselves into satellite offices for entrepreneurs and young business professionals.

> **Ding! Ding! Ding!**
> Remember, people pay others to often do what they could, but don't want to do for themselves

Look at how some people found their entrepreneurial spirit:

Brian C. gets laid-off of from his corporate job and sits at home looking for another one. Since he is home, he offers to help his neighbor take her dog out during the day. He helps her exercise her dog, and in return, she pays him $10 a day.

This sparks a thought: if his neighbor is willing to pay him $10 a day to play with her dog, how many more people can he get to pay him for exercising *their* dogs?

> The best businesses for self-employment are those where you can do things others are unwilling or unable to do for themselves

The answer: a lot! Instead of looking for a new corporate job, Brian now runs his own dog walking business. He walks them, plays with them and even feeds them. All for $10 a day.

Brian's idea has worked out so well that he now has a client list big enough to enable him to hire three employees and take care of dogs instead of crunching numbers all day.

Here's another example of entrepreneurship: A college athlete, Arthur B., graduates and returns to his former high school for a visit.

> Earn your MBA by getting a huge ROI

While he's there, a current student athlete asks for his help finding a college scholarship. He agrees to help the high school student and ends up finding and securing a nice scholarship for him.

While Arthur continues to look for a job, he agrees to help a few other students find scholarships. Eventually, he decides to start charging families for his efforts. He chooses a fee—anywhere from $400 to $1,000 dollars—and signs a contract with the families stating that if he does not find their child a scholarship at least matching his fee, then they do not have to pay him.

The genius behind Arthur's pricing is that he does not specify "athletic" scholarship to his clients. If he finds a client's kid any kind of scholarship, his job is done. Anything else is just icing on the cake. Word about his efforts and successes spread quickly and he was able to branch out into other sports and schools. Arthur has decided to pursue this opportunity full-time. Something that he started doing as a courtesy to a family at his former high school, ended up being what pays his bills and allows him to make a very healthy living.

Not convinced that you can do it? Consider this idea:

A group of business management students were faced with a project in which they had to come invent a business idea and then demonstrate to the class how to "manage" the company. The group's idea was called: Dorm Room Movers. Dorm Room Movers would be a moving company designed to help college students move the contents of their dorm rooms.

Take Your ~~Shifts~~ to ~~the Bank~~ Investors

> The only person stopping you is you!

Dorm Room Movers would, for a specified fee, pack up your dorm room in an organized and timely manner and move it to wherever you wanted—a new room, new house, storage unit, etc. The fee would be on a per-project basis dependent on factors such as distance of relocation, furniture, amount of items, and related factors.

Had the group not consisted of already time-starved student athletes, the group probably would have actualized this class project, because, let's face it: the target market is huge. The demographic of time-starved college students continues to grow with every technological advancement that we see.

You've got the plan, you've started building your business — maybe you've even gotten family and friends to buy in. Now you need to put those big plans into action, but bootstrapping isn't an option right now.

That's where business loans and investors come in. Options include venture capitalists, angel investors, and investment corporations. There are pros and cons to investors—some of the same ones as business loans.

Now is the time to really think about what we can learn from this moment of crisis. As we take our first tentative steps back out and begin to chart a new course and return to the world, what will we make of it?

How will you respond to the shifts? This is a new beginning.

As I write this book, we are not out of the "shelter-in-place" and "stay-at-home" mandates. For me, I choose to write about what the new normal could be as we recognize that there will be very little that "returns" to normal. Hopefully, this social distancing reminds all of us that we are interconnected. Leverage the wisdom of others and begin the process of recovery and reinvention.

According to Jim

- If you can figure out how to make a living doing something completely unconventional, go for it! The only person stopping you is you!
- No one is going to judge you—Make money!
- Earn your MBA (Massive Bank Account) by getting a huge ROI (Return On Ideas).
- Find time for yourself, time for relationships, time to dream and time for forgiveness.
- Only way to find the edge is by stepping over it.

You need to learn

- How to determine your best prospects!
- How to differentiate between Branding, Marketing, and Promotion.
- How to become great at being persuasive.
- How to craft your message & effectively present your products/services.

Take Your ~~Shifts~~ to ~~the Bank~~ Investors

Business loans

- 💡 **Difficult to acquire.** If you have a startup without much business credit or revenue to show, it may be tough to get a lender to fund you.
- 💡 **Can be restrictive.** You may be approved to use the funds for certain purchases only.
- 💡 **Personal credit considered.** Even if your business is doing well, you could be denied a business loan based on your personal credit.
- 💡 **Collateral.** Security in the form of business or personal assets may be required. If you default on payments, that means foreclosure on those assets.

Investors

- 💡 **Ownership.** It's entirely possible to lose the majority of ownership of your business if your equity is diluted by investors.
- 💡 **Relationship.** When something is personal, there's a higher chance of something subjective creating a divide. If an investor doesn't like a business choice you make, they can pull out.
- 💡 **No end date.** When there's no exit plan, there's no foreseeable point at which you could gain back the ownership you surrendered.
- 💡 **Long-term cost.** If you decide to sell your business down the road, your investors will need to get a payout based on their equity percentage. If you give out dividends to investors, a percentage of your profits could be diverted into the pocket of your investor indefinitely.

The Journey to Bright Ideas

When you complete your personalized coaching session, we will send you a high-resolution download of this original artwork created by Michelle Hove.

Shifts
to Avoid Thinkruptcy™

COVID-19 shifted the perspectives for almost every type of business. Consumers also shifted the way they work, travel, and interact. Muller Acura of Merrillville, IN, offered to "sanitize ANY American Honda for free." They clearly addressed the WIIFM. Changes have happened in the way we shop, spend money, use public transportation, drive, and the likelihood of attending in-person trade shows, conferences, or musical events. With these shifts and the rise of the remote workforce, new opportunities abound.

It takes hard work, determination and a genuine belief in what you are doing to succeed. Recognizing the *need*—not want—which you are bringing to others. Innovation, the ability to recognize opportunities and the knowledge and wisdom to know how to capitalize on those opportunities, will make you successful. You don't need to know *everything*. Know a lot about a little, and a little about a lot. The rest, just know where to find those answers. You don't have to be an expert of everything, but you should know where to find those experts. Build your networks, people!!!

The Secrets of Success are that, in reality, there are no secrets. Information is everywhere. In the book *Future Shock,* Alvin Tuffler predicted a world where Shift Happens so fast that people will not be able to keep up. Does that come as a surprise to you? Ever purchased anything that was better, cheaper, smaller, bigger, faster or easier, only to learn that a better, cheaper, smaller, bigger, faster or easier model was available a month later?

The secret is simple. Shift Happens every minute of every day of every week of every month of every year.

> "Act as if! Act as if you're a wealthy man, rich already, and then you'll surely become rich. Act as if you have unmatched confidence and then people will surely have confidence in you. Act as if you have unmatched experience and then people will follow your advice. And act as if you are already a tremendous success, and as sure as I stand here today—you will become successful.
>
> "And from the time I was a kid, I've had this internal monologue roaring through my head, which doesn't stop—unless I'm asleep. I'm sure every person has this; it's just that my monologue is particularly loud. And particularly troublesome. I'm constantly asking myself questions. And the problem with that is that your brain is like a computer: If you ask a question, it's programmed to respond, whether there's an answer or not. I'm constantly weighing everything in my mind and trying to predict how my actions will influence events. Or maybe manipulate events are the more appropriate words. It's like playing a game of chess with your own life!"

—Jordan Belfort, The Wolf of Wall Street

iTunes shifted the way we purchase music, Amazon's Kindle shifted the way we collect and read books, Androids cloned themselves into user-friendly cell phones and cable television competes with telephone companies to provide greater bandwidth to deliver all of our communication and entertainment.

Look around you. Did you see the shift? Are you a part of it or apart from it?

The Secret of Success is to be able to make shifts by learning from others or creating your own path. We all need to look in the mirror and say; *"I am not going to take it any more."* The right attitude greases the wheels of progress. Once you get moving, you can come up with one idea after another, and hopefully, find yourself inundated with new opportunities.

Television shows like *Shark Tank*, *The Profit*, and *The Deed: Chicago* offer stories about people like you, who—perhaps with no job and no money!—managed to turn an idea into success.

Follow their processes. They all focus on where you want to go rather than where you have been. Lori Greiner, Marcus Lemonis, Sean Conlon, and Joseph Sugarman have a GPS plan on where they want to go with their business. I have listened. I learned how they got there and their plan for the long game secret: Focus on a few things with all of their energy.

Joseph Sugarman is a legendary copywriter who started a mail-order business, JS&A Group, through the power of his pen Joe sold millions of BluBlocker Sunglasses. Sugarman was one of the first to offer his product on what were soon called, "Infomercials." He pioneered the concept of using toll-free numbers to accept credit card orders by phone before anyone else started accepting credit cards over the phone.

THE SEVEN FORCES OF SUCCESS
ACCORDING TO JOSEPH SUGARMAN

ALWAYS BE HONEST
STEP 01

LEARN FROM YOUR FAILURES
STEP 02

TURN PROBLEMS INTO OPPORTUNITIES
STEP 03

STEP 04 FOCUS YOUR ENERGY

 FOCUS ON HELPING OTHERS **STEP 05**

STEP 06 CLEAN YOUR DESK

 BE DIFFERENT **STEP 07**

Seven powerful ways to magnify your chances of winning in a competitive world.

> Get off the couch and take control of your own shift

If you want to learn more about him, The Adweek Copywriting Handbook is a great place to start. You'll learn about his style and philosophy, and you'll also learn a lot about marketing and copywriting along the way. For me it's this: "You sell on emotion, but you justify a purchase with logic."

Here are a few examples that might inspire you to create a product, idea, or modification of something in existence.

Post–COVID-19 will present new businesses and services. Cleaning, maintenance, and sanitation will see almost unlimited investors.

A new need for safety and sanitized environments will elevate janitors, maids, and cleaners to a profession.

We have been working remotely—from home—and that will continue. Office buildings will remain empty and new products and services will be targeted to home offices.

There will be less travel to conventions, trade shows, seminars, and workshops as we embrace more virtual events.

Homeschooling, alternative learning, and online training will become omnipotent with millionaires being created. Colleges and universities will have to adapt.

> The secret to success: making shifts by learning from others or creating your own path

The deterioration of "souless" bankers will continue to reduce visits to banks. More "banks" like Capital One will emerge. And community banks will see a positive reversal of previous declines.

Tele-medicine, remote testing, and online monitoring will permit "at need" information while reducing needless forms and waiting to see health-care experts.

Online shopping will continue to replace brick and mortar. Shopping centers could become virtual learning centers, indoor recreation, and fulfillment warehouses for pickup or delivery.

> The Secrets of Success are that there are no secrets

Takeout dining will continue to force a drop in business for restaurants.

All of these shifts will stimulate communities, family interaction, and even faith.

Homelessness is expected to increase since people are jobless, rent is generally not canceled (though it may be deferred in some instances), and cities are already starting to end the moratoriums on evictions.

For many, doorstep delivery services for food, medicine, grocery, packages, etc., are gaining ground. To make it safe for the recipients and riders, food delivery companies such as Deliveroo, Postmates, Instacart, and Zomato are giving options to choose contactless delivery, wherein the rider drops off the package on the doorstep.

As a result of this increase in door-to-door delivery, food banks and homeless persons have been receiving more food and clothing donations than in the past.

Since people have self-isolated to protect themselves against the COVID-19 spread, they are spending less than usual except for food, sanitation, and home entertainment). As more people stay at home in self-isolation and take quarantine measures, there is an increased use of alternate entertainment services such as games, video-on-demand, etc.

Video-streaming companies such as Netflix, Amazon Prime, Hulu, and Disney+ have experienced an increase in the number of subscribers due to COVID-19 and the possible demise of AMC Theatres.

Not surprising is that cryptocurrencies such as Bitcoin and Ethereum have experienced a major dip amid the effect of coronavirus.

If airlines don't reduce prices more people will drive to vacation locations. Getting on a plane will become a necessity only for time savings and distant locations. Hotels will become more experiential.

> "Dictionary is the only place that success comes before work. Hard work is the price we must pay for success. I think you can accomplish anything if you're willing to pay the price."
> —Vince Lombardi

Need the true secret of success? Simply look at how others did it. Read about their "rags to riches" stories. Watch them on TV or simply pick up magazines that offer these "secrets" for free. And take a small amount of time each day, just a few minutes, to ask yourself what niche you can fill.

Almost everyone that is successful has at one time been poor, unemployed and with personal and financial issues. What did they do that you can't do? Nothing. You heard me. Nothing. You breathe the same air, drink water and put on your pants one leg at a time. The only difference is they got *"mad as hell and didn't want to take it any more."*

Get a copy of *Entrepreneur, INC., Small Business Opportunities Magazine, Fortune Small Business Magazine, Get Money, Fast Company, BusinessWeek, Home Business* or go online to some of the magazines and websites that offer free information. Sign up for free webinars. Due to "stay-at-home" mandates, you can no longer drop into a hotel or meeting room and attend trade shows, but as they gravitate to virtual events there may be more access to them at little or no cost.

- Come on, in the age of Google, do we really expect there to be any secrets?
- Tap into your resources, do some research.
- There are ways to get the answers to any and every question you may ever want to ask.

According to Jim

One-On-One Coaching Registration
(Proof of hard cover book purchase will be required)

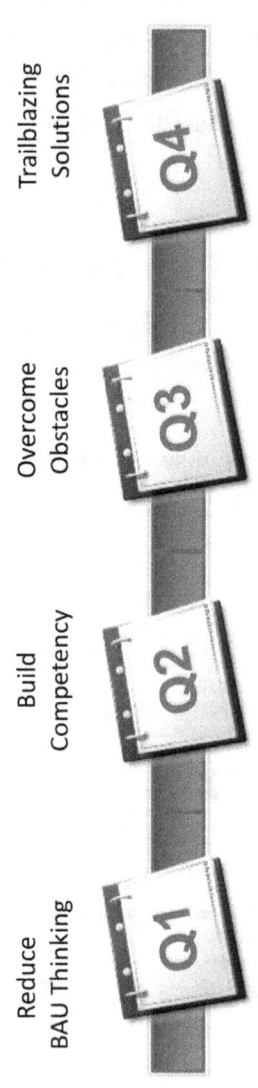

| Reduce BAU Thinking | Build Competency | Overcome Obstacles | Trailblazing Solutions |
| Q1 | Q2 | Q3 | Q4 |

Reinvent Yourself

Our team will support your efforts to create and sustain your 3D Thinking™ with our One-On-One complimentary coaching.

jfa.tips/BookRegistration

Shifting
Your Uncertainty

Soft skills will be required more than a simple change of location. It will be imperative for almost all organizations to prioritize the use of video conferences, webinars, and online education. While the younger generation grew up with many of these skills, the more mature workforce will need assistance.

Every one of us has experienced shift in some form or another. It's how we deal with our entire shift that really matters. By now, you may have started to list some shifts you want to accomplish, especially if you have No Job and No Money. **Your shifts could be:**

- Losing weight and keeping it off.
- Getting a job that you actually like. If you have lost your job, now is the perfect time to find what you love to do and get paid to do it.
- Saving money. Resolving to keep a reserve for the rainy days that could become rainy months.
- Building a personal/household budget. Study it, analyze it and then "stick to it" throughout the year.
- Cutting the fat from your household budget & spending. When the economy is lean (such as now), live according to your means—and income.
- Hiding the credit cards—for you and other household members. Resolving not to run up high monthly credit

balances—that will come due at some point. And if you don't pay them when due, your credit score will pay the price.

Like Washington crossing the Delaware, don't be afraid to look at the "other side." There could be a big victory awaiting you over there. Enrich your mind—explore and expand your household horizons.

> Surf the Internet for new services, opportunities and savings

Shift Happens!

- Let your eyeballs do the walking—surf the Internet for new services, opportunities, and savings.
- Don't become "insurance broke." Shop around for the most reasonable homeowners, auto, health, life and long-term insurance coverage.
- Save on auto gas & mileage. Make a weekly list of your shopping errands and combine several shopping trips into one weekly trip.
- Cut back on eating out and entertainment. You can eat more meals at home and find free entertainment that can save you hundreds, if not thousands, of dollars per year.
- Train your children to be thrifty at an early age. They do not need the name brand or the best of everything.
- Don't try to "keep up with the Joneses." They are often in deep debt and you don't need to go down with them.
- Learn to do simple house upkeep/repairs yourself like changing the HVAC filters in your house. It is easy and much cheaper than paying a local company to come in and do it.

- 💡 Cook your own meals. Buy foods that are on sale and freeze them if you don't want to prepare them immediately.
- 💡 Go to flea markets to find deals. Shop eBay, Craigslist, Groupon and other online discount sources.
- 💡 Compare prices and read reviews before purchasing anything of value.

The pandemic effectively confined citizens to their homes except for buying food or medicine or seeking medical treatment. One silver lining is that more time is available to research price and value for products and services you may buy in the future.

My mother used to remind me that "you get what you pay for" as she clipped coupons. In fact she organized about a dozen of her friends once a month to have a coupon-clipping and exchange party. Collectively they became experts in certain products, their competition, and importantly the reviews from actual users. She taught me to look at the ingredients label, the cost per ounce or pound, and the shelf life. Today I am avid about updating myself with the freshest dose of price/value and sharing them. The better informed you are about these comparisons, the better you become at navigating the financial and operational challenges for making educated buying decisions.

Enrich your mind

Learn from others

Every Sunday in Chicago's South Loop, there is a flea market that offers everything from fruits and vegetables to smartphone accessories and other electronics. Clothing, cosmetics, gum and candy, hardware, tools, game cartridges, software, jewelry and underwear are only a few of the myriad of products offered at huge discounts. Plus, the entire market is cash based.

There is much to learn from these flea market salespeople. In drilling into the data, I found if a product is seasonal or in short supply, the price seems to be fixed by all of the sellers. If the product is technological, out of season or in large supply the price is negotiable.

What is also amazing to me is the "wow" or "entertainment" factor from this flea market. Families make it a weekly event. Vendors make it a "must attend weather permitting" offering. The challenges of the economy are clearly presented in the essence of retailing: one-on-one selling.

> Train your children to be thrifty at an early age

Each Sunday, these vendors arrive early in the morning and set up their booths in what appears to be a "pecking" order based on seniority. I have observed how the market place adjusts for competition, how the same real estate is "owned" by the most frequent sellers, and the extremely high level of Customer service that is provided.

So how do they survive?

- Competitive Customer experience. No matter how much you buy, the experience is similar from booth to booth.
- Want a sample? No worries. Almost all of them offer samples. Get enough samples and you have a "free lunch."
- Want to negotiate? Give it a try.
- Want to return an item? No hassles as long as it is unused and in its original condition.

A trip to the flea market will help stimulate your thinking about a way to earn a few extra bucks. Talk to the vendors. Some are schoolteachers, others have nine-to-five jobs that don't pay enough to cover all of their expenses. In any case, the flea market helps them supplement their income.

> Compare prices and read reviews before purchasing anything of value

- Look at other ways to save money, like reevaluating larger bills like insurance, phone or cable service.

According to Jim

- Enrich your mind—explore and expand your household horizons.
- Read books, magazines and newspapers.
- Watch children as they try to solve a problem.
- Confusion Is not a good strategy for success.
- Learn from others.

WORK FROM HOME
essentials

A work-friendly computer or laptop with good audio and video support

High-speed internet

A proper working desk with plenty of space

Comfortable chair or sitting arrangement

Adequate lighting

Notebooks, pens and sticky notes

UPS in case of unexpected power outage

Storage area

Printer and paper shredder

Necessary office software

Fire safe box

The **Shift** Is Up to You!

This is *not* a self-help book.

It is *not* a feel good book.

It's about getting up in the morning and asking yourself:

"Am I satisfied with everything as it is?"

"What if I could be there, instead of here?"

Are you committed to making your own shifts?

At some point did you say to yourself, or better yet, others that **"I am mad and I am not going to take it anymore!"**

This book is really no different than going to a hardware store and buying a hammer. It is a tool and what you build with it is up to you.

If you Google "How To Use A Hammer" you will find over 46 million results. Certainly no one needs that much information about how to use a hammer, or do they? Would you call it self-help or instructions?

> Tools are just that . . . tools. They are simply a means to an end.

Would you use everything that is written about hammers or find what works for you and implement those ideas?

The first time you picked up a hammer, you probably didn't know how to use it, but with the proper advice and lots of practice, you could probably create something you needed or wanted. During the process you may have hit your thumb with the hammer and experienced pain, but eventually you picked up the hammer again. Why? Because a hammer is the best way to hit a nail on the head.

Toolsnob.com says, "Even many carpenters hold the hammer in the wrong place or swing it the wrong way." (https://www.prweb.com/releases/blogpire/toolsnob/prweb527851.htm) If you use a hammer a lot, doing it incorrectly can put a big strain on your body. Further, it could slow down your work and create dents all over the coffee table you just made. Learning to use ANY tool improperly can cause a lot of frustration.

Ehow.com says that you need to use the right hammer for the job. Tools are just that . . . tools. They are simply a means to an end.

Abraham Maslow, the professor of psychology and creator of Maslow's hierarchy of needs, said in 1966, "It is tempting, if the only tool you have is a hammer, to treat everything as if it were a nail."

> Don't take this book as the final answer, but the start of asking more questions

Get up in the morning and ask yourself, "What am I going to "shift" today that will get me better results than I achieved yesterday?"

Shifts are changes.

Some shift is good.

Some shift is difficult.

Shift exists and we can't always control the amount of shift we have to encounter.

It's time to find your compass and create a roadmap to guide you where you need to be to stabilize your future. And bring the hammer. You may need it.

One certainty in life is that Shift Happens! You can either let it get the best of you or bring out the best in you. It's all up to you.

> *"Most great people have achieved their greatest success just one step beyond their greatest failure."*
> **—Napoleon Hill**

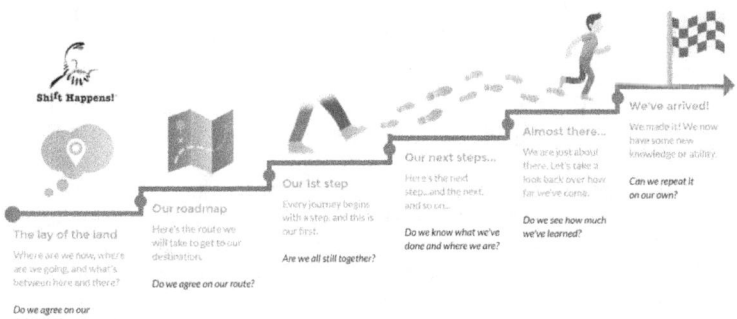

PITCH STEPS FOR ANY PRESENTATION

01 — Title
Provide attention getting title. Add in your contact information including email, mobile phone, address, your name & position.

02 — Problem/Opportunity/Pain
Write down the 'pain' you are reducing or eliminating. Think 'inside' the box.

03 — Uncork Value Proposition
Just like enjoying wine. Take your time to engage all the senses to showcase the value you provide.

04 — Smartphone or Land Line
Both allow you to communicate but one has technology, magic, effectiveness. Show your prototype or explain your breakthrough concept.

05 — Bigger Thinking Business Model
Tablets are smartphones on steroids. Leverage your idea on the bigger image to demonstrate your business model? Use high rez images and readable type.

06 — Coffee is a commodity
Explain how your idea will create a competitive differentiation without breaking the bank. Learn from Starbucks, Apple, Rolex, Zappos.

07 — USB Stick
Bring your financial projections and key metrics on a USB instead of printing them. Include your pitch deck, videos, infographics, etc. Brand your USB with your logo, etc. Also a BU of your PowerPoint in JPEG format.

08 — Competitive Analysis
It's just like chocolate. Too much is better than too little. Bring real chocolate as well.

09 — Management Team
Describe your key members and how they will consolidate and focus their wisdom to solve the problem.

10 — Future Predictions
Don't sell--tell. Detail the current status, accomplishments to date, timeline, and use of funds. Answers as many questions as possible before they are asked.

8 TIPS FOR YOUR NEXT POWERPOINT OR KEYNOTE

James D. Feldman
CSP, CPIM, CPT, CPC, CITE, PCS
The Bright Idea Guy™

Dramatically increase your chances of achieving presentation success by understanding these powerful tips. Identify ONE measurable, verifiable, unique benefit for your audience. Remember the slides are there to support you not replace you. They should help you to motivate, influence, and persuade.

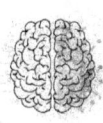

1. BIG IDEA
The opening of your presentation should grab your audience attention and establish your credibility. Do not tell them about you. Tell them about what they will learn. Reverse brainstorm from your audiences' perspective to identify their problems. Then offer solutions that are easy to understand. Summarize every major point and end your presentation with a clear call to action to ensure that Shift Happens!®

3. IMAGE IS EVERYTHING
Use royalty free images that are high resolution. Use type fonts that are san serif. Avoid bullet points-they kill presentations. Minimize your copy and use 32pt+ type size.
Your slide is a billboard not a brain dump filled with boring data or copy.

2. PERCEPTION STRENGTHS
Dress one level above the best dressed person in the room OR dress for business success. Leverage your specific presentation strength. Do your charts, graphs, and images look as professional as you do? Image is omnipotent!

4. AUDIENCE PROBLEM STATEMENT
Your presentations should have a narrative structure—just like stories—start by creating an audience journey map, with key milestones along the way. Get inputs, in advance from all relevant people before you create your presentation.

- Listen
- Find Pain Areas
- Reverse Brainstorm
- Reveal In Stages
- Collaborate with thought leaders
- Observe your audience & listen

5. NEVER READ A SCRIPT or SLIDE/SCREEN
You should know your materials and only have the script to keep you on track. Use both verbal and slide transitions to keep the presentation flow. Use "B" button to go dark. A blank screen will often 'wake up' the audience. Modulate your voice as you move through the presentation.
Bueller?... Bueller?... Bueller

6. IT'S CALLED A HANDOUT FOR A REASON
Use your slides to convey ideas and handouts to communicate details AFTER your presentation. Always get something in return such as email, business card, or charge for the handouts. You must establish their value, or you diminish your value. REMEMBER: A handout is something given freely or distributed free to those in need.
CHARGE FOR YOUR WISDOM.
If it's not worth charging for then, it's not worth giving it away for free.

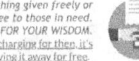

7. CREATE A COMPELLING CALL TO ACTION
If you were paid to speak normally, you could not sell from the platform. Give a website for a free ebook, infographic or your handouts. If you were not paid to speak, then you should have the rights to create an offer that has a price associated with it. Always ask permission from the planner BEFORE any offer is made.
Then FOLLOW-UP, FOLLOW-UP

MAKE THIS YOUR YEAR TO ROAR
A good public speaker with a boring slide deck may be able to maintain the attention of an audience for a few minutes, but a good public speaker with a well-planned and well-designed visual presentation can truly mesmerize an audience.

The most effective speakers have learned to wean themselves off bullet-ridden slides in favor of highly visual presentations that reinforce their words—instead of repeating them. Then you become the King Of The Presentation Jungle. Need help? Check out VISME Everything you need to tell powerful visual stories in Powerpoint presentations, Infographics, and other visual content. **http://jfa.tips/Visme**

BE VISUAL • BE VERBAL • BE RELEVANT • BE PREPARED

TOP REMOTE WORK TOOLS

SOME SAY:

The future of work is remote. The future is NOW.

Because you may be working remotely testing this new way of working is timely. We wanted to share **our top remote work tools** with you. Our team is here to help.
Contact us with any questions. inquiries@shifthappens.com

COMMUNICATION

Team communication platform for talking to team members

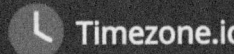

Remote work tool to track time zones and locations of team members

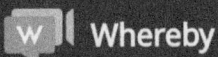

One-click video call software for team meetings

FILE SHARING

Cloud-based file sharing and storage system for teams

Collaborative file sharing with folder organization and commenting capabilities

PRODUCTIVITY

Project management software for collaborating on projects and tasks

 Notion

Project management software that allows you to build your own interface

 Hubstaff

Time tracking and productivity monitoring tool

Multi-level integration app that creates connections between tools

loom

Screen recording software for creating and sharing videos

CONTENT CREATION & DESIGN

All-in-one content creation tool with dynamic team collaboration features
http://jfa.tips/Visme

Photo editing tool for editing and cropping images

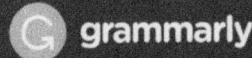

Digital writing assistant that supports clear and effective communication

Cloud-based documents for real-time content creation and collaboration

SALES & MARKETING

- Respona
- HARO (Help a Reporter Out)
- Google Alerts
- Ahrefs
- Coverage Book
- Visme
- BuzzSumo
- Business Wire
- PRWeb
- Critical Mention
- Moosend
- Anewstip
- SparkToro
- MuchRack
- Mention
- Grammarly
- NinjaOutreach
- ProfNet
- Cision
- SourceBottle
- Crystal
- Hemingway
- Mynewsdesk
- Medium
- Now Over to You

TelecommutingTips.com Appendix

Connect with the Author

Website: www.shifthappens.com
www.jfa.tips/AboutJim
Email: jfeldman@shifthappens.com
Phone: 312-527-9111
Twitter: @ShiftHappensNow
Facebook: facebook.com/jamesdfeldman *and* facebook.com/shifthappensnow
Instagram: instagram.com/thebrightideaguy
LinkedIn: linkedin.com/in/jamesfeldman
Pinterest: pinterest.com/shifthappensnow

For a full list of business resources, visit:
www.jfa.tips/BusinessResources

Magazines for Business Minds

www.forbes.com
www.fastcompany.com
www.entrepreneur.com
www.inc.com
www.smartmoney.com

www.moneywatch.com

www.prevuemeetings.com

Real-Life Examples of Innovative Businesses

www.mypetchicken.com

www.thelastlecture.com

www.stumbleupon.com

www.ideapaint.com

www.jfa.tips/GreatestShowman

Coupon Websites

www.thegrocerygame.com

www.shopittome.com

www.groupon.com

www.livingsocial.com

www.couponcabin.com

www.couponsuzy.com

Make Extra Money Selling "Stuff" On

www.ebay.com

www.craigslist.com

www.atoncer.com

www.ebid.com

www.sell.com

www.etsy.com

Barter Organizations

www.itex.com

www.imsbarter.com

www.trademedia.com

Business Building Resources

www.USPTO.gov

www.SBA.gov

www.ehow.com

www.freelogoservices.com

www.godaddy.com

www.quickbooks.com

www.jfa.tips/OutrightBookkeeping

www.taxactonline.com

www.jfa.tips/FreeMiletracker

www.waveapps.com

www.freshbooks.com

www.gusto.com

www.jfa.tips/Fundraising

www.jfa.tips/3DThinkingVideo

Business Plan Software Resources

www.jfa.tips/BusinessPlan

www.businessplanpro.com

www.planware.org

www.brs-inc.com

www.bizplandb.com
www.thebestbusinessplan.com
www.finimpact.com/writing-a-business-plan

Website Builder Resources

www.jfa.tips/Strikingly
www.smallbusiness.yahoo.com
www.netonewebdesign.com
www.yourwebdepartment.com
www.bigcommerce.com
www.interspire.com

Design, Presentations, and Marketing

www.pixabay.com
www.wordart.com
www.wordswag.co
www.creativecloud.com
www.hubspot.com
www.mailchimp.com
www.tawk.to
www.activecampaign.com
www.polarisoffice.com
www.jfa.tips/clubcalendar
www.convertkit.com
www.fliphtml5.com
www.fontsquirrel.com
www.audiojungle.net

www.compfight.com
www.jfa.tips/PresentationPro
www.presentermedia.com
www.jfa.tips/Reviews
www.slideshare.net
www.tiny.cc
www.jfa.tips/Visme
www.jfa.tips/PowerPresentations
www.whatthefont.com

Communication and Collaboration

www.jfa.tips/Welcome
www.docs.google.com
www.hangouts.google.com
www.ideaboardz.com
www.lucidchart.com/pages
www.miro.com
www.mural.co
www.otter.ai
www.trello.com
www.ziteboard.com
www.jfa.tips/YouMail
www.jfa.tips/Timezone
www.slack.com
www.pushover.net
www.fuze.com
www.addappt.com

www.zoom.us

www.jfa.tips/MailstromTrial

www.asana.com

www.dropbox.com

www.evercontact.com

Organization and Time Management

www.kanbanflow.com

www.trello.com

www.evernote.com

www.boxmeupapp.com

www.upward.net

www.tripit.com

www.omnigroup.com/omnifocus

www.myminutesapp.com

www.rescuetime.com

www.expensify.com

www.thegrizzlylabs.com

Other Resources

www.carbonite.com

www.jfawatchwinders.com

www.jfainc.espwebsite.com

www.hud.gov/topics/avoiding_foreclosure

www.charitywatch.org

www.funnyordie.com

www.dots.co

Website Appendix

www.jfa.tips/ppchecklist
www.jfa.tips/2020Outlook
www.jfa.tips/2020Vision
www.jfa.tips/3DThinking
www.jfa.tips/Advisory
www.jfa.tips/Change
www.jfa.tips/Chocolate
www.jfa.tips/Coaching
www.jfa.tips/Competence
www.jfa.tips/Covid-19Survey
www.jfa.tips/CovidDonations
www.jfa.tips/CovidMeetings
www.jfa.tips/CustomerExperienceMetrics
www.jfa.tips/CustomerJourney
www.jfa.tips/CustomerServiceAHAs
www.jfa.tips/DATING4Bars
www.jfa.tips/DATINGSlides
www.jfa.tips/DATINGYOURCUSTOMER
www.jfa.tips/Differentiation
www.jfa.tips/EventQuestionnaire
www.jfa.tips/Focus
www.jfa.tips/FreeSmiles
www.jfa.tips/GettingToYes
www.jfa.tips/GroceryCertificate
www.jfa.tips/Healthcare
www.jfa.tips/HowToThink
www.jfa.tips/JDFKeynote

www.jfa.tips/lumecube
www.jfa.tips/LaserFocus
www.jfa.tips/Leadership
www.jfa.tips/LemonadeLesson
www.jfa.tips/MeetingPlanner
www.jfa.tips/Networking
www.jfa.tips/Package
www.jfa.tips/PatientPatience
www.jfa.tips/Performance
www.jfa.tips/Professionals
www.jfa.tips/Sales
www.jfa.tips/SellingSkills
www.jfa.tips/StrategicPlanning
www.jfa.tips/Topics
www.jfa.tips/Transform
www.jfa.tips/VirtualWisdom
www.jfa.tips/Why
www.jfa.tips/YES
www.jfa.tips/RU3DThinking

Contact Information

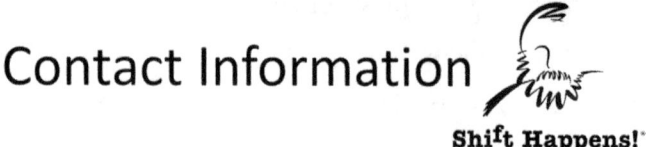

 312 527•9111   Cell 312 500•4493

 jfeldman@shifthappens.com

 www.shifthappens.com

The types of innovation cultures

Be ridiculous & willing to fail
Create a passionate & inter-connected innovation dept
Have a strong internal focus
Keep the pipeline flowing

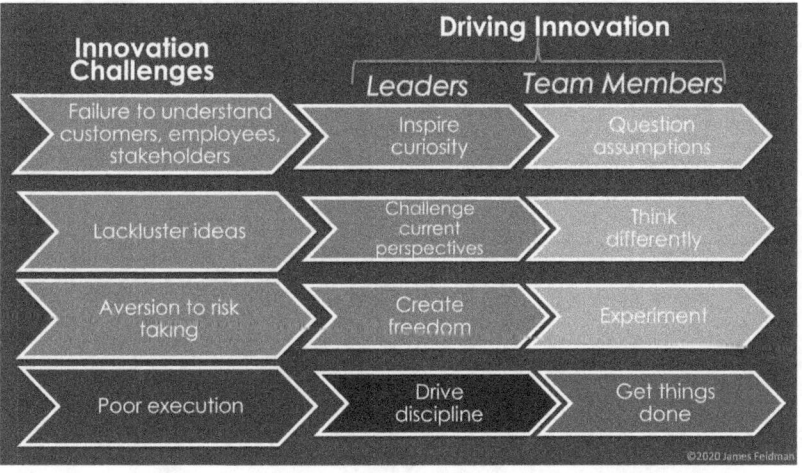

Overcoming Objections

1 Fact-driven or cultural? Understand resistance.

It's not about selling.
Selling is how you view the transaction.

It's about buying.
Your prospect is evaluating whether to buy or not to buy.

YOUR goal is not about selling but building **TRUST** and demonstrate that buying will actually be better, faster, cheaper, more pleasant, satisfying, rewarding, than not buying.

Every problem has an opportunity for those that can solve it.

2 It's all about emotions. Facts tell. Emotions Sell!

The "I" have it.
- Relate to your Customers.
- Engage your Customers.
- Sell your Customers.

It's all about what's in it for me [them] (WIIFM) that will deliver the results you want for you. Find the pain. Be the cure not another problem.

3 Address 'all' erroneous assumptions.

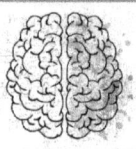

One Size Does Not Fit All.
Treat each objection as an opportunity.

4 Welcome all concerns.

Listen.
The customer maybe talking.

5 There is no point in arguing.
When a Customer expresses concern they are still engaged and open to resolution. Think of it as a gift not a punishment.

Don't talk.
The Customer may be listening. If you listen carefully the Customer will tell you how to sell them. Show interest in them and they will show interest in you.

6 Highlight your reasonableness

It's 'b-a-a-a-a-d' to

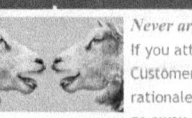

Never argue.
If you attack your Customer's logic or rationale they will go away.

7 *Be gentle. Show concern.*
Customers will remember the tone of your response more than your facts and sales points. Offer alternatives. Show them 'what it will cost to NOT do business with you.

About the Author

James Feldman is an advisor in mastering change, not only for himself, but also for his clients. He is a deep generalist with a broad perspective with selfless independence that balances his devotion to clients with objectivity and detachment. He has a history of delivering results, earning his clients' confidence, and creating groundbreaking solutions. In an era of commoditization, Jim has assisted Kodak, Microsoft, Hewlett-Packard, Apple, Hyatt Hotels and Resorts, McDonalds, Wynn Las Vegas, March of Dimes, Department of Defense, Coca-Cola, Verizon, Toyota and Frito-Lay. He has led them to create new products, retain employees and exceed the expectations of their Customers.

Jim recognizes that experts are specialists and adapts to new realities by leveraging opportunities while mitigating the risks of a changing world. With over 40 years of experience, Jim has developed a toolbox for change that offers the essential devices for a new way of thinking that harnesses the power of taking control of your own "shifts."

As an international speaker Jim has conducted presentations on mastering change, customer service, innovative problem-solving, and creating success for corporations and associations. Just to name a few (full list available at www.jfa.tips/Clients):

- 💡 Cremation Association of North America
- 💡 Association of Professional Fundraisers
- 💡 Marriott and Ritz Carlton Resorts
- 💡 Aria, Mandalay Bay, Wynn Las Vegas, Bellagio, and Foxwoods Resorts and Casinos
- 💡 Carnival Cruises
- 💡 Los Cabos Tourism Board
- 💡 Toyota, VW, Lexus, Audi, and Nissan Automotive
- 💡 San Juan Tourism

Transformation Media Books

Transformation Media Books is dedicated to publishing innovative works that nourish the body, mind, and spirit, written by authors whose ideas and messages make a difference in the world.

For more information, the latest titles or to purchase direct, please visit our website:

www.TransformationMediaBooks.com

Shift Happens

AHAs

- Shift happens when you take time to smell the roses.
- How many times do we get a present and just don't recognize it is there?
- Don't be so focused on a to-do list. Find something interesting and spend time on that.
- How to innovate: Ask what if, what's next, what's possible, and why not?
- How to innovate: Start a dialogue & move it into the strategic aspects of conversation.
- Innovative perspective: Are we going to exploit the strategic advantages that we have?
- Innovative perspective: Can we develop new capabilities using existing resources?
- Innovative perspective: Are we going to somehow create revolutionary change with these resources?
- Corporate culture today very clearly articulates the penalty for failure, but not the rewards for success.
- Someone who works to send kids to college is very risk-averse because it'll mean they're out of a job.
- How do you reverse the situation to make failure "good"?
- Pick a problem that people will pay for if it gets fixed.
- We all know people, process, and product, but we don't live it day-to-day.

- Set aside a certain part of your budget for failure, because you learn a lot from it.
- If you don't care who gets the credit, things get done.
- When you start competing internally, it becomes self-destructive.
- It's very rare for organizations to share profits with the person who brought out the idea.
- Do you feel that your organization is informative or persuasive?
- At the end of the day, it's all about making a sale.
- Change takes place in innovation, joint venture, and joint promotion.
- Is a bendable iPhone a future benefit or liability?
- What got you here today is not what's going to get you there tomorrow.
- People will pay more depending on the size of the problem you solved for them.
- It's not about attracting new clients. It's about doing more business for existing clients with new products & services.
- The speed of implementation determines success. It's innovation at the speed of opportunity.
- Steve Jobs was a master at getting ahead of the curve. Are you ahead of the curve?
- The old school organizations are not paying attention to the new school ways of doing things.
- Refer to the Apple logic of looking at things in a different way.
- Don't let what you think you know prevent you from learning what you need to know.
- "Every strike brings me closer to the next home run."

—Babe Ruth

- 💡 Life is 10% what happens to you and 90% what you do about it.
- 💡 Don't waste your time living someone else's life. Your time is limited.
- 💡 "Whether you can or you think you can't, you're right."

  —Henry Ford
- 💡 The best revenge is massive success and that's when Shift Happens!
- 💡 "Fall seven times and stand up eight."

  —Japanese proverb
- 💡 If you are offered a seat on the next trip to the moon, don't ask what seat . . . just get on board.
- 💡 Create an urgency of doing. Knowing is not enough; you must apply what you know. Being willing is not enough; you must do it.
- 💡 "I didn't fail the test. I just found 100 ways to do it wrong."

  —Benjamin Franklin
- 💡 Your commitment to success must be greater than your fear of failing. Just do it.
- 💡 Beware of distractions disguised as opportunities.
- 💡 When everything seems difficult, remember that an airplane takes off against the wind.
- 💡 "INNOVATE or die" should be displayed to make sure nobody forgets how painful it can be to change the rules of the game.
- 💡 Make it. Master it. Make it matter. Discover the best.
- 💡 Dream what could be. Design what should be. Destiny is what will be.
- 💡 Innovation is the product of discomfort. Find the pain. Provide the cure. Get paid for it.

- 💡 Change people's lives instead of their experiences.
- 💡 Think about "clear and present" opportunities and become a solution provider.
- 💡 Time is the only inventory we can't replace. Create a need so strong that clients say, "I need you in my life."
- 💡 To overcome the roadblocks to your success you have to go from failure to failure without losing any of your determination.
- 💡 Tomorrow we wake up to everything imagined by Jules Verne, DaVinci, Edison, Steve Jobs. WHAT DID YOU IMAGINE TODAY?
- 💡 Unclutter yourself. Get rid of disposable crutches. Focus on doing one thing better than anyone else.
- 💡 Volunteer for a charity, visit hospitals, so you can look in the mirror and say you have given back. It will create a positive shift.
- 💡 We cannot survive the 21st century with the INNOVATIONS from the 20th Century. Shift Happens! and we need to embrace it.
- 💡 We must react to the forces around us and determine if we can overcome the challenge and be more productive.
- 💡 Wealth is not gained by perfecting the known, but by seizing the unknown by taking charge of your own destiny.
- 💡 The biggest challenge is the rate of change and our resistance to it.
- 💡 Determine how you will solve the problem. Determination is the reason most companies don't impact their bottom line.
- 💡 Many people often solve problems, identify opportunities, resolve conflicts—in their mind—and never act.
- 💡 Set small, measurable, attainable steps. Imagine achieving that goal. Get people to share that success.

- A superior thinker accurately predicts the consequences of doing or not doing something while remaining focused on the long-term goal.
- The way of evaluating the significance of a task is how you determine what your next priority really is.
- What are my highest-value activities?
- What can I do that will make a real difference?
- What is the most valuable use of my time?
- The potential consequences of any task or activity are the key determinants of how important it really is to you and to your company.
- "The things that matter most must never be at the mercy of the things that matter least."

—Johann Wolfgang von Goethe

> The way to OUTSELL your competition isn't just OUTWORK your competition, but to OUTTHINK your competition

How to kill Big Innovative Solutions Ideas in 10 small steps

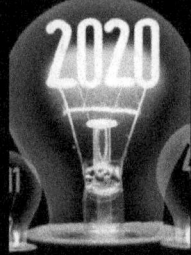

1. The *Great! Let's roll!* Department
2. The *Send me that mail again...* Department
3. The *Did you send it? I didn't get it.* Department
4. The *The client won't like it.* Department
5. The *Let's Do It Diffently* Department
6. The *It's Not The Right Timing* Department
7. The *It's Not In My Budget* Department
8. The *Yes, But We Haven't Done That Before*
9. The *Yes, But Let's do it differently* Department
10. The Innovation Is For Big Businesses Department

Jim's Reading List

- *All I Really Need to Know I Learned in Kindergarten* by Robert Fulghum
- *Change Your Thoughts, Change Your Life* by Wayne W. Dyer
- *Changing the Channel* by Michael Masterson & Mary Ellen Tribby
- *Clients for Life* by Jagdish Sheth and Andrew Sobel
- *Competitive Differentiation* by Jaynie L. Smith
- *Creative Solution Finding* by Gerald Nadler, PhD and Shozo Hibino, PhD
- *Creativity for Leaders* by Gary Fellers
- *D-A-T-I-N-G Your Customers®* by James D. Feldman (jfa.tips/CustomerService)
- *Dare to Win* by Jack Canfield
- *Debt Cures II* by Kevin Trudeau
- *Discover Your Genius* by Michael Gelb
- *Excuses Begone!* by Wayne W. Dyer
- *Find A Job Through Social Networking* by Diane Crompton and Ellen Sautter
- *Good to Great* by Jim Collins
- *How to Be a Great Communicator* by Nido R. Qubein
- *How to Think Like Leonardo da Vinci* by Michael Gelb
- *Imagine* by Jonah Lehrer
- *Innovation to the Core* by Peter Skarzynski and Rowan Gibson

- *Innovative Mind* by Gene N. Landrum, PhD
- *Kick Start Your Success: Four Powerful Steps to Get What You Want...* by Romanus Wolter
- *Live Your Dreams* by Les Brown
- *No Excuses!: The Power of Self-Discipline* by Brian Tracy
- *Now What?! Finding Your Way from Job-Loss Crisis to Career Resilience* by Jean Baur
- *Poke the Box* by Seth Godin
- *Profiting from Uncertainty* by Paul Schomemaker
- *Reality Check* by Guy Kawasaki
- *Scaling Up* by Verne Harnish
- *Secrets Banks & Lenders Don't Want You to Know* by Richard Weathington & Beth M. Ley
- *Secrets of Real Estate Millionaires* by Tom Nardone
- *The 7 Habits of Highly Effective People* by Stephen R. Covey
- *The 9 Steps to Financial Freedom* by Suze Orman
- *The Answer: Grow Any Business, Achieve Financial Freedom, and Live an Extraordinary Life* by John Assaraf & Murray Smith
- *The Art of War* by Sun Tzu, comments from Gary Gagliardi
- *The Big Moo* by Seth Godin
- *The Brand Called You* by Peter Montoya
- *The Courage to Be Rich* by Mark Victor Hansen
- *The Creative Problem Solver's Toolbox* by Richard Forbes
- *The Dip: A Little Book That Teaches You When To Quit (and When to Stick)* by Seth Godin
- *The Experience Economy* by Joseph Pine II and James Gilmore
- *The Fine Art of Doing Better* by John D. Hammond
- *The Laws of Lifetime Growth* by Dan Sullivan
- *The Millionaire Mind* by Thomas J. Stanley, PhD

- 💡 *The One Minute Millionaire* by Mark Victor Hansen & Robert Allen
- 💡 *The Road to Wealth* by Suze Orman
- 💡 *The Secret* by Rhonda Bryne
- 💡 *The Seven Forces of Success* by Joseph Sugarman
- 💡 *Triggers: 30 Sales Tools You Can Use to Control the Mind of Your Prospect...* by Joseph Sugarman
- 💡 *Unleashing the Ideavirus* by Seth Godin
- 💡 Wall Street Journal *Guide to Planning Your Financial Future* by Kenneth M. Morris, Alan M. Siegel, Virgina B. Morris
- 💡 *50 Books to Help You Shift Your Thinking* by Peter McWilliams & John Roger

Use these Resources to refine your big picture thinking.

www.ingramcontent.com/pod-product-compliance
Lightning Source LLC
Chambersburg PA
CBHW060105230426
43661CB00033B/1419/J